Sources of
THE MAKING OF THE WEST

PEOPLES AND CULTURES

A CONCISE HISTORY

Volume I: To 1740

Sources of

THE MAKING OF THE WEST

PEOPLES AND CULTURES

A CONCISE HISTORY

Volume I: To 1740

Katharine J. Lualdi

University of Southern Maine

BEDFORD / ST. MARTIN'S   Boston   ◆   New York

For Bedford/St. Martin's

Publisher for History: Patricia A. Rossi
Executive Editor for History: Elizabeth M. Welch
Production Editor: Lori Chong Roncka
Production Supervisor: Maria R. Gonzalez
Marketing Manager: Jenna Bookin Barry
Editorial Assistant: Brianna Germain
Production Assistants: Thomas P. Crehan, Courtney Jossart, Kendra LeFleur
Copyeditor: Patricia Herbst
Text Design: Wanda Kossak
Cover Design: Donna Dennison
Cover Art: Christine de Pisan presenting her book. By permission of the British Library. Ms Harley 4431.f.3.
Composition: TechBooks
Printing and Binding: R.R. Donnelley & Sons Company

President: Joan E. Feinberg
Director of Marketing: Karen Melton
Director of Editing, Design, and Production: Marcia Cohen
Managing Editor: Elizabeth M. Schaaf

7 6 5 4 3 2
f e d c b a

For information, write: Bedford/St. Martin's, 75 Arlington Street, Boston, MA 02116 (617-399-4000)

ISBN: 0–312–40718–1 (Vol. I)
      0–312–40719–X (Vol. II)

Acknowledgments

Chapter 1
    King Hammurabi. *The Code of Hammurabi* (early 18th century B.C.). From *Ancient Near Eastern Texts Relating to the Old Testament*, edited by James B. Pritchard. Copyright © 1969 by James B. Pritchard. Reprinted with the permission of the publishers.

Preface for Instructors

Sources of The Making of the West: A Concise History is a collection of firsthand accounts intended to provide depth and breadth to the discussion of important events, ideas, and experiences discussed in *The Making of the West: Peoples and Cultures, A Concise History,* the text for which it was specifically compiled. Organized chapter by chapter to parallel the textbook, these sources offer teachers varied opportunities to ignite a dialogue in the classroom between the past and present.

Together, these documents yield a rich array for such a dialogue within the strong, succinct framework of *The Making of the West: A Concise History.* For example, when the textbook discusses the European slave trade, students can experience it for themselves in the source collection through the eyes of Olaudah Equiano, the African slave who survived to tell his story (Document 44). Information and ideas thus come alive with the emotions, opinions, and observations of contemporaries, revealing to students the relationship between narrative history and original sources and showing them that history is not a fixed set of immutable facts but rather an ongoing process of evaluation and interpretation. *Sources of* The Making of the West: A Concise History provides the raw materials for this process.

Inspired by and tailored to *The Making of the West,* the criteria governing the selection of documents naturally reflect historians' changing understanding of Western civilization. Although traditional political sources are included, these views are broadened by less conventional documents illuminating not only social and cultural life but also Europe's increasing interconnectedness with the larger world. Women's voices received special attention in the selection process because of their crucial and often underappreciated role in shaping the course of Western history from both within and outside the corridors of power. The documents were also selected based on their accessibility and appeal to students. For this reason, I edited each primary source to speak to specific themes without impairing its overall sense and tone.

To assist students with their journey into the past, I prepared with equal care the wide range of learning aids that appear in the sourcebook. Each chapter opens with a short introduction that situates the documents within the broader historical context and addresses their relationship to one another. An explanatory headnote accompanies each document to provide fundamental background information on the author and the source while highlighting its significance. Discussion questions are also included to help students examine the key points and issues in greater depth and to suggest topics for discussion or writing assignment. Although these editorial features intentionally strengthen the coherency of each chapter as a unit, they also allow instructors to choose documents and questions that best suit their specific teaching goals and methods.

Acknowledgments

I owe many people thanks for helping to bring this project to fruition. First among them are the authors of *The Making of the West: A Concise History*, Lynn Hunt, Thomas R. Martin, Barbara H. Rosenwein, R. Po-chia Hsia, and Bonnie G. Smith, who provided invaluable suggestions, advice, and insight. I would also like to thank Larissa Juliet Taylor, Julia O'Brien, Megan Armstrong, and David K. Smith for their help and encouragement, as well as my development editor, Molly Kalkstein, for her careful eye and enthusiasm. Those at Bedford/St. Martin's also helped make this book possible: in particular, my thanks to Joan E. Feinberg, President; Charles H. Christensen, former President; Patricia A. Rossi, Publisher for History; Elizabeth M. Welch, Executive Editor for History; John Amburg, Assistant Managing Editor; Maria R. Gonzalez, Production Supervisor; and Lori Chong Roncka, Production Editor.

I also owe a debt of gratitude to the staff of the University of Maine library system who patiently endured my seemingly endless requests for books and articles. Without them, compiling this collection would not have been possible.

Last and above all, I thank my husband, John, for his sense of humor and understanding as I lost myself in books and Post-it notes.

Introduction for Students

Your textbook, *The Making of the West: Peoples and Cultures, A Concise History,* provides an essential chronological and thematic framework for understanding the development of the West as a cultural and geographic entity. Yet the process of historical inquiry extends beyond the text into the thoughts, words, and experiences of people living at the time. Firsthand accounts—that is, primary sources—expose the world that their writers inhabited, revealing the ideas, emotions, and beliefs of contemporary historical actors. Primary-source collections like this one allow you to observe, analyze, and interpret the past as it unfolds before you; unlike other sourcebooks, however, this reader's thorough integration with your textbook reveals the relationship between historical narrative and the original sources that inform it.

As the main title of your textbook, *The Making of the West,* suggests, history is not a static collection of names, facts, and dates. Rather, it is an ongoing attempt to make sense of the past and its relationship to the present, usually through the lens of primary sources. *Sources of* THE MAKING OF THE WEST: A CONCISE HISTORY provides this lens for you, with firsthand accounts representing a wide range of the documents historians use—from Egyptian chronicles and Greek poems to English feminist tracts and German political memoirs. When combined, the documents reflect historians' appreciation of the need to examine Western civilization from a variety of conceptual angles (political, social, cultural, economic) and geographic viewpoints. The composite picture that emerges as a result reveals a variety of historical experiences shaping each era from both within and outside Europe. Furthermore, the documents demonstrate that the most historically significant of these experiences are not always those of people in formal positions of power. Women, minorities, and everyday folk likewise influenced profoundly the course of Western history.

The sources in this reader were selected with an eye to their ability not only to capture the multifaceted dimensions of the past but also to ignite your historical imagination. Each document is a unique product of human endeavor and as such is often colored by the author's personal concerns, biases, and objectives. Among the most exciting challenges facing you is to sift through such nuances for what they reveal about the source and its links to the broader historical context.

Understanding how each document is connected to its author and to larger historical issues is key to the study of history. To this end, as you read each document, you should keep a series of questions at the front of your mind, just like a reporter investigating a breaking news story: Who wrote the document, when, for whom, why, and where? Each of these questions represents a crucial piece of the puzzle of the past and is an essential means of meeting every historian's basic goal, to chart change and continuity over time.

A Nazi propaganda pamphlet written in 1930 (Document 67) offers an instructive example. The author of the pamphlet, Joseph Goebbels, was the propaganda chief of Adolf Hitler, the leader of the Nazi party. Similar political goals and beliefs bound both men, including virulent anti-Semitism. At the time Goebbels wrote the document, Germany was mired in economic recession. Capitalizing on the downhearted mood of the day with promises of a better life, he successfully used pamphlets such as this one to broaden the Nazis' popular support on the eve of Hitler's rise to power. All of these factors—Goebbels's position within the Nazi party, what he was writing, for whom, when, and why—shaped the document's content, and thus should inform your interpretation of what it suggests about the Nazis and Germany in this period. By contrast, the recollections of Jews who were the victims of this propaganda (Document 69) offer a far different view of the Nazis and the human impact of their regime. This difference can be attributed not only to the nature of the sources themselves but also to the opposing perspectives they represent.

Mining documents for their multiple layers of meaning thus requires a careful balancing act, first between fact and interpretation, and second between the content of the document and the larger historical backdrop. To aid you with this process, *Sources of THE MAKING OF THE WEST: A CONCISE HISTORY* was compiled to use directly alongside your textbook. Each chapter in the collection contains three or four documents illustrative of the central ideas, issues, and events discussed in the corresponding textbook chapter, where cross-references link the narrative to the readings. In addition, *Sources of THE MAKING OF THE WEST: A CONCISE HISTORY* includes a variety of useful learning aids that supplement the materials offered in the textbook. An introduction linking the documents to the historical period in which they were written opens each chapter, and each document has an explanatory headnote that provides essential information about the author and the source and why the document is historically significant. Finally, three or four questions conclude each document to help you probe beneath the surface to understand what each document communicates and to see the similarities and differences among them.

The documents included in *Sources of THE MAKING OF THE WEST: A CONCISE HISTORY* invite you to become an active participant in discovering how history was actually lived over time by an array of different people in an array of different places. They are meant to offer snapshots of the past that, when viewed and interpreted together within the broader historical context found in the textbook, will help you paint a colorful and interconnected picture of the historical development of Western civilization—while learning that history, unlike a picture, is never finished.

Contents

Preface for Instructors   v
Introduction for Students   vii

CHAPTER 1
Foundations of Western Civilization, to 500 B.C.   1

  1. King Hammurabi, *The Code of Hammurabi* (Early Eighteenth Century B.C.)   1
  2. *The Book of Exodus, Chapters 19–24* (c. Tenth to Sixth Centuries B.C.)   8
  3. Tyrtaeus of Sparta and Solon of Athens, *Poems* (Seventh to Sixth Centuries B.C.)   13
  4. Sappho of Lesbos, *Poems* (Sixth Century B.C.)   15

CHAPTER 2
The Greek Golden Age, c. 500–400 B.C.   19

  5. Lysias, *A Husband Speaks in His Own Defense* (c. 400 B.C.)   19
  6. Plato, *The Apology of Socrates* (399 B.C.)   24
  7. Thucydides, *The Funeral Oration of Pericles* (429 B.C.)   28

CHAPTER 3
From the Classical to the Hellenistic World, c. 400–30 B.C.   31

  8. Zenon, Egyptian Official, *Records* (259–250 B.C.)   31
  9. *Funerary Inscriptions and Epitaphs* (Fifth to First Centuries B.C.)   34
10. Polybius, *The Histories* (Second Century B.C.)   37

CHAPTER 4
The Rise of Rome, c. 753–44 B.C.   39

11. Livy, *Roman Women Demonstrate against the Oppian Law* (195 B.C.)   39
12. *The Twelve Tables* (451–449 B.C.)   42
13. Cicero, *On the Commonwealth* (54 B.C.)   47

CHAPTER 5
The Roman Empire, c. 44 B.C.–A.D. 284   51

14. Augustus, *The Accomplishments of Augustus* (A.D. 14)   51
15. *Notices and Graffiti from Pompeii* (First Century A.D.)   55
16. Pliny the Younger, *Letters* (A.D. 111–113)   57

CHAPTER 6
The Transformation of the Roman Empire, A.D. 284–c. 600   61

17. St. Jerome, *Letter 107* (A.D. 403)   61
18. *The Burgundian Code* (c. 475–525)   64
19. Procopius, *Buildings* (c. 553–554)   68

CHAPTER 7
The Heirs of the Roman Empire, 600–750   71

20. *Islamic Terms of Peace* (633–643)   71
21. *The Life of Lady Balthild, Queen of the Franks* (Late Seventh Century)   74
22. Pope Gregory the Great, *Letters* (598–601)   76

CHAPTER 8
Unity and Diversity in Three Societies, 750–1050   79

23. *Digenis Akritas* (Tenth or Eleventh Century)   79
24. Ahmad al-Ya'qūbī, *Kitāb al-buldān* (Ninth Century)   81
25. *General Capitulary for the* Missi (802)   84

CHAPTER 9
Renewal and Reform, 1050–1200   89

26. *Urban Charters of Jaca, Spain* (c. 1077) and *Lorris, France* (1155)   89
27. Emperor Henry IV and Pope Gregory VII, *Letters of the Investiture Conflict* (1076)   92
28. Hildegard of Bingen, *Selected Writings* (Twelfth Century)   94
29. Saints Francis and Clare of Assisi, *Selected Writings* (Thirteenth Century)   98

CHAPTER 10
An Age of Confidence, 1200–1340   103

30. Hadewijch of Brabant, *Letters and Poems of a Female Mystic* (1220–1240)   103
31. *Medieval University Life* (Twelfth to Early Thirteenth Centuries)   105
32. Dante Alighieri, *Human and Divine Love* (Late Thirteenth to Early Fourteenth Centuries)   109

CHAPTER 11
Crisis and Renaissance, 1340–1500   115

33. *The Black Death* (Fourteenth Century)   115
34. Christine de Pisan, *Lament on the Evils of the Civil War* (1410)   118
35. Giovanni Pico della Mirandola, *Oration on the Dignity of Man* (1496)   120
36. Alessandra Strozzi, *Letters from a Widow and Matriarch of a Great Family* (1450–1465)   122

CHAPTER 12
Struggles over Beliefs, 1500–1648   125

37. Argula von Grumbach and John Hooker, *Women's Actions in the Reformation*
    (1520s–1530s)   125
38. Henry IV, *Edict of Nantes* (1598)   128
39. Saint Ignatius of Loyola, *A New Kind of Catholicism* (1546, 1549, 1553)   131
40. Galileo Galilei, *Letter to the Grand Duchess Christina* (1615)   133

CHAPTER 13
State Building and the Search for Order, 1648–1690   137

41. Louis de Rouvroy, Duke of Saint-Simon, *Memoirs* (1694–1723)   137
42. Ludwig Fabritius, *The Revolt of Stenka Razin* (1670)   139
43. British Parliament, *The English Bill of Rights* (1689)   141

CHAPTER 14
The Atlantic System and Its Consequences, 1690–1740   145

44. Olaudah Equiano, *The Interesting Narrative of the Life of Olaudah Equiano,
    Written by Himself* (1789)   145
45. Montesquieu, *Persian Letters: Letter 37* (1721)   147
46. Mary Astell, *Reflections upon Marriage* (1706)   149

Sources of
THE MAKING OF THE WEST

PEOPLES AND CULTURES

A CONCISE HISTORY

Volume I: To 1740

CHAPTER I

Foundations of Western Civilization, to 500 B.C.

The roots of Western culture extend across distant lands and ancient societies. The four documents in this chapter expose the fundamental features of these early civilizations as they developed between the eighteenth and sixth centuries B.C. The evidence reveals that on the one hand, peoples then living in the Near East, Africa, and the Mediterranean developed their own distinctive beliefs, customs, and sense of identity. On the other, they shared many attributes, such as urban populations, the use of writing, devotion to religion, and economies based on trade and agriculture. This unique mixture of cross-cultural similarities and differences forged the path for the future. The last two documents reveal that Greece did not rely on the past alone to forge its future. Instead, it created innovative social, political, and cultural forms—ranging from the city-state to lyric poetry—that left permanent imprints on Western civilization.

1. King Hammurabi, *The Code of Hammurabi* (Early Eighteenth Century B.C.)

The law code promulgated by King Hammurabi (r. c. 1792–1750 B.C.) of Babylon elucidates the inner workings of Mesopotamian society, the cradle of the world's first civilization. The copy of the code excerpted here is inscribed on a stone pillar, crowned by a bas-relief depicting the god of justice commissioning Hammurabi to write the laws. This image embodies the Mesopotamian belief that kings were divinely appointed and thereby responsible for imparting justice and promoting their subjects' well-being. As a messenger of the divine will, King Hammurabi influenced both the public and the private lives of his people. As the following selection reveals, he was especially concerned with protecting property rights and the social hierarchy, with slaves at the bottom and free persons at the top. By codifying laws in writing, Hammurabi helped set an enduring precedent in the Western tradition.

When lofty Anum,[1] king of the Anunnaki,[2]
(and) Enlil, lord of heaven and earth,
the determiner of the destinies of the land,

---

[1] The sky-god, the leader of the pantheon, worshiped especially in the temple of Eanna in Uruk, along with the goddess Inanna.

[2] In this inscription the Anunnaki are the lesser gods attendant upon Anum, and the Igigi are the lesser gods attendant on Enlil.

From *Ancient Near Eastern Texts Relating to the Old Testament*, ed. James B. Pritchard, 3d ed. (Princeton, N.J.: Princeton University Press, 1969), 164–78.

1

determined for Marduk,[3] the first-born of Enki,[4]
the Enlil functions over all mankind,
made him great among the Igigi,[5]
called Babylon by its exalted name,
made it supreme in the world,
established for him in its midst an enduring kingship,
whose foundations are as firm as heaven and earth—
at that time Anum and Enlil named me
to promote the welfare of the people,[6]
me, Hammurabi, the devout, god-fearing prince,
to cause justice to prevail in the land,
to destroy the wicked and the evil,
that the strong might not oppress the weak,
to rise like the sun over the black-headed (people),[7]
and to light up the land. . . .

(v)

When Marduk commissioned me to guide the people aright,
to direct the land,
I established law and justice in the language of the land,
thereby promoting the welfare of the people.
At that time (I decreed):

THE LAWS

If a seignior[8] accused a(nother) seignior and brought a charge of murder against him, but has
not proved it, his accuser shall be put to death.[9]

If a seignior brought a charge of sorcery against a(nother) seignior, but has not proved it,
the one against whom the charge of sorcery was brought, upon going to the river,[10] shall throw
himself into the river, and if the river has then overpowered him, his accuser shall take over his

---

[3]The storm-god, the chief executive of the pantheon, worshiped especially in the temple of Ekur in Nippur
in central Babylonia, modern Nuffar.

[4]The son of Enki and consort of Sarpanit; the god of Babylon and in Hammurabi's time the god of the Baby-
lonian Empire with the functions of Enlil delegated to him; worshiped especially in the temple of Esagila in
Babylon.

[5]Lord of the earth and the mass of life-giving waters within it, issuing in streams and fountains; the father
of Marduk; worshiped especially in the temple of Eabzu in Eridu, in southern Babylonia, modern Abu
Shahrein.

[6]Lit., "to make good the flesh of the people."   [7]The late-Sumerian expression for men in general.

[8]The word awēlum, used here, is literally "man," but in the legal literature it seems to be used in at least three
senses: (1) sometimes to indicate a man of the higher class, a noble; (2) sometimes a free man of any class,
high or low; and (3) occasionally a man of any class, from king to slave. For the last I use the inclusive word
man, but for the first two, since it is seldom clear which of the two is intended in a given context, I follow
the ambiguity of the original and use the rather general term seignior in Italian and Spanish, to indicate any
free man of standing, and not in the strict feudal sense, although the ancient Near East did have something
approximating the feudal system, and that is another reason for using seignior.

[9]With this law and the three following, cf. Deut. 5:20, 19:16 ff.; Exod. 23:1–3.

[10]The word for "river" throughout this section has the determinative of deity, indicating that the river (the
Euphrates) as judge in the case was regarded as god.

estate; if the river has shown that seignior to be innocent and he has accordingly come forth safe, the one who brought the charge of sorcery against him shall be put to death, while the one who threw himself into the river shall take over the estate of his accuser.

If a seignior came forward with false testimony in a case, and has not proved the word which he spoke, if that case was a case involving life, that seignior shall be put to death. . . .

If a seignior has purchased or he received for safe-keeping either silver or gold or a male slave or a female slave or an ox or a sheep or an ass or any sort of thing from the hand of a seignior's son or a seignior's slave without witnesses and contracts, since that seignior is a thief, he shall be put to death.

If a seignior stole either an ox or a sheep or an ass or a pig or a boat, if it belonged to the church (or) if it belonged to the state, he shall make thirtyfold restitution; if it belonged to a private citizen, he shall make good tenfold. If the thief does not have sufficient to make restitution, he shall be put to death. . . .

If a seignior has stolen the young son of a(nother) seignior, he shall be put to death.[11]

If a seignior has helped either a male slave of the state or a female slave of the state or a male slave of a private citizen or a female slave of a private citizen to escape through the city-gate, he shall be put to death.

If a seignior has harbored in his house either a fugitive male or female slave belonging to the state or to a private citizen and has not brought him forth at the summons of the police, that householder shall be put to death. . . .

If a seignior made a breach in a house, they shall put him to death in front of that breach and wall him in.[12]

If a seignior committed robbery and has been caught, that seignior shall be put to death.

If the robber has not been caught, the robbed seignior shall set forth the particulars regarding his lost property in the presence of god, and the city and governor, in whose territory and district the robbery was committed, shall make good to him his lost property.

If it was a life (that was lost), the city and governor shall pay one mina[13] of silver to his people. . . .[14]

If a seignior rented a field for cultivation, but has not produced grain in the field, they shall prove that he did no work on the field and he shall give grain to the owner of the field on the basis of those adjoining it.

If he did not cultivate the field, but has neglected (it), he shall give grain to the owner of the field on the basis of those adjoining it; furthermore, the field which he neglected he shall break up with mattocks, harrow and return to the owner of the field. . . .

If a shepherd has not come to an agreement with the owner of a field to pasture sheep on the grass, but has pastured sheep on the field without the consent of the owner of the field, when the owner of the field harvests his field, the shepherd who pastured the sheep on the field without the consent of the owner of the field shall give in addition twenty *kur* of grain per eighteen *iku* to the owner of the field. . . .

If a merchant lent grain, wool, oil, or any goods at all to a trader to retail, the trader shall write down the value and pay (it) back to the merchant, with the trader obtaining a sealed receipt for the money which he pays to the merchant.

If the trader has been careless and so has not obtained a sealed receipt for the money which he paid to the merchant, the money with no sealed receipt may not be credited to the account.

---

[11]Cf. Exod. 21:16; Deut. 24:7.   [12]Cf. Exod. 22:2, 3a.

[13]A weight of about 500 grams, divided into 60 shekels.   [14]For this and the preceding law, cf. Deut. 21:1 ff.

If a trader borrowed money from a merchant and has then disputed (the fact) with his merchant, that merchant in the presence of god and witnesses shall prove that the trader borrowed the money and the trader shall pay to the merchant threefold the full amount of money that he borrowed.

When a merchant entrusted (something) to a trader and the trader has returned to his merchant whatever the merchant gave him, if the merchant has then disputed with him whatever the trader gave him, that trader shall prove it against the merchant in the presence of god and witnesses and the merchant shall pay to the trader sixfold whatever he received because he had a dispute with his trader.

If a woman wine seller, instead of receiving grain for the price of a drink, has received money by the large weight and so has made the value of the drink less than the value of the grain, they shall prove it against that wine seller[15] and throw her into the water.

If outlaws have congregated in the establishment of a woman wine seller and she has not arrested those outlaws and did not take them to the palace, that wine seller shall be put to death. . . .

If a seignior pointed the finger at a nun or the wife of a(nother) seignior, but has proved nothing, they shall drag that seignior into the presence of the judges and also cut off half his (hair).

If a seignior acquired a wife, but did not draw up the contracts for her, that woman is no wife.

If the wife of a seignior has been caught while lying with another man, they shall bind them and throw them into the water. If the husband[16] of the woman wishes to spare his wife, then the king in turn may spare his subject.[17]

If a seignior bound the (betrothed) wife of a(nother) seignior, who had had no intercourse with[18] a male and was still living in her father's house, and he has lain in her bosom and they have caught him, that seignior shall be put to death, while that woman shall go free.[19]

If a seignior's wife was accused by her husband,[20] but she was not caught while lying with another man, she shall make affirmation by god and return to her house.

If the finger was pointed at the wife of a seignior because of another man, but she has not been caught while lying with the other man, she shall throw herself into the river[21] for the sake of her husband.[22]

If a seignior was taken captive, but there was sufficient to live on in his house, his wife [shall not leave her house, but she shall take care of her person by not] entering [the house of another].[23]

If that woman did not take care of her person, but has entered the house of another, they shall prove it against that woman and throw her into the water.[24]

If the seignior was taken captive and there was not sufficient to live on in his house, his wife may enter the house of another, with that woman incurring no blame at all.

If, when a seignior was taken captive and there was not sufficient to live on in his house, his wife has then entered the house of another before his (return) and has borne children, (and) later her husband has returned and has reached his city, that woman shall return to her first husband, while the children shall go with their father.

If, when a seignior deserted his city and then ran away, his wife has entered the house of another after his (departure), if that seignior has returned and wishes to take back his wife, the wife of the fugitive shall not return to her husband because he scorned his city and ran away. . . .

---

[15]This has also been translated as "they shall bind that wine seller."
[16]Lit., "owner, master."   [17]Lit., "his slave." With this law cf. Deut. 22:22.   [18]Lit., "had not known."
[19]Cf. Deut. 22:23–27.   [20]Lit., "If with respect to a seignior's wife (*casus pendens*) her husband accused her."
[21]I.e., submit to the water ordeal, with the river as divine judge; cf. note 10.   [22]Cf. Num. 5:11–31.
[23]I.e., in order to live there as another man's wife.   [24]I.e., to be drowned.

If a seignior wishes to divorce his wife who did not bear him children, he shall give her money to the full amount of her marriage-price and he shall also make good to her the dowry which she brought from her father's house and then he may divorce her.

If there was no marriage-price, he shall give her one mina of silver as the divorce-settlement. If he is a peasant,[25] he shall give her one-third mina of silver.

If a seignior's wife, who was living in the house of the seignior, has made up her mind to leave in order that she may engage in business, thus neglecting her house (and) humiliating her husband, they shall prove it against her; and if her husband has then decided on her divorce, he may divorce her, with nothing to be given her as her divorce-settlement upon her departure.[26] If her husband has not decided on her divorce, her husband may marry another woman, with the former woman[27] living in the house of her husband like a maidservant.

If a woman so hated her husband that she has declared, "You may not have me," her record shall be investigated at her city council, and if she was careful and was not at fault, even though her husband has been going out and disparaging her greatly, that woman, without incurring any blame at all, may take her dowry and go off to her father's house.

If she was not careful, but was a gadabout, thus neglecting her house (and) humiliating her husband, they shall throw that woman into the water. . . .

When a seignior married a woman and a fever[28] has then seized her, if he has made up his mind to marry another, he may marry (her), without divorcing his wife whom the fever seized; she shall live in the house which he built and he shall continue to support her as long as she lives.

If that woman has refused to live in her husband's house, he shall make good her dowry to her which she brought from her father's house and then she may leave.

If a seignior, upon presenting a field, orchard, house, or goods to his wife, left a sealed document with her, her children may not enter a claim against her after (the death of) her husband, since the mother may give her inheritance to that son of hers whom she likes, (but) she may not give (it) to an outsider. . . .

If a seignior's wife has brought about the death of her husband because of another man, they shall impale that woman on stakes. . . .

If, when a seignior acquired a wife, she bore him children and that woman has then gone to (her) fate, her father may not lay claim to her dowry, since her dowry belongs to her children.

If a seignior acquired a wife and that woman has gone to (her) fate without providing him with children, if his father-in-law has then returned to him the marriage-price which that seignior brought to the house of his father-in-law, her husband may not lay claim to the dowry of that woman, since her dowry belongs to her father's house. . . .

If a member of the artisan class[29] took a son as a foster child and has taught him his handicraft, he may never be reclaimed. . . .

If a son has struck his father, they shall cut off his hand.[30]

---

[25]The word is *muškēnum.*   [26]Lit., "her journey," a noun in the adverbial accusative of manner.

[27]Lit., "that woman."   [28]The exact meaning of the word used here, *la'bum,* is not known.

[29]Lit., "the son of an artisan," where "son" is used in the technical sense of "belonging to the class of, species of," so common in the Semitic languages.

[30]Cf. Exod. 21:15. For the whole collection of laws dealing with personal injuries (laws 195–214), cf. the similiar collection in Exod. 21:12–27.

If a seignior has destroyed the eye of a member of the aristocracy,[31] they shall destroy his eye.[32]

If he has broken a(nother) seignior's bone, they shall break his bone.[33]

If he has destroyed the eye of a commoner or broken the bone of a commoner, he shall pay one mina of silver.

If he has destroyed the eye of a seignior's slave or broken the bone of a seignior's slave, he shall pay one-half his value.

If a seignior has knocked out a tooth of a seignior of his own rank, they shall knock out his tooth.[34]

If he has knocked out a commoner's tooth, he shall pay one-third mina of silver.

If a seignior has struck the cheek of a seignior who is superior to him, he shall be beaten sixty (times) with an oxtail whip in the assembly.

If a member of the aristocracy has struck the cheek of a(nother) member of the aristocracy who is of the same rank as[35] himself, he shall pay one mina of silver.

If a commoner has struck the cheek of a(nother) commoner, he shall pay ten shekels of silver.

If a seignior's slave has struck the cheek of a member of the aristocracy, they shall cut off his ear.

If a seignior has struck a(nother) seignior in a brawl and has inflicted an injury on him, that seignior shall swear, "I did not strike him deliberately";[36] and he shall also pay for the physician.

If he has died because of his blow, he shall swear (as before), and if it was a member of the aristocracy, he shall pay one-half mina of silver.

If it was a member of the commonalty, he shall pay one-third mina of silver.

If a seignior struck a(nother) seignior's daughter and has caused her to have a miscarriage,[37] he shall pay ten shekels of silver for her fetus.

If that woman has died, they shall put his daughter to death.

If by a blow he has caused a commoner's daughter to have a miscarriage, he shall pay five shekels of silver.

If that woman has died, he shall pay one-half mina of silver.

If he struck a seignior's female slave and has caused her to have a miscarriage, he shall pay two shekels of silver.

If that female slave has died, he shall pay one-third mina of silver. . . .

If an ox, when it was walking along the street, gored a seignior to death,[38] that case is not subject to claim.

---

[31]Lit., "the son of a man," with "son" used in the technical sense already explained and "man" clearly in the sense of "noble, aristocrat." Or it is possible that "son" here is to be taken in its regular sense to indicate a person younger than the assailant.

[32]Cf. Exod. 21:23–25.

[33]Cf. Lev. 24:19f.

[34]Cf. Deut. 19:21.

[35]Lit., "who is like."

[36]Lit., "while I was aware of (it)."

[37]Lit., "caused her to drop that of her womb (her fetus)." With this and the following five laws, cf. Exod. 21:22–25.

[38]Lit., "and has caused his death."

If a seignior's ox was a gorer and his city council made it known to him that it was a gorer, but he did not pad its horns (or) tie up his ox, and that ox gored to death a member of the aristocracy, he shall give one-half mina of silver.[39]

If it was a seignior's slave, he shall give one-third mina of silver. . . .

The Epilogue

The laws of justice, which Hammurabi, the efficient king, set up,
and by which he caused the land to take the right way and have good government.
I, Hammurabi, the perfect king,
was not careless (or) neglectful of the black-headed (people),
whom Enlil had presented to me,
(and) whose shepherding Marduk had committed to me;
I sought out peaceful regions for them;
I overcame grievous difficulties;
I caused light to rise on them.
With the mighty weapon which Zababa and Inanna entrusted to me,
with the insight that Enki allotted to me,
with the ability that Marduk gave me,
I rooted out the enemy above and below;
I made an end of war;
I promoted the welfare of the land;
I made the peoples rest in friendly habitations;
I did not let them have anyone to terrorize them.
The great gods called me,
so I became the beneficent shepherd whose scepter is righteous;
my benign shadow is spread over my city.
In my bosom I carried the peoples of the land of Sumer and Akkad;
they prospered under my protection;
I always governed them in peace;
I sheltered them in my wisdom.
In order that the strong might not oppress the weak,
that justice might be dealt the orphan (and) the widow,
in Babylon, the city whose head Anum and Enlil raised aloft,
in Esagila, the temple whose foundations stand firm like heaven and earth,
I wrote my precious words on my stela,
and in the presence of the statue of me, the king of justice,
I set (it) up in order to administer the law of the land,
to prescribe the ordinances of the land,
to give justice to the oppressed.

■ Discussion Questions

1. What do the Prologue and Epilogue indicate about the status of Mesopotamian rulers?
2. What values or ideals governing the code do you see underlying these excerpts?
3. What does the code reveal in particular about women's position in Mesopotamian society?
4. Historians traditionally view cities, formal political systems, knowledge of writing, and diverse crafts as defining features of civilization. Which of these features are reflected in the code?

---

[39]Cf. Exod. 21:28–36.

2. The Book of Exodus, Chapters 19–24
(c. Tenth to Sixth Centuries B.C.)

This excerpt from Exodus, the second book of the Hebrew Bible, exposes an important trait shared by Hammurabi's Code and other ancient laws: perpetrators of acts defined as unlawful must endure a specified punishment. In its account of the Hebrews' flight from Egypt in the thirteenth century B.C., the book of Exodus includes the first proclamation by their God, Yahweh, of the divine laws governing his relations with them and their relations with one another. The Hebrews agreed to follow the rules in exchange for God's promise to make them his chosen people. Although they did not yet deny the existence of other gods, their covenant was a crucial stage in the development of monotheism. The biblical story casts the Hebrew leader Moses in much the same role as that of Hammurabi in his code: both are agents of divine justice and protection.

19 On the third new moon after the people of Israel had gone forth out of the land of Egypt, on that day they came into the wilderness of Sinai. And when they set out from Rephidim and came into the wilderness of Sinai, they encamped in the wilderness; and there Israel encamped before the mountain. And Moses went up to God, and the LORD called him out of the mountain, saying, "Thus you shall say to the house of Jacob, and tell the people of Israel: You have seen what I did to the Egyptians, and how I bore you on eagles' wings and brought you to myself. Now therefore, if you will obey my voice and keep my covenant, you shall be my own possession among all peoples; for all the earth is mine, and you shall be to me a kingdom of priests and a holy nation. These are the words which you shall speak to the children of Israel."

So Moses came and called the elders of the people, and set before them all these words which the LORD had commanded him. And all the people answered together and said, "All that the LORD has spoken we will do." And Moses reported the words of the people to the LORD. And the LORD said to Moses, "Lo, I am coming to you in a thick cloud, that the people may hear when I speak with you, and may also believe you for ever."

Then Moses told the words of the people to the LORD. And the LORD said to Moses, "Go to the people and consecrate them today and tomorrow, and let them wash their garments, and be ready by the third day; for on the third day the LORD will come down upon Mount Sinai in the sight of all the people. And you shall set bounds for the people round about, saying, 'Take heed that you do not go up into the mountain or touch the border of it; whoever touches the mountain shall be put to death; no hand shall touch him, but he shall be stoned or shot; whether beast or man, he shall not live.' When the trumpet sounds a long blast, they shall come up to the mountain." So Moses went down from the mountain to the people, and consecrated the people; and they washed their garments. And he said to the people, "Be ready by the third day; do not go near a woman."

On the morning of the third day there were thunders and lightnings, and a thick cloud upon the mountain, and a very loud trumpet blast, so that all the people who were in the camp trembled. Then Moses brought the people out of the camp to meet God; and they took their stand at the foot of the mountain. And Mount Sinai was wrapped in smoke, because the LORD descended upon it in fire; and the smoke of it went up like the smoke of a kiln, and the whole mountain quaked greatly. And as the sound of the trumpet grew louder and louder, Moses spoke, and God answered him in thunder. And the LORD came down upon Mount Sinai, to the top of the mountain; and the LORD called Moses to the top of the mountain, and Moses went up. And

From *The Holy Bible, Authorized King James Version* (Oxford: Oxford University Press, 1960), 67–72.

the Lord said to Moses, "Go down and warn the people, lest they break through to the Lord to gaze and many of them perish. And also let the priests who come near to the Lord consecrate themselves, lest the Lord break out upon them." And Moses said to the Lord, "The people cannot come up to Mount Sinai; for thou thyself didst charge us, saying, 'Set bounds about the mountain, and consecrate it.'" And the Lord said to him, "Go down, and come up bringing Aaron with you; but do not let the priests and the people break through to come up to the Lord, lest he break out against them." So Moses went down to the people and told them.

20 And God spoke all these words, saying,

"I am the Lord your God, who brought you out of the land of Egypt, out of the house of bondage.

"You shall have no other gods before me.

"You shall not make yourself a graven image, or any likeness of anything that is in heaven above, or that is in the earth beneath, or that is in the water under the earth; you shall not bow down to them or serve them; for I the Lord your God am a jealous God, visiting the iniquity of the fathers upon the children to the third and the fourth generation of those who hate me, but showing steadfast love to thousands of those who love me and keep my commandments.

"You shall not take the name of the Lord your God in vain; for the Lord will not hold him guiltless who takes his name in vain.

"Remember the sabbath day, to keep it holy. Six days you shall labor, and do all your work; but the seventh day is a sabbath to the Lord your God; in it you shall not do any work, you, or your son, or your daughter, your manservant, or your maidservant, or your cattle, or the so-journer who is within your gates; for in six days the Lord made heaven and earth, the sea, and all that is in them, and rested the seventh day; therefore the Lord blessed the sabbath day and hallowed it.

"Honor your father and your mother, that your days may be long in the land which the Lord your God gives you.

"You shall not kill.

"You shall not commit adultery.

"You shall not steal.

"You shall not bear false witness against your neighbor.

"You shall not covet your neighbor's house; you shall not covet your neighbor's wife, or his manservant, or his maidservant, or his ox, or his ass, or anything that is your neighbor's."

Now when all the people perceived the thunderings and the lightnings and the sound of the trumpet and the mountain smoking, the people were afraid and trembled; and they stood afar off, and said to Moses, "You speak to us, and we will hear; but let not God speak to us, lest we die." And Moses said to the people, "Do not fear; for God has come to prove you, and that the fear of him may be before your eyes, that you may not sin."

And the people stood afar off, while Moses drew near to the thick cloud where God was. And the Lord said to Moses, "Thus you shall say to the people of Israel: 'You have seen for yourselves that I have talked with you from heaven. You shall not make gods of silver to be with me, nor shall you make for yourselves gods of gold. An altar of earth you shall make for me and sacrifice on it your burnt offerings and your peace offerings, your sheep and your oxen; in every place where I cause my name to be remembered I will come to you and bless you. And if you make me an altar of stone, you shall not build it of hewn stones; for if you wield your tool upon it you profane it. And you shall not go up by steps to my altar, that your nakedness be not exposed on it.'

21 "Now these are the ordinances which you shall set before them. When you buy a Hebrew slave, he shall serve six years, and in the seventh he shall go out free, for nothing. If he comes in single, he shall go out single; if he comes in married, then his wife shall go out with him. If his master gives him a wife and she bears him sons or daughters, the wife and her children shall be

her master's and he shall go out alone. But if the slave plainly says, 'I love my master, my wife, and my children; I will not go out free,' then his master shall bring him to God, and he shall bring him to the door or the doorpost; and his master shall bore his ear through with an awl; and he shall serve him for life.

"When a man sells his daughter as a slave, she shall not go out as the male slaves do. If she does not please her master, who has designated her for himself, then he shall let her be redeemed; he shall have no right to sell her to a foreign people, since he has dealt faithlessly with her. If he designates her for his son, he shall deal with her as with a daughter. If he takes another wife to himself, he shall not diminish her food, her clothing, or her marital rights. And if he does not do these three things for her, she shall go out for nothing, without payment of money.

"Whoever strikes a man so that he dies shall be put to death. But if he did not lie in wait for him, but God let him fall into his hand, then I will appoint for you a place to which he may flee. But if a man willfully attacks another to kill him treacherously, you shall take him from my altar, that he may die.

"Whoever strikes his father or his mother shall be put to death.

"Whoever steals a man, whether he sells him or is found in possession of him, shall be put to death.

"Whoever curses his father or his mother shall be put to death.

"When men quarrel and one strikes the other with a stone or with his fist and the man does not die but keeps his bed, then if the man rises again and walks abroad with his staff, he that struck him shall be clear; only he shall pay for the loss of his time, and shall have him thoroughly healed.

"When a man strikes his slave, male or female, with a rod and the slave dies under his hand, he shall be punished. But if the slave survives a day or two, he is not to be punished; for the slave is his money.

"When men strive together, and hurt a woman with child, so that there is a miscarriage, and yet no harm follows, the one who hurt her shall be fined, according as the woman's husband shall lay upon him; and he shall pay as the judges determine. If any harm follows, then you shall give life for life, eye for eye, tooth for tooth, hand for hand, foot for foot, burn for burn, wound for wound, stripe for stripe.

"When a man strikes the eye of his slave, male or female, and destroys it, he shall let the slave go free for the eye's sake. If he knocks out the tooth of his slave, male or female, he shall let the slave go free for the tooth's sake.

"When an ox gores a man or a woman to death, the ox shall be stoned, and its flesh shall not be eaten; but the owner of the ox shall be clear. But if the ox has been accustomed to gore in the past, and its owner has been warned but has not kept it in, and it kills a man or a woman, the ox shall be stoned, and its owner also shall be put to death. If a ransom is laid on him, then he shall give for the redemption of his life whatever is laid upon him. If it gores a man's son or daughter, he shall be dealt with according to this same rule. If the ox gores a slave, male or female, the owner shall give to their master thirty shekels of silver, and the ox shall be stoned.

"When a man leaves a pit open, or when a man digs a pit and does not cover it, and an ox or an ass falls into it, the owner of the pit shall make it good; he shall give money to its owner, and the dead beast shall be his.

"When one man's ox hurts another's, so that it dies, then they shall sell the live ox and divide the price of it; and the dead beast also they shall divide. Or if it is known that the ox has been accustomed to gore in the past, and its owner has not kept it in, he shall pay ox for ox, and the dead beast shall be his.

22 "If a man steals an ox or a sheep, and kills it or sells it, he shall pay five oxen for an ox, and four sheep for a sheep. He shall make restitution; if he has nothing, then he shall be sold for

his theft. If the stolen beast is found alive in his possession, whether it is an ox or an ass or a sheep, he shall pay double.

"If a thief is found breaking in, and is struck so that he dies, there shall be no bloodguilt for him; but if the sun has risen upon him, there shall be bloodguilt for him.

"When a man causes a field or vineyard to be grazed over, or lets his beast loose and it feeds in another man's field, he shall make restitution from the best in his own field and in his own vineyard.

"When fire breaks out and catches in thorns so that the stacked grain or the standing grain or the field is consumed, he that kindled the fire shall make full restitution.

"If a man delivers to his neighbor money or goods to keep, and it is stolen out of the man's house, then, if the thief is found, he shall pay double. If the thief is not found, the owner of the house shall come near to God, to show whether or not he has put his hand to his neighbor's goods.

"For every breach of trust, whether it is for ox, for ass, for sheep, for clothing, or for any kind of lost thing, of which one says, 'This is it,' the case of both parties shall come before God; he whom God shall condemn shall pay double to his neighbor.

"If a man delivers to his neighbor an ass or an ox or a sheep or any beast to keep, and it dies or is hurt or is driven away, without any one seeing it, an oath by the LORD shall be between them both to see whether he has not put his hand to his neighbor's property; and the owner shall accept the oath, and he shall not make restitution. But if it is stolen from him, he shall make restitution to its owner. If it is torn by beasts, let him bring it as evidence; he shall not make restitution for what has been torn.

"If a man borrows anything of his neighbor, and it is hurt or dies, the owner not being with it, he shall make full restitution. If the owner was with it, he shall not make restitution; if it was hired, it came for its hire.

"If a man seduces a virgin who is not betrothed, and lies with her, he shall give the marriage present for her, and make her his wife. If her father utterly refuses to give her to him, he shall pay money equivalent to the marriage present for virgins.

"You shall not permit a sorceress to live.

"Whoever lies with a beast shall be put to death.

"Whoever sacrifices to any god, save to the LORD only, shall be utterly destroyed.

"You shall not wrong a stranger or oppress him, for you were strangers in the land of Egypt. You shall not afflict any widow or orphan. If you do afflict them, and they cry out to me, I will surely hear their cry; and my wrath will burn, and I will kill you with the sword, and your wives shall become widows and your children fatherless.

"If you lend money to any of my people with you who is poor, you shall not be to him as a creditor, and you shall not exact interest from him. If ever you take your neighbor's garment in pledge, you shall restore it to him before the sun goes down; for that is his only covering, it is his mantle for his body; in what else shall he sleep? And if he cries to me, I will hear, for I am compassionate.

"You shall not revile God, nor curse a ruler of your people.

"You shall not delay to offer from the fulness of your harvest and from the outflow of your presses.

"The first-born of your sons you shall give to me. You shall do likewise with your oxen and with your sheep: seven days it shall be with its dam; on the eighth day you shall give it to me.

"You shall be men consecrated to me; therefore you shall not eat any flesh that is torn by beasts in the field; you shall cast it to the dogs.

23 "You shall not utter a false report. You shall not join hands with a wicked man, to be a malicious witness. You shall not follow a multitude to do evil; nor shall you bear witness in a

suit, turning aside after a multitude, so as to pervert justice; nor shall you be partial to a poor man in his suit.

"If you meet your enemy's ox or his ass going astray, you shall bring it back to him. If you see the ass of one who hates you lying under its burden, you shall refrain from leaving him with it, you shall help him to lift it up.

"You shall not pervert the justice due to your poor in his suit. Keep far from a false charge, and do not slay the innocent and righteous, for I will not acquit the wicked. And you shall take no bribe, for a bribe blinds the officials, and subverts the cause of those who are in the right.

"You shall not oppress a stranger; you know the heart of a stranger, for you were strangers in the land of Egypt.

"For six years you shall sow your land and gather in its yield; but the seventh year you shall let it rest and lie fallow, that the poor of your people may eat; and what they leave the wild beasts may eat. You shall do likewise with your vineyard, and with your olive orchard.

"Six days you shall do your work, but on the seventh day you shall rest; that your ox and your ass may have rest, and the son of your bondmaid, and the alien, may be refreshed. Take heed to all that I have said to you; and make no mention of the names of other gods, nor let such be heard out of your mouth.

"Three times in the year you shall keep a feast to me. You shall keep the feast of unleavened bread; as I commanded you, you shall eat unleavened bread for seven days at the appointed time in the month of Abib, for in it you came out of Egypt. None shall appear before me empty-handed. You shall keep the feast of harvest, of the first fruits of your labor, of what you sow in the field. You shall keep the feast of ingathering at the end of the year, when you gather in from the field the fruit of your labor. Three times in the year shall all your males appear before the LORD God.

"You shall not offer the blood of my sacrifice with leavened bread, or let the fat of my feast remain until the morning.

"The first of the first fruits of your ground you shall bring into the house of the LORD your God.

"You shall not boil a kid in its mother's milk.

"Behold, I send an angel before you, to guard you on the way and to bring you to the place which I have prepared. Give heed to him and hearken to his voice, do not rebel against him, for he will not pardon your transgression; for my name is in him.

"But if you hearken attentively to his voice and do all that I say, then I will be an enemy to your enemies and an adversary to your adversaries.

"When my angel goes before you, and brings you in to the Amorites, and the Hittites, and the Perizzites, and the Canaanites, the Hivites, and the Jebusites, and I blot them out, you shall not bow down to their gods, nor serve them, nor do according to their works, but you shall utterly overthrow them and break their pillars in pieces. You shall serve the LORD your God, and I will bless your bread and your water; and I will take sickness away from the midst of you. None shall cast her young or be barren in your land; I will fulfil the number of your days. I will send my terror before you, and will throw into confusion all the people against whom you shall come, and I will make all your enemies turn their backs to you. And I will send hornets before you, which shall drive out Hivite, Canaanite, and Hittite from before you. I will not drive them out from before you in one year, lest the land become desolate and the wild beasts multiply against you. Little by little I will drive them out from before you, until you are increased and possess the land. And I will set your bounds from the Red Sea to the sea of the Philistines, and from the wilderness to the Euphrates; for I will deliver the inhabitants of the land into your hand, and you shall drive them out before you. You shall make no covenant with them or with their gods. They shall not dwell in your land, lest they make you sin against me; for if you serve their gods, it will surely be a snare to you."

24 And he said to Moses, "Come up to the LORD, you and Aaron, Nadab, and Abihu, and seventy of the elders of Israel, and worship afar off. Moses alone shall come near to the LORD; but the others shall not come near, and the people shall not come up with him."

Moses came and told the people all the words of the LORD and all the ordinances; and all the people answered with one voice, and said, "All the words which the LORD has spoken we will do." And Moses wrote all the words of the LORD. And he rose early in the morning, and built an altar at the foot of the mountain, and twelve pillars, according to the twelve tribes of Israel. And he sent young men of the people of Israel, who offered burnt offerings and sacrificed peace offerings of oxen to the LORD. And Moses took half of the blood and put it in basins, and half of the blood he threw against the altar. Then he took the book of the covenant, and read it in the hearing of the people; and they said, "All that the LORD has spoken we will do, and we will be obedient." And Moses took the blood and threw it upon the people, and said, "Behold the blood of the covenant which the LORD has made with you in accordance with all these words."

Then Moses and Aaron, Nadab, and Abihu, and seventy of the elders of Israel went up, and they saw the God of Israel; and there was under his feet as it were a pavement of sapphire stone, like the very heaven for clearness. And he did not lay his hand on the chief men of the people of Israel; they beheld God, and ate and drank.

The LORD said to Moses, "Come up to me on the mountain, and wait there; and I will give you the tables of stone, with the law and the commandment, which I have written for their instruction." So Moses rose with his servant Joshua, and Moses went up into the mountain of God. And he said to the elders, "Tarry here for us, until we come to you again; and, behold, Aaron and Hur are with you; whoever has a cause, let him go to them."

Then Moses went up on the mountain, and the cloud covered the mountain. The glory of the LORD settled on Mount Sinai, and the cloud covered it six days; and on the seventh day he called to Moses out of the midst of the cloud. Now the appearance of the glory of the LORD was like a devouring fire on the top of the mountain in the sight of the people of Israel. And Moses entered the cloud, and went up on the mountain. And Moses was on the mountain forty days and forty nights.

■ Discussion Questions

1. What does God mean by his "covenant," and what is its significance for the Hebrew people?
2. What do the Ten Commandments and the other laws delineated in this selection reveal about the Hebrews' way of life?
3. How does the Book of Exodus cast light on the development of Hebrew monotheism?

3. Tyrtaeus of Sparta and Solon of Athens, *Poems* (Seventh to Sixth Centuries B.C.)

Among the most remarkable products of Greece's recovery from its Dark Age was the creation of a new social and political entity, the city-state. These poems elucidate the values shaping two of these communities, Sparta and Athens. The author of the first, Tyrtaeus of Sparta (originally from Athens, according to some ancient sources), was active when Sparta launched the Second Messenian War in

From *The Greek Polis,* ed. Arthur W. H. Adkins and Peter White, vol. 1, *University of Chicago Readings in Western Civilization* (Chicago: University of Chicago Press, 1986), 23–26.

the mid-sixth century B.C. His poem reveals the preeminent importance of military glory to the Spartans' communal identity. The author of the second work, the Athenian statesman Solon, emphasizes shared justice as the ideal basis of society. Democratic reforms instituted in the late sixth century B.C. transformed his vision into reality. Both poems were written in the elegiac meter, a style often used at the time to instruct the public.

TYRTAEUS

Beautiful-and-honorable [kalon] it is for a brave [agathos] warrior to die, fallen among the foremost fighters, in battle for his native land; but to leave his polis and rich fields and beg—that is most painful of all, as he wanders with his dear mother and aged father, his small children and wedded wife. Detested he will be in the eyes of all those to whom he comes, constrained by need and hateful poverty. He shames his birth and belies his glorious appearance; dishonor and misery are his companions. If no account is taken of a warrior who is a wanderer, if there is no respect for him or his family in the future, then let us fight with all our hearts for this land and die for our children, no longer hesitating to risk our lives. Young men, stand firm beside each other and fight. Do not begin shameful flight or fear. Rather create a mighty, valorous spirit in your breasts, and do not show love for your lives when you are fighting with warriors. Do not flee, abandoning the older men, whose knees are no longer nimble. For shameful-and-ugly [aischron] it is for an older warrior to fall among the foremost fighters and lie out ahead of the young men—a man whose hair is already white and his beard gray—as he breathes out his valorous spirit in the dust, holding his bloody genitals in his own hands, his body laid bare. Shameful-and-ugly [aischra] is this to the eyes, and a cause of resentment to look upon. But to the young men all is seemly, while the glorious flower of lovely youth is theirs. To men the young man is admirable to look upon, and to women lovable while he lives, and beautiful-and-honorable when he lies among the foremost fighters. So let a man take a firm stance and stand fast, with both feet planted upon the ground, biting his lip with his teeth.

SOLON

Our polis will never perish as a result of the apportionment of Zeus and the intentions of the blessed immortal gods; for such a great-hearted guardian, daughter of a mighty father, Pallas Athena, holds her hands in protection over it. But the citizens themselves, persuaded by wealth, are willing to destroy a mighty polis by their follies, and the mind of the leaders of the people is unjust. For the leaders it is prepared that they should suffer many griefs as a result of their great hubris. For they do not know how to restrain the excesses sprung from satiety or how to discipline in peaceful quiet the present merriments of the feast. . . . They grow wealthy, relying on unjust deeds. . . . Sparing neither sacred nor public property, they steal by snatching, one from one source, one from another, nor do they reverence the august abode where justice is set, she who in silence knows what is happening, and what has occurred in the past, and in time at all events comes to exact requital.

This is now coming upon the whole polis as an inescapable wound, and it comes swiftly to grievous slavery, which stirs up civic strife among the people and sleeping [civil?] war, which destroys the lovely prime of many. For by the action of enemies a much-beloved polis is swiftly brought to hardship in meetings by those who wrong their friends. These woes go to and fro in the land; and, of the poor, many arrive at another land, sold and bound in unseemly fetters. . . . Thus a woe of the people comes home to each individual, and the courtyard gates are no longer willing to shut it out, but it leaps over the high fence and finds a man nonetheless, even if he is in flight in a corner of his chamber.

These things my heart bids me tell the Athenians: that *dusnomia*[1] causes very many woes to a polis. *Eunomia* shows forth everything orderly and appropriate and often puts shackles on the unjust; she makes the rough smooth, ends the insolence of satiety, dims hubris, and dries up the growing blossoms of infatuation, straightens crooked judgments, and tames proud deeds; she ends the deeds of civil conflict, ends the wrath of grievous strife, and all things among mankind are appropriate and prudent under her rule.

▪ Discussion Questions

1. What does Tyrtaeus reveal about the values and comportment that Spartan hoplites were expected to uphold?
2. How does Tyrtaeus describe warriors who do not live up to these expectations? What do his criticisms reveal about Spartan culture?
3. Why does Solon think Athenian citizens pose a threat to the polis?
4. What message does Solon seek to convey to them in this poem?

4. Sappho of Lesbos, *Poems*   (Sixth Century B.C.)

The poetry of Sappho of Lesbos allows us the opportunity to hear a woman's voice emanating from Greece during the Archaic Age. Although little is known about her life, her legacy endures in her lyric poems, almost all of which have survived only in fragments. In both their rhythmic form and emphasis on inner, personal emotions, her poems reflect the cultural innovation characteristic of the period. As these selections reveal, Sappho used her poetry to express her innermost feelings of love and longing as a woman living in a male-dominated society. Her poems were revered throughout the ancient world, and they established an influential precedent for later lyric poets.

To Aphrodite (Fr. 1. G)

Aphrodite on your intricate throne, immortal, daughter of Zeus, weaver of plots, I beg you, do not tame me with pain or my heart with anguish

but come here, as once before when I asked you, you heard my words from afar and listened, and left your father's golden house and came

you yoked your chariot, and lovely swift sparrows brought you, fast whirling over the dark earth from heaven through the midst of the bright air

---

[1] *Eunomia* and *dusnomia* cannot be neatly rendered. *Nomos*, at least in somewhat later Greek, can mean "law," and the words have been supposed to characterize states of affairs in which the laws are good and bad, respectively, or states of affairs in which the laws are obeyed or disobeyed. But *eunomia* and *dusnomia* are derived from the root *nem*, "to apportion," and can readily mean, respectively, states of affairs in which everything is shared out well or badly—a sense that is not irrelevant to Solon's political program. None of the possible senses needs to be excluded: The words were as imprecise in Solon's day as they appear to us. They are political slogans and, like many political slogans since, combine a high emotive charge with a vague denotation.

From *Women's Life in Greece and Rome,* ed. Mary R. Lefkowitz and Maureen B. Fant, 2d ed. (Baltimore: Johns Hopkins University Press, 1992), 2–4.

and soon they arrived. And you, O blessed goddess, smiled with your immortal face and asked what was wrong with me, and why did I call now,

and what did I most want in my maddened heart to have for myself. "Whom now am I to persuade to your love, who, Sappho, has done you wrong? For if she flees, soon she'll pursue you, and if she won't take gifts, soon she'll give them, and if she won't love, soon she will love you, even if she doesn't want to."

Come to me now again, release me from my cruel anxiety, accomplish all that my heart wants accomplished. You yourself join my battle.

WHEN I LOOK AT YOU (FR. 31. G)

The man seems to me strong as a god, the man who sits across from you and listens to your sweet talk nearby

and your lovely laughter—which, when I hear it, strikes fear in the heart in my breast. For whenever I glance at you, it seems that I can say nothing at all

but my tongue is broken in silence, and that instant a light fire rushes beneath my skin, I can no longer see anything in my eyes and my ears are thundering,

and cold sweat pours down me, and shuddering grasps me all over, and I am greener than grass, and I seem to myself to be little short of death

But all is endurable, since even a poor man . . .

ANACTORIA (FR. 16. G)

Some would say an army of cavalry, others of infantry, others of ships, is the fairest thing on the dark earth, but I say it's whatever you're in love with

It's completely easy to make this clear to everyone, for Helen, who far surpassed other people in beauty, left behind the most aristocratic

of husbands and went to Troy. She sailed away, and did not remember at all her daughter or her beloved parents, but [Aphrodite] took her aside

(3 lines missing) which makes me remember Anactoria who is no longer near,

her lovely step and the brilliant glancing of her face I would rather see than the Lydians' chariots or their infantry fighting in all their armour.

PARTING (FR. 94. G)

"The truth is, I wish I were dead." She left me, weeping often, and she said this, "Oh what a cruel fate is ours, Sappho, yes, I leave you against my will."

And I answered her: "Farewell, go and remember me, for you know how we cared for you.

"If you do remember, I want to remind you . . . and were happy . . . of violets . . . you set beside me and with woven garlands made of flowers around your soft neck

"and with perfume, royal, rich . . . you anointed yourself and on soft beds you would drive out your passion

"and then . . . sanctuary . . . was . . . from which we were away . . ."

REMEMBERING THE GIRL ATTHIS (FR. 96. G)

... you, like a goddess renowned, in your song she took most joy. Now she is unique among Lydian women, as the moon once the sun sets

stands out among all the stars, and her light grasps both the salt sea and the flowering meadows

and fair dew flows forth, and soft roses and chervil and fragrant melilot bloom.

Often as she goes out, she remembers gentle Atthis, and her tender heart is eaten by grief ...

THE WEDDING OF HECTOR AND ANDROMACHE (FR. 44. G)

"... Hector and his comrades are bringing a girl with dark eyes from holy Thebes and ... Plakia, soft Andromache in their ships across the salt sea; many curved bands of gold and purple robes and intricate playthings, countless silver cups and ivory." So he spoke. And [Hector's] beloved father quickly got up, and the story went out to his friends throughout the city [of Troy] with its wide dancing places. Then the Trojan women led mules to wheeled carts and a crowd of women came out, and also of . . . -ankled maidens, and separately the daughters of Priam and men brought horses with chariots (*unknown number of lines missing*) . . . and the sweet-sounding *aulos* was mixed with the noise of castanets, and the maidens sang a sacred song and the holy sound reached heaven ... bowls and goblets ... perfume and cassia and incense were mixed and all the older women shouted out, and all the men cried out a fair loud song, calling on Paean, the far-shooter, the lyre player, to sing of Hector and Andromache, who were like gods ...

▪ Discussion Questions

1. Do you think that Sappho's status as a woman shaped the content of her poetry? Who seem to be the principal objects of her affections?
2. What do Sappho's poems suggest about Greek notions of love at the time?
3. Aside from aspects of love, what else do the images and themes used by Sappho reveal about Greek society?

CHAPTER 2
The Greek Golden Age, c. 500–400 B.C.

In the fifth century B.C., Athens entered a period of extraordinary prosperity and achievement. Its economy was booming and its culture flourishing while at the same time its male citizens developed the first democracy in history. Under their guidance, Athens became the leader of the Greek world. As the first document demonstrates, a woman's status was inextricably linked to her roles as wife and mother. To put either in jeopardy threatened the very foundations of Athenian society. The last two documents elucidate the dynamism of the times in a variety of related arenas, all of which attest to Athens's enduring legacy to Western civilization. They also reveal that even as innovation fueled the city-state's rise to glory, the pull of traditional beliefs remained strong. Such beliefs were especially influential in demarcating the boundaries of the lives of Athenian women.

5. Lysias, *A Husband Speaks in His Own Defense* (c. 400 B.C.)

In contrast to the trial of Socrates (Document 6), that of an ordinary Athenian illuminates the mundane aspects of life in fifth-century B.C. Athens. It also indicates that despite the momentous changes of the age, ancient traditions retained their grip on much of society, especially women. The testimony is that of a man named Euphiletus who was put on trial for murdering his wife's lover. He presented the following arguments in his own defense, as prepared by the speechwriter Lysias (c. 440–380 B.C.). The outcome of the trial is unknown. Nevertheless, Euphiletus's testimony opens a window onto domestic routines at the time and the ways in which they were expected to serve as the anchor of a woman's identity and her husband's honor.

I would give a great deal, members of the jury, to find you, as judges of this case, taking the same attitude towards me as you would adopt towards your own behaviour in similar circumstances. I am sure that if you felt about others in the same way as you did about yourselves, not one of you would fail to be angered by these deeds, and all of you would consider the punishment a small one for those guilty of such conduct.

Moreover, the same opinion would be found prevailing not only among you, but everywhere throughout Greece. This is the one crime for which, under any government, democratic or exclusive, equal satisfaction is granted to the meanest against the mightiest, so that the least of them receives the same justice as the most exalted. Such is the detestation, members of the jury, in which this outrage is held by all mankind.

From *The Murder of Herodes and Other Trials from the Athenian Law Courts,* ed. Kathleen Freeman (London: MacDonald & Co., 1946), 43–52.

Concerning the severity of the penalty, therefore, you are, I imagine, all of the same opinion: not one of you is so easy-going as to believe that those guilty of such great offences should obtain pardon, or are deserving of a light penalty. What I have to prove, I take it, is just this: that Eratosthenes seduced my wife, and that in corrupting her he brought shame upon my children and outrage upon me, by entering my home; that there was no other enmity between him and me except this; and that I did not commit this act for the sake of money, in order to rise from poverty to wealth, nor for any other advantage except the satisfaction allowed by law.

I shall expound my case to you in full from the beginning, omitting nothing and telling the truth. In this alone lies my salvation, I imagine—if I can explain to you everything that happened.

Members of the jury: when I decided to marry and had brought a wife home, at first my attitude towards her was this: I did not wish to annoy her, but neither was she to have too much of her own way. I watched her as well as I could, and kept an eye on her as was proper. But later, after my child had been born, I came to trust her, and I handed all my possessions over to her, believing that this was the greatest possible proof of affection.

Well, members of the jury, in the beginning she was the best of women. She was a clever housewife, economical and exact in her management of everything. But then, my mother died; and her death has proved to be the source of all my troubles, because it was when my wife went to the funeral that this man Eratosthenes saw her; and as time went on, he was able to seduce her. He kept a look out for our maid who goes to market; and approaching her with his suggestions, he succeeded in corrupting her mistress.

Now first of all, gentlemen, I must explain that I have a small house which is divided into two—the men's quarters and the women's—each having the same space, the women upstairs and the men downstairs.

After the birth of my child, his mother nursed him; but I did not want her to run the risk of going downstairs every time she had to give him a bath, so I myself took over the upper storey, and let the women have the ground floor. And so it came about that by this time it was quite customary for my wife often to go downstairs and sleep with the child, so that she could give him the breast and stop him from crying.

This went on for a long while, and I had not the slightest suspicion. On the contrary, I was in such a fool's paradise that I believed my wife to be the chastest woman in all the city.

Time passed, gentlemen. One day, when I had come home unexpectedly from the country, after dinner, the child began crying and complaining. Actually it was the maid who was pinching him on purpose to make him behave so, because—as I found out later—this man was in the house.

Well, I told my wife to go and feed the child, to stop his crying. But at first she refused, pretending that she was so glad to see me back after my long absence. At last I began to get annoyed, and I insisted on her going.

"Oh, yes!" she said. "To leave *you* alone with the maid up here! You mauled her about before, when you were drunk!"

I laughed. She got up, went out, closed the door—pretending that it was a joke—and locked it. As for me, I thought no harm of all this, and I had not the slightest suspicion. I went to sleep, glad to do so after my journey from the country.

Towards morning, she returned and unlocked the door.

I asked her why the doors had been creaking during the night. She explained that the lamp beside the baby had gone out, and that she had then gone to get a light from the neighbours.

I said no more. I thought it really was so. But it did seem to me, members of the jury, that she had done up her face with cosmetics, in spite of the fact that her brother had died only a month before. Still, even so, I said nothing about it. I just went off, without a word.

After this, members of the jury, an interval elapsed, during which my injuries had progressed, leaving me far behind. Then, one day, I was approached by an old hag. She had been sent by a woman—Eratosthenes' previous mistress, as I found out later. This woman, furious because he no longer came to see her as before, had been on the look-out until she had discovered the reason. The old crone, therefore, had come and was lying in wait for me near my house.

"Euphiletus," she said, "please don't think that my approaching you is in any way due to a wish to interfere. The fact is, the man who is wronging you and your wife is an enemy of ours. Now if you catch the woman who does your shopping and works for you, and put her through an examination, you will discover all. The culprit," she added, "is Eratosthenes from Oea. Your wife is not the only one he has seduced—there are plenty of others. It's his profession."

With these words, members of the jury, she went off.

At once I was overwhelmed. Everything rushed into my mind, and I was filled with suspicion. I reflected how I had been locked into the bedroom. I remembered how on that night the middle and outer doors had creaked, a thing that had never happened before; and how I had had the idea that my wife's face was rouged. All these things rushed into my mind, and I was filled with suspicion.

I went back home, and told the servant to come with me to market. I took her instead to the house of one of my friends; and there I informed her that I had discovered all that was going on in my house.

"As for you," I said, "two courses are open to you: either to be flogged and sent to the treadmill, and never be released from a life of utter misery; or to confess the whole truth and suffer no punishment, but win pardon from me for your wrong-doing. Tell me no lies. Speak the whole truth."

At first she tried denial, and told me that I could do as I pleased—she knew nothing. But when I named Eratosthenes to her face, and said that he was the man who had been visiting my wife, she was dumbfounded, thinking that I had found out everything exactly. And then at last, falling at my feet and exacting a promise from me that no harm should be done to her, she denounced the villain. She described how he had first approached her after the funeral, and then how in the end she had passed the message on, and in course of time my wife had been overpersuaded. She explained the way in which he had contrived to get into the house, and how when I was in the country my wife had gone to a religious service with this man's mother, and everything else that had happened. She recounted it all exactly.

When she had told all, I said:

"See to it that nobody gets to know of this; otherwise the promise I made you will not hold good. And furthermore, I expect you to show me this actually happening. I have no use for words. I want the *fact* to be exhibited, if it really is so."

She agreed to do this.

Four or five days then elapsed, as I shall prove to you by important evidence. But before I do so, I wish to narrate the events of the last day.

I had a friend and relative named Sôstratus. He was coming home from the country after sunset when I met him. I knew that as he had got back so late, he would not find any of his own people at home; so I asked him to dine with me. We went home to my place, and going upstairs to the upper storey, we had dinner there. When he felt restored, he went off; and I went to bed.

Then, members of the jury, Eratosthenes made his entry; and the maid wakened me and told me that he was in the house.

I told her to watch the door; and going downstairs, I slipped out noiselessly.

I went to the houses of one man after another. Some I found at home; others, I was told, were out of town. So collecting as many as I could of those who were there, I went back. We procured torches from the shop near by, and entered my house. The door had been left open by arrangement with the maid.

We forced the bedroom door. The first of us to enter saw him still lying beside my wife. Those who followed saw him standing naked on the bed.

I knocked him down, members of the jury, with one blow. I then twisted his hands behind his back and tied them. And then I asked him why he was committing this crime against me, of breaking into my house.

He answered that he admitted his guilt; but he begged and besought me not to kill him— to accept a money-payment instead.

But I replied:

"It is not I who shall be killing you, but the law of the State, which you, in transgressing, have valued less highly than your own pleasures. You have preferred to commit this great crime against my wife and my children, rather than to obey the law and be of decent behaviour."

Thus, members of the jury, this man met the fate which the laws prescribe for wrong-doers of his kind.

Eratosthenes was not seized in the street and carried off, nor had he taken refuge at the altar, as the prosecution alleges. The facts do not admit of it: he was struck in the bedroom, he fell at once, and I bound his hands behind his back. There were so many present that he could not possibly escape through their midst, since he had neither steel nor wood nor any other weapon with which he could have defended himself against all those who had entered the room.

No, members of the jury: you know as well as I do how wrong-doers will not admit that their adversaries are speaking the truth, and attempt by lies and trickery of other kinds to excite the anger of the hearers against those whose acts are in accordance with Justice.

(*To the Clerk of the Court*):

Read the Law.

(*The Law of Solon is read, that an adulterer may be put to death by the man who catches him.*)

He made no denial, members of the jury. He admitted his guilt, and begged and implored that he should not be put to death, offering to pay compensation. But I would not accept his estimate. I preferred to accord a higher authority to the law of the State, and I took that satisfaction which you, because you thought it the most just, have decreed for those who commit such offences.

Witnesses to the preceding, kindly step up.

(*The witnesses come to the front of the Court, and the Clerk reads their depositions. When the Clerk has finished reading, and the witnesses have agreed that the depositions are correct, the defendant again addresses the Clerk*):

Now please read this further law from the pillar of the Court of the Areopagus:

(*The Clerk reads another version of Solon's law, as recorded on the pillar of the Areopagus Court.*)

You hear, members of the jury, how it is expressly decreed by the Court of the Areopagus itself, which both traditionally and in your own day has been granted the right to try cases of murder, that no person shall be found guilty of murder who catches an adulterer with his wife and inflicts this punishment. The Lawgiver was so strongly convinced of the justice of these provisions in the case of married women, that he applied them also to concubines, who are of less importance. Yet obviously, if he had known of any greater punishment than this for cases where married women are concerned, he would have provided it. But in fact, as it was impossible for him to invent any more severe penalty for corruption of wives, he decided to provide the same punishment as in the case of concubines.

(To the Clerk of the Court):

Please read me this Law also.

(The Clerk reads out further clauses from Solon's laws on rape.)

You hear, members of the jury, how the Lawgiver ordains that if anyone debauch by force a free man or boy, the fine shall be double that decreed in the case of a slave. If anyone debauch a woman—in which case it is *permitted* to kill him—he shall be liable to the same fine. Thus, members of the jury, the Lawgiver considered violators deserving of a lesser penalty than seducers: for the latter he provided the death-penalty; for the former, the doubled fine. His idea was that those who use force are loathed by the persons violated, whereas those who have got their way by persuasion corrupt women's minds, in such a way as to make other men's wives more attached to themselves than to their husbands, so that the whole house is in their power, and it is uncertain who is the children's father, the husband or the lover. These considerations caused the Lawgiver to affix death as the penalty for seduction.

And so, members of the jury, in my case the laws not only hold me innocent, but actually order me to take this satisfaction; but it depends on you whether they are to be effective or of no moment. The reason, in my opinion, why all States lay down laws is in order that, whenever we are in doubt on any point, we can refer to these laws and find out our duty. And therefore it is the laws which in such cases enjoin upon the injured party to exact this penalty. I exhort you to show yourselves in agreement with them; otherwise you will be granting such impunity to adulterers that you will encourage even burglars to declare themselves adulterers, in the knowledge that if they allege this reason for their action and plead that this was their purpose in entering other men's houses, no one will lay a finger on them. They will all realize that they need not bother about the law on adultery, but need only fear your verdict, since this is the supreme authority in the State.

Consider, members of the jury, their accusation that it was I who on that day told the maid to fetch the young man. In my opinion, gentlemen, I should have been justified in using any means to catch the seducer of my wife. If there had been only words spoken and no actual offence, I should have been doing wrong; but when by that time they had gone to all lengths and he had often gained entry into my house, I consider that I should have been within my rights whatever means I employ to catch him. But observe that this allegation of the prosecution is also false. You can easily convince yourselves by considering the following:

I have already told you how Sôstratus, an intimate friend of mine, met me coming in from the country around sunset, and dined with me, and when he felt refreshed, went off. Now in the first place, gentlemen, ask yourselves whether, if on that night I had had designs on Eratosthenes, it would have been better for me that Sôstratus should dine elsewhere, or that I should take a guest home with me to dinner. Surely in the latter circumstances Eratosthenes would have been less inclined to venture into the house. Further, does it seem to you probable that I would have let my guest go, and been left alone, without company? Would I not rather have urged him to stay, so that he could help me to punish the adulterer?

Again, gentlemen, does it not seem to you probable that I would have passed the word round among my friends during the daytime, and told them to assemble at the house of one of my friends who lived nearest, rather than have started to run round at night, as soon as I found out, without knowing whom I should find at home and whom away? Actually, I called for Harmodius and certain others who were out of town—I did not know it—and others, I found, were not at home, so I went along taking with me whomever I could. But if I had known beforehand, does it not seem to you probable that I would have arranged for servants and passed the word round to my friends, so that I myself could go in with the maximum of safety—

for how did I know whether he too might not have had a dagger or something?—and also in order that I might exact the penalty in the presence of the greatest number of witnesses? But in fact, since I knew nothing of what was going to happen on that night, I took with me whomever I could get.

Witnesses to the preceding, please step up.

(Further witnesses come forward, and confirm their evidence as read out by the Clerk.)

You have heard the witnesses, members of the jury. Now consider the case further in your own minds, inquiring whether there had ever existed between Eratosthenes and myself any other enmity but this. You will find none. He never brought any malicious charge against me, nor tried to secure my banishment, nor prosecuted me in any private suit. Neither had he knowledge of any crime of which I feared the revelation, so that I desired to kill him; nor by carrying out this act did I hope to gain money. So far from ever having had any dispute with him, or drunken brawl, or any other quarrel, I had never even set eyes on the man before that night. What possible object could I have had, therefore, in running so great a risk, except that I had suffered the greatest of all injuries at his hands? Again, would I myself have called in witnesses to my crime, when it was possible for me, if I desired to murder him without justification, to have had no confidants?

It is my belief, members of the jury, that this punishment was inflicted not in my own interests, but in those of the whole community. Such villains, seeing the rewards which await their crimes, will be less ready to commit offences against others if they see that you too hold the same opinion of them. Otherwise it would be far better to wipe out the existing laws and make different ones, which will penalise those who keep guard over their own wives, and grant full immunity to those who criminally pursue them. This would be a far more just procedure than to set a trap for citizens by means of the laws, which urge the man who catches an adulterer to do with him whatever he will, and yet allow the injured party to undergo a trial far more perilous than that which faces the law-breaker who seduces other men's wives. Of this, I am an example—I, who now stand in danger of losing life, property, everything, because I have obeyed the laws of the State.

■ Discussion Questions

1. What does Euphiletus's testimony reveal about the role women were expected to play in Athenian society?
2. How does the husband justify his actions?
3. Why does the husband feel that adultery is especially worthy of severe punishment?

6. Plato, *The Apology of Socrates*   (399 B.C.)

Political innovation was not the only distinctive feature of fifth-century B.C. Athens. Socrates' views on ethics and morality challenged conventional values while steering Greek philosophy in new directions. Unlike the sophists, Socrates (469–399 B.C.) offered no classes and did not write his ideas down. He relied instead on conversation and critical questioning to draw people into his way of thinking. In this document, we hear Socrates speaking for himself before a jury as described by his pupil Plato.

From *Dialogues of Plato*, trans. Benjamin Jowett, ed. J. D. Kaplan (New York: Pocket Books, 1950), 5–14, 21–24, 39–40.

At the time, Socrates was on trial for impiety, and he spoke these words to convince his fellow citizens of his innocence. His efforts were in vain; he was convicted and sentenced to death.

How you, O Athenians, have been affected by my accusers, I cannot tell; but I know that they almost made me forget who I was—so persuasively did they speak; and yet they have hardly uttered a word of truth. But of the many falsehoods told by them, there was one which quite amazed me;—I mean when they said that you should be upon your guard and not allow yourselves to be deceived by the force of my eloquence. To say this, when they were certain to be detected as soon as I opened my lips and proved myself to be anything but a great speaker, did indeed appear to me most shameless—unless by the force of eloquence they mean the force of truth; for if such is their meaning, I admit that I am eloquent. But in how different a way from theirs! Well, as I was saying, they have scarcely spoken the truth at all; but from me you shall hear the whole truth: not, however, delivered after their manner in a set oration duly ornamented with words and phrases. No, by heaven! but I shall use the words and arguments which occur to me at the moment; for I am confident in the justice of my cause. . . .

I will begin at the beginning, and ask what is the accusation which has given rise to the slander of me, and in fact has encouraged Meletus to prefer this charge against me. Well, what do the slanderers say? They shall be my prosecutors, and I will sum up their words in an affidavit: "Socrates is an evildoer, and a curious person, who searches into things under the earth and in heaven, and he makes the worse appear the better cause; and he teaches the aforesaid doctrines to others." Such is the nature of the accusation: it is just what you have yourselves seen in the comedy of Aristophanes, who has introduced a man whom he calls Socrates, going about and saying that he walks in air, and talking a deal of nonsense concerning matters of which I do not pretend to know either much or little—not that I mean to speak disparagingly of any one who is a student of natural philosophy. I should be very sorry if Meletus could bring so grave a charge against me. But the simple truth is, O Athenians, that I have nothing to do with physical speculations. Very many of those here present are witnesses to the truth of this, and to them I appeal. . . .

Men of Athens, this reputation of mine has come of a certain sort of wisdom which I possess. If you ask me what kind of wisdom, I reply, wisdom such as may perhaps be attained by man, for to that extent I am inclined to believe that I am wise; whereas the persons of whom I was speaking have a superhuman wisdom, which I may fail to describe, because I have it not myself; and he who says that I have, speaks falsely, and is taking away my character. And here, O men of Athens, I must beg you not to interrupt me, even if I seem to say something extravagant. For the word which I will speak is not mine. I will refer you to a witness who is worthy of credit; that witness shall be the God of Delphi—he will tell you about my wisdom, if I have any, and of what sort it is. You must have known Chaerephon; he was early a friend of mine, and also a friend of yours, for he shared in the recent exile of the people, and returned with you. Well, Chaerephon, as you know, was very impetuous in all his doings, and he went to Delphi and boldly asked the oracle to tell him whether—as I was saying, I must beg you not to interrupt—he asked the oracle to tell him whether any one was wiser than I was, and the Pythian prophetess answered, that there was no man wiser. Chaerephon is dead himself; but his brother, who is in court, will confirm the truth of what I am saying.

Why do I mention this? Because I am going to explain to you why I have such an evil name. When I heard the answer, I said to myself, What can the God mean? and what is the interpretation of his riddle? for I know that I have no wisdom, small or great. What then can he mean when he says that I am the wisest of men? And yet he is a god, and cannot lie; that would be against his nature. After long consideration, I thought of a method of trying the question. I reflected that if I could only find a man wiser than myself, then I might go to the god with a refutation in my hand. I should say to him, "Here is a man who is wiser than I am; but you said that

I was the wisest." Accordingly I went to one who had the reputation of wisdom, and observed him—his name I need not mention; he was a politician whom I selected for examination—and the result was as follows: When I began to talk with him, I could not help thinking that he was not really wise, although he was thought wise by many, and still wiser by himself; and thereupon I tried to explain to him that he thought himself wise, but was not really wise; and the consequence was that he hated me, and his enmity was shared by several who were present and heard me. So I left him, saying to myself, as I went away: Well, although I do not suppose that either of us knows anything really beautiful and good, I am better off than he is,—for he knows nothing, and thinks that he knows; I neither know nor think that I know. In this latter particular, then, I seem to have slightly the advantage of him. Then I went to another who had still higher pretensions to wisdom, and my conclusion was exactly the same. Whereupon I made another enemy of him, and of many others besides him.

Then I went to one man after another, being not unconscious of the enmity which I provoked, and I lamented and feared this: but necessity was laid upon me,—the word of God, I thought, ought to be considered first. And I said to myself, Go I must to all who appear to know, and find out the meaning of the oracle. And I swear to you, Athenians, by the dog I swear!— for I must tell you the truth—the result of my mission was just this: I found that the men most in repute were all but the most foolish; and that others less esteemed were really wiser and better. I will tell you the tale of my wanderings and of the "Herculean" labours, as I may call them, which I endured only to find at last the oracle irrefutable. After the politicians, I went to the poets; tragic, dithyrambic, and all sorts. And there, I said to myself, you will be instantly detected; now you will find out that you are more ignorant than they are. Accordingly I took them some of the most elaborate passages in their own writings, and asked what was the meaning of them— thinking that they would teach me something. Will you believe me? I am almost ashamed to confess the truth, but I must say that there is hardly a person present who would not have talked better about their poetry than they did themselves. Then I knew that not by wisdom do poets write poetry, but by a sort of genius and inspiration; they are like diviners or soothsayers who also say many fine things, but do not understand the meaning of them. The poets appeared to me to be much in the same case; and I further observed that upon the strength of their poetry they believed themselves to be the wisest of men in other things in which they were not wise. So I departed, conceiving myself to be superior to them for the same reason that I was superior to the politicians.

At last I went to the artisans, I was conscious that I knew nothing at all, as I may say, and I was sure that they knew many fine things; and here I was not mistaken, for they did know many things of which I was ignorant, and in this they certainly were wiser than I was. But I observed that even the good artisans fell into the same error as the poets;—because they were good workmen they thought that they also knew all sorts of high matters, and this defect in them overshadowed their wisdom; and therefore I asked myself on behalf of the oracle, whether I would like to be as I was, neither having their knowledge nor their ignorance, or like them in both; and I made answer to myself and to the oracle that I was better off as I was.

This inquisition has led to my having many enemies of the worst and most dangerous kind, and has given occasion also to many calumnies. And I am called wise, for my hearers always imagine that I myself possess the wisdom which I find wanting in others: but the truth is, O men of Athens, that God only is wise; and by his answer he intends to show that the wisdom of men is worth little or nothing; he is not speaking of Socrates, he is only using my name by way of illustration, as if he said, He, O men, is the wisest, who, like Socrates, knows that his wisdom is in truth worth nothing. And so I go about the world obedient to the god, and search and make enquiry into the wisdom of any one, whether citizen or stranger, who appears to be wise; and if he is not wise, then in vindication of the oracle I show him that he is not wise; and my occupation quite absorbs me, and I have no time to give either to any public matter of interest or to any concern of my own, but I am in utter poverty by reason of my devotion to the god.

There is another thing:—young men of the richer classes, who have not much to do, come about me of their own accord; they like to hear the pretenders examined, and they often imitate me, and proceed to examine others; there are plenty of persons, as they quickly discover, who think that they know something, but really know little or nothing; and then those who are examined by them instead of being angry with themselves are angry with me: This confounded Socrates, they say; this villainous misleader of youth!—and then if somebody asks them, Why, what evil does he practise or teach? they do not know, and cannot tell; but in order that they may not appear to be at a loss, they repeat the ready-made charges which are used against all philosophers about teaching things up in the clouds and under the earth, and having no gods, and making the worse appear the better cause; for they do not like to confess that their pretence of knowledge has been detected—which is the truth; and as they are numerous and ambitious and energetic, and are drawn up in battle array and have persuasive tongues, they have filled your ears with their loud and inveterate calumnies. And this is the reason why my three accusers, Meletus and Anytus and Lycon, have set upon me; Meletus, who has a quarrel with me on behalf of the poets; Anytus, on behalf of the craftsmen and politicians; Lycon, on behalf of the rhetoricians: and, as I said at the beginning, I cannot expect to get rid of such a mass of calumny all in a moment. And this, O men of Athens, is the truth and the whole truth; I have concealed nothing, I have dissembled nothing. And yet, I know that my plainness of speech makes them hate me, and what is their hatred but a proof that I am speaking the truth? Hence has arisen the prejudice against me; and this is the reason of it. . . .

Some one will say: And are you not ashamed, Socrates, of a course of life which is likely to bring you to an untimely end? To him I may fairly answer: There you are mistaken: a man who is good for anything ought not to calculate the chance of living or dying; he ought only to consider whether in doing anything he is doing right or wrong—acting the part of a good man or of a bad. . . .

For the fear of death is indeed the pretence of wisdom, and not real wisdom, being a pretence of knowing the unknown; and no one knows whether death, which men in their fear apprehend to be the greatest evil, may not be the greatest good. Is not this ignorance of a disgraceful sort, the ignorance which is the conceit that a man knows what he does not know? And in this respect only I believe myself to differ from men in general, and may perhaps claim to be wiser than they are:—that whereas I know but little of the world below, I do not suppose that I know: but I do know that injustice and disobedience to a better, whether God or man, is evil and dishonourable, and I will never fear or avoid a possible good rather than a certain evil. And therefore if you let me go now, and are not convinced by Anytus, who said that since I had been prosecuted I must be put to death; (or if not that I ought never to have been prosecuted at all); and that if I escape now, your sons will all be utterly ruined by listening to my words—if you say to me, Socrates, this time we will not mind Anytus, and you shall be let off, but upon one condition, that you are not to enquire and speculate in this way any more, and that if you are caught doing so again you shall die;—if this was the condition on which you let me go, I should reply: Men of Athens, I honour and love you; but I shall obey God rather than you, and while I have life and strength I shall never cease from the practice and teaching of philosophy, exhorting any one whom I meet and saying to him after my manner: You, my friend,—a citizen of the great and mighty and wise city of Athens,—are you not ashamed of heaping up the greatest amount of money and honour and reputation, and caring so little about wisdom and truth and the greatest improvement of the soul, which you never regard or heed at all? And if the person with whom I am arguing, says: Yes, but I do care; then I do not leave him or let him go at once; but I proceed to interrogate and examine and cross-examine him, and if I think that he has no virtue in him, but only says that he has, I reproach him with undervaluing the greater, and overvaluing the less. And I shall repeat the same words to every one whom I meet, young and old, citizen and alien, but especially to the citizens, inasmuch as they are my brethren. For know that this is the command of God; and I believe that no greater good has ever happened in the State than my service to the God. For I do nothing but go about persuading you all, old and young alike, not to take thought for your persons or your properties, but first and chiefly to care about the greatest improvement of the soul. I tell you that virtue is not given by money, but that from virtue comes money and every other good of man, public as well as private. This is my teaching, and if this is the doctrine which corrupts the youth, I am a mischievous person. But if any one says that this is not my teaching, he is speaking an untruth. Wherefore, O men of Athens, I say to you, do as Anytus bids or not as Anytus bids, and either acquit me or not; but whichever you do, understand that I shall never alter my ways, not even if I have to die many times. . . .

Wherefore, O judges, be of good cheer about death, and know of a certainty, that no evil can happen to a good man, either in life or after death. He and his are not neglected by the gods; nor has my own approaching end happened by mere chance. But I see clearly that the time had arrived when it was better for me to die and be released from trouble; wherefore the oracle gave no sign. For which reason, also, I am not angry with my condemners, or with my accusers; they have done me no harm, although they did not mean to do me any good; and for this I may gently blame them.

Still, I have a favour to ask of them. When my sons are grown up, I would ask you, O my friends, to punish them; and I would have you trouble them, as I have troubled you, if they seem to care about riches, or anything, more than about virtue; or if they pretend to be something when they are really nothing,—then reprove them, as I have reproved you, for not caring about that for which they ought to care, and thinking that they are something when they are really nothing. And if you do this, both I and my sons will have received justice at your hands.

The hour of departure has arrived, and we go our ways—I to die, and you to live. Which is better God only knows.

■ Discussion Questions

1. According to Socrates, what accusations have been levied against him, and why?
2. In refuting these accusations, what does Socrates reveal about his fundamental intellectual beliefs and methods?
3. Why do you think many of Socrates' contemporaries found his views so threatening?
4. What impressions do Socrates' words give you of him as a man?

7. Thucydides, *The Funeral Oration of Pericles* (429 B.C.)

The most renowned Athenian politician in his day, Pericles (c. 495–429 B.C.) contributed greatly to the brilliance of Athens's Golden Age. Not only did he help to build the city-state's empire abroad, but he also devoted much of his career to strengthening democracy at home. In his History of the Peloponnesian War, *Thucydides brings Pericles to life in a description of a speech he delivered to honor those who had died in the first year of fighting. The Peloponnesian War pitted Athens against its authoritarian rival, Sparta, from 431 to 404 B.C., ending ultimately with Athens's defeat. Pericles' words reveal, however, that at the time of his speech, Athens was still brimming with confidence in the greatness of its people and government.*

From Thucydides, *History of the Peloponnesian War,* trans. Benjamin Jowett (New York: Twayne Publishers, 1963), 65–72.

During the same winter, in accordance with traditional custom, the funeral of those who first fell in this war was celebrated by the Athenians at the public charge. . . .

Over the first who were buried, Pericles was chosen to speak. At the fitting moment he advanced from the sepulcher to a lofty stage, which had been erected in order that he might be heard as far away as possible by the crowd, and spoke somewhat as follows: . . .

"I will speak of our ancestors first, for it is right and seemly that on such an occasion as this we should also render this honor to their memory. Men of the same stock, ever dwelling in this land, in successive generations to this very day, by their valor handed it down as a free land. They are worthy of praise, and still more are our fathers, who added to their inheritance, and after many a struggle bequeathed to us, their sons, the great empire we possess. . . . But before I praise the dead, I shall first proceed to show by what kind of practices we attained to our position, and under what kind of institutions and manner of life our empire became great. For I conceive that it would not be unsuited to the occasion that this should be told, and that this whole assembly of citizens and foreigners may profitably listen to it.

"Our institutions do not emulate the laws of others. We do not copy our neighbors: rather, we are an example to them. Our system is called a democracy, for it respects the majority and not the few; but while the law secures equality to all alike in their private disputes, the claim of excellence is also recognized; and when a citizen is in any way distinguished, he is generally preferred to the public service, not in rotation, but for merit. Nor again is there any bar in poverty and obscurity of rank to a man who can do the state some service. It is as free men that we conduct our public life, and in our daily occupations we avoid mutual suspicions; we are not angry with our neighbor if he does what he likes; we do not put on sour looks at him which, though harmless, are not pleasant. While we give no offense in our private intercourse, in our public acts we are prevented from doing wrong by fear; we respect the authorities and the laws, especially those which are ordained for the protection of the injured as well as those unwritten laws which bring upon the transgressor admitted dishonor.

"Furthermore, none have provided more relaxations for the spirit from toil; we have regular games and sacrifices throughout the year; our homes are furnished with elegance; and the delight which we daily feel in all these things banishes melancholy. Because of the greatness of our city, the fruits of the whole earth flow in upon us so that we enjoy the goods of other countries as freely as our own.

"Then, again, in military training we are superior to our adversaries, as I shall show. Our city is thrown open to the world, and we never expel a foreigner or prevent him from seeing or learning anything which, if not concealed, it might profit an enemy to see. We rely not so much upon preparations or stratagems, as upon our own courage in action. And in the matter of education, whereas from early youth they are always undergoing laborious exercises which are to make them brave, we live at ease and yet are equally ready to face perils to which our strength is equal. And here is the evidence. The Lacedaemonians march against our land not by themselves, but with all their allies: we invade a neighbor's country alone; and although our opponents are fighting for their homes and we are on a foreign soil, we seldom have any difficulty in overcoming them. . . .

"Nor is this the only cause for marveling at our city. We are lovers of beauty without extravagance and of learning without loss of vigor. Wealth we employ less for talk and ostentation than when there is a real use for it. To avow poverty with us is no disgrace: the true disgrace is in doing nothing to avoid it. The same persons attend at once to the concerns of their households and of the city, and men of diverse employments have a very fair idea of politics. If a man takes no interest in public affairs, we alone do not commend him as quiet but condemn him as useless; and if few of us are originators, we are all sound judges of a policy. In our opinion action does not suffer from discussion but, rather, from the want of that instruction which is gained by discussion preparatory to the action required. For we have an exceptional gift of acting with audacity after calculating the prospects of our enterprises, whereas other men are bold from ignorance but hesitate upon reflection. But it would be right to esteem those men bravest in spirit who have the clearest understanding of the pains and pleasures of life and do not on that account shrink from danger. . . .

"This is why I have dwelt upon the greatness of Athens, showing you that we are contending for a higher prize than those who enjoy no like advantages, and establishing by manifest proof the merit of these men whom I am now commemorating. Their loftiest praise has been already spoken; for in descanting on [speaking about] the city, I have honored the qualities which earned renown for them and for men such as they. And of how few Hellenes can it be said as of them, that their deeds matched their fame! In my belief an end such as theirs proves a man's worth; it is at once its first revelation and final seal. For even those who come short in other ways may justly plead the valor with which they have fought for their country; they have blotted out evil with good, and their public services have outweighed the harm they have done in their private actions. . . . And when the moment for fighting came, they held it nobler to suffer death than to yield and save their lives; it was the report of dishonor from which they fled, but on the battlefield their feet stood fast; and while for a moment they were in the hands of fortune, at the height, less of terror than of glory, they departed.

"Such was the conduct of these men; they were worthy of Athens. The rest of us must pray for a safer issue to our courage and yet disdain to show any less daring towards our enemies. We must not consider only what words can be uttered on the utility of such a spirit. Anyone might discourse to you at length on all the advantages of resisting the enemy bravely, but you know them just as well yourselves. It is better that you should actually gaze day by day on the power of the city until you are filled with the love of her; and when you are convinced of her greatness, reflect that it was acquired by men of daring who knew their duty and feared dishonor in the hour of action, men who if they ever failed in an enterprise, even then disdained to deprive the city of their prowess but offered themselves up as the finest contribution to the common cause. . . .

"To you who are the sons and brothers of the departed, I see that the struggle to emulate them will be arduous. For all men praise the dead; and, however preeminent your virtue may be, you would hardly be thought their equals, but somewhat inferior. The living have their rivals and detractors; but when a man is out of the way, the honor and good will which he receives is uncontested. And, if I am also to speak of womanly virtues to those of you who will now be widows, let me sum them up in one short admonition: 'Your glory will be great if you show no more than the infirmities of your nature, a glory that consists in being least the subjects of report among men, for good or evil.'

"I have spoken in obedience to the law, making use of such fitting words as I had. The tribute of deeds has been paid in part, for the dead have been honorably interred; it remains only that their children shall be maintained at the public charge until they are grown up: this is the solid prize with which, as with a garland, Athens crowns these men and those left behind after such contests. For where the rewards of virtue are greatest, there men do the greatest services to their cities. And now, when you have duly lamented, everyone his own dead, you may depart."

■ Discussion Questions

1. According to Pericles, what sets Athens apart from its neighbors and adversaries?
2. As described in this document, what are the guiding principles of Athenian democracy?
3. How does Pericles characterize his fellow Athenians and their contributions to the city's glory?
4. What obligations does Pericles believe Athenian citizens have to the state?

CHAPTER 3

From the Classical to the Hellenistic World, c. 400–30 B.C.

After the Peloponnesian War ended in 404 B.C., the Greek city-states fell victim to internal squabbling and disunity as each vied to dominate Greece. In the first document, we see the Hellenistic world through the eyes of an official working in one of its hubs, Egypt. The second document allows us to understand better where women fit into this new landscape, which was colored by both change and tradition. Against this backdrop, the once-mighty Greek city-states became second-rate powers, prompting many Greek thinkers, such as Polybius (Document 10), to reexamine the roles of fate and chance in human life.

8. Zenon, Egyptian Official, *Records* (259–250 B.C.)

Alexander the Great's imperial glory was short-lived. After his death in 323 B.C., his army commanders divided his empire into separate kingdoms over which they assumed control. To rule effectively, these new kings and their successors relied on a bureaucracy staffed by Greeks and local administrators. This document illuminates the busy life of one such official, a Greek named Zenon, who was an agent for Apollonius, the financial minister to Ptolemy Philadelphus of Egypt (r. 285–246 B.C.). At the time, Egypt was full of both Greeks and local peoples, who created a vibrant urban culture and economy. These excerpts include instructions from Apollonius, requests for favors and help, to-do lists, and other records.

LETTER FROM HIEROCLES (257 B.C.)

Hierocles to Zenon greeting. If you are well, it would be excellent. I too am in good health. You wrote to me about Pyrrhus, telling me to train[1] him if I am quite certain of his success, but if not, to avoid incurring useless expense and distracting him from his studies. Now as for my being certain, the gods should know best, but it seems to Ptolemaeus, as far as a man can tell, that Pyrrhus is much better than those now being trained, though they started long before him, and that in a very short time he will be far ahead of them; moreover he is pursuing his other studies as well; and to speak with the gods' leave, I hope to see you crowned. Make haste to send him a bathing-apron, and if possible let it be of goatskin or, if not, of thin sheepskin, and a tunic and cloak, and the mattress, coverlet and pillows, and the honey. You wrote to me that you were

---

[1]For competition in the public games.

From *Select Papyri*, trans. A. S. Hunt and C. C. Edgar, vol. 1 (London and New York: William Heinemann Ltd., 1932), 269–77, 397–99, 409–15.

surprised at my not understanding that all these things are subject to toll. I know it, but you are well able to arrange for them to be sent in perfect security.[2] (Addressed) To Zenon. (Docketed) Hierocles about Pyrrhus. Year 29, Xandicus 3, at Memphis.

LETTER FROM PROMETHION (256 B.C.)

Promethion[3] to Zenon greeting. I suffered anxiety when I heard of your long protracted illness, but now I am delighted to hear that you are convalescent and already on the point of recovery. I myself am well. I previously gave your agent Heraclides 150 drachmae in silver from your account, as you wrote to me to do, and he is bringing you now 10 *hins* of perfume in 21 vases which have been sealed with my finger-ring. For though Apollonius wrote to me to buy and give him also 300 wild pomegranate wreaths, I did not manage to give him these at the same time, as they were not ready, but Pa . . . will bring them to him at Naucratis; for they will be finished before the 30th. I have paid the price both of these and of the perfume from your account, as Apollonius wrote. I have also paid a charge of 10 drachmae in copper for the boat in which he is sailing up. And 400 drachmae in silver have been paid to Iatrocles for the papyrus rolls which are being manufactured in Tanis for Apollonius. Take note then that these affairs have been settled thus. And please write yourself if ever you need anything here. Goodbye. Year 29, Choiach 28. (Addressed) To Zenon. (Docketed) Year 29, Peritius 3. Promethion about what he has paid.

LETTER FROM APOLLONIUS THE DIOECETES (256 B.C.)

Apollonius to Zenon greeting. From the dry wood put on board a boat as many of the thickest logs as possible and send them immediately to Alexandria that we may be able to use them for the festival of Isis. Goodbye. Year 30, Dius 3, Phaophi 23. (Addressed) To Zenon. At once.[4] (Docketed by Zenon) Year 30, Dius 18, Hathur 18. Apollonius about wood for the Isis festival. (Docketed by sender) Wood for the Isis festival.

LETTER FROM PLATON (255 B.C.)

Platon to Zenon greeting. The father of Demetrius the bearer of this letter happens, it seems, to be residing in the Arsinoite nome,[5] and the lad therefore wishes to find employment there himself. On hearing of your kindly disposition some of his friends asked me to write to you about him, begging you to give him a post in your service. Please then do me a favour and provide some employment for him, whatever you may think suitable, and otherwise look after him, if you find him useful. As a token (of goodwill) I have sent you, from Sosus, 2 artabae[6] of chickpeas bought at 5 drachmae each, and if there are any at Naucratis, I will try to buy you about 20 artabae more and bring them up to you myself. Goodbye. Year 31, Dius 12. (Addressed) To Zenon.

LETTER FROM ARTEMIDORUS (252 B.C.)

Artemidorus[7] to Zenon greeting. If you are well, it would be excellent. I too am well and Apollonius is in good health and other things are satisfactory. As I write this, we have just arrived in

---

[2]That is, by using his influence as an agent of the financial minister.   [3]A banker in Mendes.
[4]An admonition to the persons concerned to send the letter immediately.   [5]**Nome** means region. [ED.]
[6]**Artabae** means baskets. [ED.]   [7]A physician in the service of the dioecetes.

Sidon after escorting the princess[8] to the frontier, and I expect that we shall soon be with you. Now you will do me a favour by taking care of your own health and writing to me if you want anything done that I can do for you. And kindly buy me, so that I may get them when I arrive, 3 metretae[9] of the best honey and 600 artabae of barley for the animals, and pay the cost of them out of the produce of the sesame and croton,[10] and also see to the house in Philadelphia in order that I may find it roofed when I arrive. Try also as best you can to keep watch on the oxen and the pigs and the geese and the rest of the stock there; I shall have a better supply of provisions if you do. Also see to it that the crops are harvested somehow, and if any outlay is required, do not hesitate to pay what is necessary. Goodbye. Year 33, intercalary Peritius 6. (Addressed) To Zenon. To Philadelphia. (Docketed) Year 33, Phamenoth 6. Artemidorus.

Letter from an Invalid (259–257 b.c.)

Memorandum to Zenon from Cydippus. If in accordance with the doctors' orders I could have purchased any of the following things in the market, I should not have troubled you; but as it is I have written you a note of what I require, as Apollonius thought I ought to do. So if you have them in store, send me a jar of wine, either Lesbian or Chian, of the very sweetest, and if possible a chous[11] of honey or, if not, as much as you can; and order them to fill me the vessel with salt fish. For both these things they consider to be most needful. And if my health improves and I go abroad to Byzantium, I will bring you back some excellent salt fish. (On the back) Memorandum from Cydippus.

Letter from a House-Painter (c. 255 b.c.)

Memorandum to Zenon from Theophilus the . . . About the work in the house of Diotimus: for the portico, [I undertake] to have the cornice painted with a purple border, the upper part of the wall variegated, the lower course like vetch-seed,[12] and the pediment with circular veining, providing myself with all materials, for 30 drachmae. For the dining-room with seven couches, I will do the vault according to the pattern which you saw, and give the lower course an agreeable tint and paint the Lesbian cornice, providing myself with all materials, for 20 drachmae. And for the dining-rooms with five couches, I will paint the cornices, providing myself with all materials, for 3 drachmae. The sum total is 53 drachmae. But if you provide everything, it will come to 30 drachmae. Goodbye.

Zenon's Agenda (c. 250 b.c.)

To ask Herodotus about the goat hair. To ask Aminias at how much the mina he sold it. The letter to Dioscurides about the boat. To make an agreement with Timaeus about the pigs. To draft the contract with Apollodorus and write to him to hand over. To load the boat with wool. To write to Jason to let Dionysius put the wool on board and take it down the river when cleaned; the fourth part of the Arabian wool; to let him take down the sour wine. To write to Meliton to plant shoots of the *bumastus* vine belonging to Neoptolemus, and to Alcimus to do likewise if he approves. To Theogenes about twelve yokes of bulls. To give Apollodorus and Callippus . . . From

---

[8]The princess Berenice, who was escorted to Syria by Apollonius on the occasion of her marriage to Antiochus II.
[9]**Metretae** means jars. [Ed.]
[10]The two oils chiefly used in Egypt at this period were made from sesame and croton (the castor-oil plant), the former for food and the latter for lamps.
[11]**Chous** means container. [Ed.]   [12]**Vetch-seed** is pea-colored. [Ed.]

Metrodorus to Athenagoras about the same year's produce. To Theophilus granting a favour and about the state of the work. To write about corn to Iatrokles and Theodorus before the water from the canal . . .

ZENON'S AGENDA (c. 250 B.C.)

To get the olive kernels. The oil from Heragoras. To buy for the horses 4 strigils, 4 rubbing cloths, 4 scrapers, and for Phatres 1 strigil. To get shoots of the walnut trees. To ascertain the registration of the wine carried down, for which nome it has been registered. To receive Hermon's boy.

LIST OF FOREIGN GOODS (257 B.C.)

Year 29, Xandicus 11, at Hermopolis.[13] We have left behind these articles which Charmus has handed over to Apollodotus: in a basket 5 small bags of nard sealed and 1 small wallet sealed, 1 small wallet, sealed, containing dice of gazelle bone; purple dye in one pillow-case; 1 strip of variegated cloth; 3 half-strips of variegated cloth; 2 strips of white cloth; 4 strips of purple cloth; 3 bags and 1 small bag of frankincense sealed; 3 small bags of myrrh sealed; 1 wallet containing dice of gazelle bone; 1 small wallet of purple dye sealed; 1 small wallet of saffron sealed.

LIST OF ZENON'S CLOTHES (c. 257 B.C.)

Zenon's trunk in which are contained: 1 linen wrap, washed; 1 clay-coloured cloak, for winter, washed, and 1 worn, 1 for summer, half-worn, 1 natural-coloured, for winter, washed, and 1 worn, 1 vetch-coloured, for summer, new; 1 white tunic for winter, with sleeves, washed, 1 natural-coloured, for winter, with sleeves, worn, 1 natural-coloured, for winter, worn, 2 white, for winter, washed, and 1 half-worn, 3 for summer, white, new, 1 unbleached, 1 half-worn; 1 outer garment, white, for winter, washed; 1 coarse mantle; 1 summer garment, white, washed, and 1 half-worn; 1 pair of Sardian pillow-cases; 2 pairs of socks, clay-coloured, new, 2 pairs of white, new; 2 girdles, white, new. (Endorsed) From Pisicles, a list of Zenon's clothes.

■ Discussion Questions

1. If you had to write a job description for Zenon based on these records, what responsibilities would it include?
2. What do Zenon's records reveal about the local economy?
3. What evidence do you find in Zenon's records of cross-cultural influences within the Hellenistic world?

9. *Funerary Inscriptions and Epitaphs* (Fifth to First Centuries B.C.)

These inscriptions and epitaphs provide a glimpse of women's place in the Classical and Hellenistic worlds as described by family members and admirers after their deaths. The words preserved in this form do not simply mark each woman's passing from this world to the next, but they hold her up as an exemplar of female behavior. As in the past, a woman's identity revolved principally around her

---

[13]Hermopolis Parva in the Delta.

From *Women's Life in Greece and Rome,* ed. Mary R. Lefkowitz and Maureen B. Fant, 2d ed. (Baltimore: Johns Hopkins University Press, 1992), 16–17, 190, 206, 219, 221–22, 263, 266–67, 274.

roles as daughter, wife, and mother. Yet not all women's lives were confined to domestic duties. Some were royal attendants, priestesses, and even physicians, whose daily activities extended into the public sphere.

ARCHEDICE, ATHENS, FIFTH CENTURY B.C.

This dust hides Archedice, daughter of Hippias, the most important man in Greece in his day. But though her father, husband, brothers, and children were tyrants, her mind was never carried away into arrogance.

ASPASIA, CHIOS, C. 400 B.C.

Of a worthy wife this is the tomb—here, by the road that throngs with people—of Aspasia, who is dead; in response to her noble disposition Euopides set up this monument for her; she was his consort.

DIONYSIA, ATHENS, FOURTH CENTURY B.C.

It was not clothes, it was not gold that this woman admired during her lifetime; it was her husband and the good sense that she showed in her behaviour. But in return for the youth you shared with him, Dionysia, your tomb is adorned by your husband Antiphilus.

CLAUDIA, ROME, SECOND CENTURY B.C.

Friend, I have not much to say; stop and read it. This tomb, which is not fair, is for a fair woman. Her parents gave her the name Claudia. She loved her husband in her heart. She bore two sons, one of whom she left on earth, the other beneath it. She was pleasant to talk with, and she walked with grace. She kept the house and worked in wool. That is all. You may go.

AN ACCOMPLISHED WOMAN, SARDIS, FIRST CENTURY B.C.

[An inscription set up by the municipality of Sardis in honour of Menophila, daughter of Hermagenes.] This stone marks a woman of accomplishment and beauty. Who she is the Muses' inscriptions reveal: Menophila. Why she is honoured is shown by a carved lily and an alpha, a book and a basket, and with these a wreath. The book shows that you were wise, the wreath that you wore on your head shows that you were a leader; the letter alpha that you were an only child; the basket is a sign of your orderly excellence; the flower shows the prime of your life, which Fate stole away. May the dust lie light on you in death. Alas; your parents are childless; to them you have left tears.

POSILLA SENENIA, MONTELEONE SABINO, FIRST CENTURY B.C.

Posilla Senenia, daughter of Quartus and Quarta Senenia, freedwoman of Gaius.

Stranger, stop and, while you are here, read what is written: that a mother was not permitted to enjoy her only daughter, whose life, I believe, was envied by some god.

Since her mother was not allowed to adorn her while she was alive, she does so just the same after death; at the end of her time, [her mother] with this monument honours her whom she loved.

XENOCLEA, PIRAEUS, 360? B.C.

Leaving two young girls, Xenoclea, daughter of Nicarchus, lies here dead; she mourned the sad end of her son, Phoenix, who died out at sea when he was eight years old.

There is no one so ignorant of grief, Xenoclea, that he doesn't pity your fate. You left behind two young girls and died of grief for your son, who has a pitiless tomb where he lies in the dark sea.

HANDIWORK, ATHENS, AFTER 350 B.C.

I worked with my hands; I was a thrifty woman, I, Nicarete who lie here.

A STOREROOM ATTENDANT, CAPE ZOSTER, NEAR ATHENS, 56–55 B.C.

[An epitaph by a mother for a daughter who worked for Cleopatra at the royal court of Alexandria.] Her mother, an Athenian woman, raised her to be an attendant of foreign storerooms. She too rushed for her child's sake to come to the palace of the king who had set her over his rich possessions. Yet still she could not bring her daughter back alive. But the daughter has a tomb in Athens instead of on Libyan sand.

EPITAPH FOR A WOMAN WHO DIED WHILE PREGNANT, EGYPT, SECOND–FIRST CENTURIES B.C.

Dosithea, daughter of —. Look at these letters on the polished rock. Thallo's son Chaeremon married me in his great house. I die in pain, escaping the pangs of childbirth, leaving the breath of life when I was 25 years old; from a disease which he died of before, I succumbed after. I lie here in Schedia. Wayfarers, as you go by, all of you, say: "Beloved Dosithea, stay well, also among the dead."

A MIDWIFE AND PHYSICIAN, ATHENS, FOURTH CENTURY B.C.

[The memorial tablet represents two women, one seated, one standing, surrounded by infants of both sexes.] Phanostrate, a midwife and physician, lies here. She caused pain to none, and all lamented her death.

A NURSE, ATHENS, AFTER 350 B.C.

[Epitaph for] Apollodorus the immigrant's daughter, Melitta, a nurse. Here the earth covers Hippostrate's good nurse; and Hippostrate still misses you. "I loved you while you were alive, nurse, I love you still now even beneath the earth and now I shall honour you as long as I live. I know that for you beneath the earth also, if there is reward for the good, honours will come first to you, in the realm of Persephone and of Pluto."

EPITAPH FOR A PRIESTESS, MILETUS, THIRD CENTURY B.C.

Bacchae[1] of the City, say, "Farewell you holy priestess." This is what a good woman deserves. She led you to the mountain and carried all the sacred objects and implements, marching in procession before the whole city. Should some stranger ask for her name: Alcmeonis, daughter of Rhodius, who knew her share of the blessings.

■ Discussion Questions

1. Given these texts, what particular qualities did people admire in women, and why?
2. Scholars have described Greek society at the time as patriarchal. Do the epitaphs and

---

[1]Women worshipers of Dionysus. [ED.]

inscriptions support this view? What do they reveal about the social and economic standing of the women they describe?

3. What do these sources suggest about contemporary attitudes toward death?

10. Polybius, *The Histories*   (Second Century B.C.)

The rise of the Macedonian and Hellenistic kings forever crippled the Greek city-states' political independence. At the same time, a new power, Rome, was vying for supremacy. Polybius (203? B.C.– c. 120 B.C.) was a Greek statesman and historian who witnessed these changes firsthand while working at home and abroad, including in Rome, where he spent many years as a private tutor. He observed the city's institutions and people with a keen eye for detail, laying the groundwork for his forty-volume Histories. *This excerpt is remarkable for its discussion of a prominent concern among contemporary thinkers striving to explain the tumultuous and seemingly random course of recent Greek history: the relationship between human affairs and the power of Luck and Chance. In arguing that inexplicable phenomena are caused by Fate, not by human action, Polybius reveals the influence on his views of Stoicism, one of the leading new philosophical schools of his day.*

For my part, says Polybius, in finding fault with those who ascribe public events and incidents in private life to Fate and Chance, I now wish to state my opinion on this subject as far as it is admissible to do so in a strictly historical work. Now indeed as regards things the causes of which it is impossible or difficult for a mere man to understand, we may perhaps be justified in getting out of the difficulty by setting them down to the action of a god or of chance, I mean such things as exceptionally heavy and continuous rain or snow, or on the other hand the destruction of crops by severe drought or frost, or a persistent outbreak of plague or other similar things of which it is not easy to detect the cause. So in regard to such matters we naturally bow to popular opinion, as we cannot make out why they happen, and attempting by prayer and sacrifice to appease the heavenly powers, we send to ask the gods what we must do and say, to set things right and cause the evil that afflicts us to cease. But as for matters the efficient and final cause of which it is possible to discover we should not, I think, put them down to divine action. For instance, take the following case. In our own time the whole of Greece has been subject to a low birth-rate and a general decrease of the population, owing to which cities have become deserted and the land has ceased to yield fruit, although there have neither been continuous wars nor epidemics. If, then, any one had advised us to send and ask the gods about this, and find out what we ought to say or do, to increase in number and make our cities more populous, would it not seem absurd, the cause of the evil being evident and the remedy being in our own hands? For as men had fallen into such a state of pretentiousness, avarice, and indolence that they did not wish to marry, or if they married to rear the children born to them, or at most as a rule but one or two of them, so as to leave these in affluence and bring them up to waste their substance, the evil rapidly and insensibly grew. For in cases where of one or two children the one was carried off by war and the other by sickness, it is evident that the houses must have been left unoccupied, and as in the case of swarms of bees, so by small degrees cities became resourceless and feeble. About this it was of no use at all to ask the gods to suggest a means of deliverance from such an evil. For any ordinary man will tell you that the most effectual cure had to be men's own action, in

From Polybius, *The Histories*, trans. W. R. Paton, vol. 6 (Cambridge, Mass.: Harvard University Press, 1960), 383–87.

either striving after other objects, or if not, in passing laws making it compulsory to rear children. Neither prophets nor magic were here of any service, and the same holds good for all particulars. But in cases where it is either impossible or difficult to detect the cause the question is open to doubt. One such case is that of Macedonia. For the Macedonians had met with many signal favours from Rome; the country as a whole had been delivered from the arbitrary rule and taxation of autocrats, and, as all confessed, now enjoyed freedom in place of servitude, and the several cities had, owing to the beneficent action of Rome, been freed from serious civil discord and internecine massacres. . . . But now they witnessed in quite a short time more of their citizens exiled, tortured and murdered by this false Philip than by any of their previous real kings. . . . But while they were defeated by the Romans in fighting for Demetrius and Perseus, yet now fighting for a hateful man and displaying great valour in defence of his throne, they worsted the Romans. How can anyone fail to be nonplused by such an event? for here it is most difficult to detect the cause. So that in pronouncing on this and similar phenomena we may well say that the thing was a heaven-sent infatuation, and that all the Macedonians were visited by the wrath of God, as will be evident from what follows.

■ Discussion Questions

1. Does Polybius believe that humans have control over their lives?
2. How does Polybius distinguish between the power of divine action and human action to dictate the course of events on earth?
3. What does Polybius reveal about Hellenistic religious beliefs and practices? How did people typically seek to solve the evils and troubles of human existence?

CHAPTER 4
The Rise of Rome, c. 753–44 B.C.

When the Roman republic was founded in 509 B.C., few could have foreseen its transformation into a mighty imperialist state. At the time, Greece was on the threshold of its Golden Age, which was soon followed by Macedonia's meteoric rise to power. Yet throughout this period, the Romans gradually expanded their territories and wealth, so that by the end of the second century B.C., they controlled most of southern Europe, North Africa, Greece, and Asia Minor. Victory came at a price, however, as Roman politicians and military leaders came to value their individual successes more than that of the republic. The documents in this chapter help us chart the republic's development from several different angles. Together, they reveal the pillars of the republic—law, tradition, and communal values—while providing a glimpse of their ultimate demise.

11. Livy, *Roman Women Demonstrate against the Oppian Law* (195 B.C.)

Women in ancient Rome were most valued as wives and mothers, yet sometimes they stepped outside the boundaries of family life to make their voices heard. In his History of Rome, *the Roman historian Livy (59 B.C.–A.D. 17) reconstructs a heated debate that erupted on one such occasion. In 195 B.C., upper-class women from the city and its environs joined together to demonstrate publicly against the Oppian law, which had been passed during wartime and restricted the amount of finery women could wear and their use of carriages in an effort to reduce friction between rich and poor. Their demand for the law's repeal so that they could once again display their elite status sparked both disdain and sympathy among various leaders, to whom they appealed for support. Each camp, represented here by the consul, Cato, and the tribune, Valerius, claimed to have tradition on its side.*

Amid the anxieties of great wars, either scarce finished or soon to come, an incident occurred, trivial to relate, but which, by reason of the passions it aroused, developed into a violent contention. Marcus Fundanius and Lucius Valerius, tribunes of the people, proposed to the assembly the abrogation of the Oppian law. The tribune Gaius Oppius had carried this law in the heat of the Punic War, in the consulship of Quintus Fabius and Tiberius Sempronius, that no woman should possess more than half an ounce of gold or wear a parti-coloured garment or ride in a carriage in the City or in a town within a mile thereof, except on the occasion of a religious festival. The tribunes Marcus and Publius Iunius Brutus were supporting the Oppian law, and averred that

From Livy, *History of Rome*, trans. Evan T. Sage, vol. 9 (Cambridge, Mass.: Harvard University Press, 1961), 413–21, 425–39.

they would not permit its repeal; many distinguished men came forward to speak for and against it; the Capitoline was filled with crowds of supporters and opponents of the bill. The matrons could not be kept at home by advice or modesty or their husbands' orders, but blocked all the streets and approaches to the Forum, begging the men as they came down to the Forum that, in the prosperous condition of the state, when the private fortunes of all men were daily increasing, they should allow the women too to have their former distinctions restored. The crowd of women grew larger day by day; for they were now coming in from the towns and rural districts. Soon they dared even to approach and appeal to the consuls, the praetors, and the other officials, but one consul, at least, they found adamant, Marcus Porcius Cato, who spoke thus in favour of the law whose repeal was being urged.

"If each of us, citizens, had determined to assert his rights and dignity as a husband with respect to his own spouse, we should have less trouble with the sex as a whole; as it is, our liberty, destroyed at home by female violence, even here in the Forum is crushed and trodden underfoot, and because we have not kept them individually under control, we dread them collectively. . . .

"For myself, I could not conceal my blushes a while ago, when I had to make my way to the Forum through a crowd of women. Had not respect for the dignity and modesty of some individuals among them rather than of the sex as a whole kept me silent, lest they should seem to have been rebuked by a consul, I should have said, 'What sort of practice is this, of running out into the streets and blocking the roads and speaking to other women's husbands? Could you not have made the same requests, each of your own husband, at home? Or are you more attractive outside and to other women's husbands than to your own? And yet, not even at home, if modesty would keep matrons within the limits of their proper rights, did it become you to concern yourselves with the question of what laws should be adopted in this place or repealed.' Our ancestors permitted no woman to conduct even personal business without a guardian to intervene in her behalf;[1] they wished them to be under the control of fathers, brothers, husbands; we (Heaven help us!) allow them now even to interfere in public affairs, yes, and to visit the Forum and our informal and formal sessions. What else are they doing now on the streets and at the corners except urging the bill of the tribunes and voting for the repeal of the law? Give loose rein to their uncontrollable nature and to this untamed creature and expect that they will themselves set bounds to their licence; unless you act, this is the least of the things enjoined upon women by custom or law and to which they submit with a feeling of injustice. It is complete liberty or, rather, if we wish to speak the truth, complete licence that they desire.

"If they win in this, what will they not attempt? Review all the laws with which your forefathers restrained their licence and made them subject to their husbands; even with all these bonds you can scarcely control them. What of this? If you suffer them to seize these bonds one by one and wrench themselves free and finally to be placed on a parity with their husbands, do you think that you will be able to endure them? The moment they begin to be your equals, they will be your superiors. . . . No law is entirely convenient for everyone; this alone is asked, whether it is good for the majority and on the whole. If every law which harms anyone in his private affairs is to be repealed and discarded, what good will it do for all the citizens to pass laws which those at whom they are aimed will at once annul? . . . What pretext, respectable even to mention, is now given for this insurrection of the women? 'That we may glitter with gold and purple,' says one, 'that we may ride in carriages on holidays and ordinary days, that we may be borne through the city as if in triumph over the conquered and vanquished law and over the votes which we have captured and wrested from you; that there may be no limits to our spending and our luxury.' . . .

---

[1] A woman was never *sui iuris* and was not a person in the legal sense. If she was not under the *potestas* (power) of a father or the *manus* (control) of a husband, a *tutor* was appointed to act for her in legal matters.

"She who can buy from her own purse will buy; she who cannot will beg her husband. Poor wretch that husband, both he who yields and he who yields not, since what he will not himself give he will see given by another man. Now they publicly address other women's husbands, and, what is more serious, they beg for a law and votes, and from sundry men they get what they ask. In matters affecting yourself, your property, your children, you, Sir, can be importuned; once the law has ceased to set a limit to your wife's expenditures you will never set it yourself. Do not think, citizens, that the situation which existed before the law was passed will ever return. It is safer for a criminal to go unaccused than to be acquitted; and luxury, left undisturbed, would have been more endurable then than it will be now, when it has been, like a wild beast, first rendered angry by its very fetters and then let loose. My opinion is that the Oppian law should on no account be repealed; whatever is your decision, I pray that all the gods may prosper it."

After this the tribunes of the people who had declared that they would veto the bill spoke briefly to the same effect, and then Lucius Valerius argued thus for the measure which he had proposed: . . . "Now, since that most influential man, the consul Marcus Porcius, has attacked our proposal not only with his authority, which unexpressed would have had enough of weight, but also in a long and carefully-prepared speech, it is necessary to make a brief reply. And yet he used up more words in reproving the matrons than he did in opposing our bill, and, in fact, left it in doubt whether the conduct for which he rebuked the matrons was spontaneous or inspired by us. I propose to defend the measure rather than ourselves, at whom the consul directed his insinuations, more to have something to say than to make a serious charge. This gathering of women he called a sedition and sometimes 'a female secession,' because the matrons, in the streets, had requested you to repeal, in a time of peace and in a rich and prosperous commonwealth, a law that was passed against them in the trying days of a war. . . .

"What new thing, pray, have the matrons done in coming out into the streets in crowds in a case that concerned them? Have they never before this moment appeared in public? Let me unroll your own *Origines* against you.[2] Hear how often they have done it and always, indeed, for the general good. . . . These cases, you say, are different. It is not my purpose to prove them similar; it suffices if I prove that this is nothing new. But what no one wonders that all, men and women alike, have done in matters that concern them, do we wonder that the women have done in a case peculiarly their own? What now have they done? We have proud ears, upon my word, if, although masters do not scorn to hear the petitions of slaves, we complain that we are appealed to by respectable women. . . .

"Laws passed in time of peace, war frequently annuls, and peace those passed in times of war, just as in handling a ship some means are useful in fair weather and others in a storm. Since they are so distinguished by nature, to which class, I ask, does the law which we are trying to repeal seem to belong? Well? Is it an ancient regal law, born with the City itself, or, what is next to that, one inscribed on the twelve tables by the decemvirs appointed to codify the law? Is it a law without which our ancestors held that a matron's virtue could not be preserved, and which we too must fear to repeal lest along with it we repeal the modesty and purity of our women? Who is there, then, who does not know that this is a new law, passed twenty years ago, in the consulship of Quintus Fabius and Tiberius Sempronius? Since for so many years our matrons lived virtuous lives without it, what danger is there that when it is repealed they will rush into riotous luxury? . . .

---

[2]Valerius quotes or pretends to quote from Cato's own historical work, which treated early Roman history. The *Origines* had not actually been written at the time of the feminist agitation. The scroll form of the ancient book explains the choice of the verb "unroll."

"Who fails to see that the poverty and distress of the state wrote that law, since all private property had to be diverted to public use, and that the law was to remain in force so long as the cause of its enactment lasted?[3]

"All other orders, all men, will feel the change for the better in the state; shall our wives alone get no enjoyment from national peace and tranquillity? . . . By Hercules, there is mourning and anger among all when they see the wives of allies of the Latin confederacy permitted the ornaments which are refused to them, when they see them decked out in gold and purple, when they see them riding through the city, and themselves following on foot, as if dominion resided in the Latin towns and not in Rome. A thing like this would hurt the feelings even of men: what do you think is its effect upon weak women, whom even little things disturb? No offices, no priesthoods, no triumphs, no decorations, no gifts, no spoils of war can come to them; elegance of appearance, adornment, apparel—these are the woman's badges of honour; in these they rejoice and take delight; these our ancestors called the woman's world. What else do they lay aside in times of mourning than purple and jewellery? What do they put on when they have finished their time of mourning? What do they add save more splendid jewels in times of congratulations and thanksgiving? Of course, if you repeal the Oppian law, you will have no authority if you wish to forbid any of these things which now the law forbids; daughters, wives, even sisters of some will be less under control—never while their males survive is feminine slavery shaken off; and even they abhor the freedom which loss of husbands and fathers gives.[4] They prefer to have their finery under your control and not the law's; you too should keep them in control and guardianship and not in slavery, and should prefer the name of father or husband to that of master." . . .

When these speeches against and for the bill had been delivered, the next day an even greater crowd of women appeared in public, and all of them in a body beset the doors of the Bruti, who were vetoing their colleagues' proposal, and they did not desist until the threat of veto was withdrawn by the tribunes. After that there was no question that all the tribes would vote to repeal the law. The law was repealed twenty years after it was passed.

■ Discussion Questions

1. Why did Cato object to repealing the Oppian law? What was the basis of his objections?
2. How did Valerius counter Cato's assertions? What evidence did he use?
3. What do Valerius and Cato reveal about contemporary attitudes toward women and their place in the republic?
4. What does this excerpt show about the republic's government?

12. *The Twelve Tables*   (451–449 B.C.)

Although Rome's elite successfully overthrew the Roman monarchy and established the republic in 509 B.C., more challenges lay ahead. For the next two centuries, the city's patricians and the rest of its citizens battled over the course the new government should take and their respective roles in it.

---

[3]Valerius argues that the Oppian law was merely one of a series of emergency measures by which all elements in the state were affected. To leave this one law in force would mean continued discrimination against one element, the women, after the other methods had been abandoned.

[4]Under the stricter Roman law, a woman was throughout life under the *potestas* of her father or his representative or the *manus* of her husband. Valerius makes the point that this domestic authority will be resumed in full with the repeal of the law, and that the same restrictions that the law provided can be enforced if desired.

From *Ancient Rome Statutes,* trans. Allan Chester Johnson et al. (Austin: University of Texas Press, 1961), 9–17.

Promulgated between 451 and 449 B.C., the Twelve Tables were a turning point in this struggle, marking the republic's first step toward establishing a fair system of justice. Surviving in fragments, this code, the earliest Roman laws, was based on custom. The following excerpts illuminate not only the social and economic landscape of early Rome but also the foundation of Roman jurisprudence.

TABLE I. PROCEEDINGS PRELIMINARY TO TRIAL

If the plaintiff summons the defendant to court the defendant shall go. If the defendant does not go the plaintiff shall call a witness thereto. Only then the plaintiff shall seize the defendant.

If the defendant attempts evasion or takes flight the plaintiff shall lay hand on him.

If sickness or age is an impediment he who summons the defendant to court shall grant him a vehicle. If he does not wish he shall not spread a carriage with cushions.

For a freeholder[1] a freeholder shall be surety;[2] for a proletary[3] anyone who wishes shall be surety.

There shall be the same right of bond and of conveyance with the Roman people for a steadfast person and for a person restored to allegiance.[4]

When the parties agree on the matter the magistrate shall announce it.

If they agree not on terms the parties shall state their case before the assembly in the meeting place or before the magistrate in the market place before noon. Both parties being present shall plead the case throughout together.

If one of the parties does not appear the magistrate shall adjudge the case, after noon, in favor of the one present.

If both parties are present sunset shall be the time limit of the proceedings. . . .

TABLE II. TRIAL

The penal sum[5] in an action by solemn deposit shall be either 500 asses or 50 asses.[6] . . . It shall be argued by solemn deposit with 500 asses, when the property is valued at 1,000 asses or more, but with 50 asses, when the property is valued at less than 1,000 asses. But if the controversy is about the freedom of a person, although the person may be very valuable, yet the case shall be argued by a solemn deposit of 50 asses. . . .

TABLE III. EXECUTION OF JUDGMENT

Thirty days shall be allowed by law for payment of confessed debt and for settlement of matters adjudged in court.

After this time the creditor shall have the right of laying hand on the debtor. The creditor shall hale the debtor into court.

---

[1] A taxpayer whose fortune is valued at not less than 1,500 asses (bronze coins).

[2] That is, for his appearance at trial.

[3] A proletary is a nontaxpayer whose fortune is rated at less than a freeholder's.

[4] Apparently this allows the Latin allies who had revolted and afterward returned into allegiance to enjoy the same rights and to use the same legal formulas in contractual matters and in transferring property as those who had remained loyal.

[5] Each litigant deposited a sum with the court as a kind of "wager on oath" that his cause was right. The defeated party forfeited his deposit to the state. On account of the desire to show special favor to persons illegally held as slaves and claiming their freedom, the law made the deposit for them very low, only fifty asses in such cases.

[6] Bronze coins. [ED.]

Unless the debtor discharges the debt adjudged or unless someone offers surety for him in court the creditor shall take the debtor with him. He shall bind him either with a thong or with fetters of not more than fifteen pounds in weight, or if he wishes he shall bind him with fetters of more than this weight.

If the debtor wishes he shall live on his own means. If he does not live on his own means the creditor who holds him in bonds shall give him a pound of grits daily. If he wishes he shall give him more.

. . . Meanwhile they shall have the right to compromise, and unless they make a compromise the debtors shall be held in bonds for sixty days. During these days they shall be brought to the praetor[7] into the meeting place on three successive market days, and the amount for which they have been judged liable shall be declared publicly. Moreover, on the third market day they shall suffer capital punishment or shall be delivered for sale abroad across the Tiber River.

On the third market day the creditors shall cut shares. If they have cut more or less than their shares it shall be without prejudice.

TABLE IV. PATERNAL POWER

A notably deformed child shall be killed immediately.

To a father . . . shall be given over a son the power of life and death.

If a father thrice surrenders a son for sale the son shall be free from the father.[8]

To repudiate his wife her husband shall order her . . . to have her own property for herself, shall take the keys, shall expel her.[9]

A child born within ten months of the father's death shall enter into the inheritance. . . .

TABLE V. INHERITANCE AND GUARDIANSHIP

. . . Women, even though they are of full age,[10] because of their levity of mind shall be under guardianship . . . except vestal virgins, who . . . shall be free from guardianship. . . .

The conveyable possessions of a woman who is under guardianship of male agnates[11] shall not be acquired by prescriptive right unless they are transferred by the woman herself with the authorization of her guardian. . . .

According as a person has made bequest regarding his personal property or the guardianship of his estate so shall be the law.

If anyone who has no direct heir dies intestate the nearest male agnate shall have the estate.

---

[7]A *praetor* is a high elected official. [ED.] This statute comes from Gellius, who gives *praetorem* for (the expected) *consulem*. Because the praetorship was not instituted till 367 B.C., Gellius is guilty of anachronism, unless he was enough of an antiquarian to remember that *praetor* was an early equivalent for *consul* or unless *consules* were still called *praetores* in the time of the Twelve Tables.

[8]In the early days of Rome a Roman father could sell his son into slavery. If the buyer freed the son the son reentered his father's control (*patria potestas*).

[9]The formula for a valid repudiation (*repudium*) of the other by either the husband or the wife is said to have contained the words *tuas res tibi habeto* or *agito* (have [*or* manage] your own property for yourself). Dissolution of marriage by mutual consent is divorce (*divortium*). In either event an essential feature is the husband's return of the wife's dowry, if any, whose investment he had controlled during marriage.

[10]For females "full age" is twenty-five years. According to the law of this period, a woman never has legal independence: if she is not in her father's power (*potestas*), she is dependent on her husband's control (*manus*) or, if unmarried and fatherless, she is subject to her guardian's governance (*tutela*).

[11]**Agnates** are relatives from the father's family. [ED.]

If there is not a male agnate the male clansmen shall have the estate.

Persons for whom by will . . . a guardian is not given, for them . . . their male agnates shall be guardians.

If a person is insane authority over him and his personal property shall belong to his male agnates and in default of these to his male clansmen. . . .

If a Roman citizen freedman dies intestate without a direct heir, to his patron shall fall the inheritance . . . from said household . . . into said household. . . .

TABLE VI. OWNERSHIP AND POSSESSION

. . . If any woman is unwilling to be subjected in this manner[12] to her husband's marital control she shall absent herself for three successive nights in every year and by this means shall interrupt his prescriptive right of each year.[13] . . .

One shall not take from framework timber fixed in buildings or in vineyard. . . . One shall be permitted neither to remove nor to claim stolen timber fixed in buildings or in vineyards, . . . but against the person who is convicted of having fixed such timber there an action for double damages shall be given. . . .

TABLE VII. REAL PROPERTY

If a watercourse conducted through a public place does damage to a private person the said person shall have the right to bring an action . . . that security against damage may be given to the owner.

. . . Branches of a tree shall be pruned all around to a height of fifteen feet.

If a tree from a neighbor's farm has been felled by the wind over one's farm, . . . one rightfully can take legal action for that tree to be removed.

. . . It shall be lawful to gather fruit falling upon another's farm. . . .

A slave is ordered in a will to be a free man under this condition: "if he has given 10,000 asses to the heir"; although the slave has been alienated by the heir, yet the slave by giving the said money to the buyer shall enter into his freedom. . . .

TABLE VIII. TORTS OR DELICTS

. . . If anyone sings or composes an incantation that can cause dishonor or disgrace to another . . . he shall suffer a capital penalty.[14]

If anyone has broken another's limb there shall be retaliation in kind unless he compounds for compensation with him.

. . . If a person breaks a bone of a freeman with hand or by club, he shall undergo a penalty of 300 asses; or of 150 asses, if of a slave.

If one commits an outrage against another the penalty shall be twenty-five asses.

. . . One has broken. . . . One shall make amends.

---

[12]That is, by prescriptive right (*usus*).

[13]This method, the so-called *ius trinoctii* (right of three nights; that is, the right acquired by an absence of three successive nights), enabled a wife to remain married to her husband and yet neither to come into nor to remain in his marital control (*manus*). If the prescriptive right (*usus*) has been interrupted for three consecutive nights annually, the time of *usus* must commence afresh, because the husband's previous possession is considered to be canceled.

[14]The infliction of this penalty perhaps may have included clubbing (to death), according to one ancient account.

If a quadruped is said to have caused damage an action shall lie therefor . . . either for surrendering that which did the damage to the aggrieved person . . . or for offering an assessment of the damage.

If fruit from your tree falls onto my farm and if I feed my flock off it by letting the flock onto it . . . no action can lie against me either on the statute concerning pasturage of a flock, because it is not being pastured on your land, or on the statute concerning damage caused by an animal. . . .

If anyone pastures on or cuts by night another's crops obtained by cultivation the penalty for an adult shall be capital punishment and after having been hung up, death as a sacrifice to Ceres. . . . A person below the age of puberty at the praetor's decision shall be scourged and shall be judged as a person either to be surrendered to the plaintiff for damage done or to pay double damages.

Whoever destroys by burning a building or a stack of grain placed beside a house . . . shall be bound, scourged, burned to death, provided that knowingly and consciously he has committed this crime; but if this deed is by accident, that is, by negligence, either he shall repair the damage or if he is unable he shall be corporally punished more lightly.

Whoever fells unjustly another's trees shall pay twenty-five asses for each tree.

If a thief commits a theft by night, if the owner kills the thief, the thief shall be killed lawfully.

By daylight . . . if a thief defends himself with a weapon . . . and the owner shall shout.

In the case of all other . . . thieves caught in the act freemen shall be scourged and shall be adjudged as bondsmen to the person against whom the theft has been committed provided that they have done this by daylight and have not defended themselves with a weapon; slaves caught in the act of theft . . . shall be whipped with scourges and shall be thrown from the rock;[15] but children below the age of puberty shall be scourged at the praetor's decision and the damage done by them shall be repaired. . . .

If a patron defrauds a client he shall be accursed.[16]

Unless he speaks his testimony whoever allows himself to be called as a witness or is a scales-bearer shall be dishonored and incompetent to give or obtain testimony. . . .

If anyone pastures on or cuts stealthily by night . . . another's crops . . . the penalty shall be capital punishment, and, after having been hung up, death as a sacrifice to Ceres, a punishment more severe than in homicide. . . .

TABLE IX. PUBLIC LAW

Laws of personal exception shall not be proposed. Laws concerning capital punishment of a citizen shall not be passed . . . except by the Greatest Assembly. . . .

. . . Whoever incites a public enemy or whoever betrays a citizen to a public enemy shall be punished capitally.

For anyone whomsoever to be put to death without a trial and unconvicted . . . is forbidden.

---

[15]A southern spur of the Capitoline Hill, which overlooks the Forum.

[16]That is, declared forfeited to the nether gods and liable to be slain by anyone with impunity.

Table X. Sacred Law

A dead person shall not be buried or burned in the city.[17] . . .

. . . Expenses of a funeral shall be limited to three mourners wearing veils and one mourner wearing an inexpensive purple tunic and ten flutists. . . .

Women shall not tear their cheeks or shall not make a sorrowful outcry on account of a funeral.

A dead person's bones shall not be collected that one may make a second funeral.

An exception is for death in battle and on foreign soil. . . .

Table XI. Supplementary Laws

. . . There shall not be intermarriage between plebeians and patricians.

Table XII. Supplementary Laws

It is forbidden to dedicate for consecrated use a thing concerning whose ownership there is a controversy; otherwise a penalty of double the value involved shall be suffered. . . .

▪ Discussion Questions

1. What are the tables' principal concerns?
2. What do these concerns suggest about Roman society at the time?
3. In what ways did these laws represent a triumph for the plebeian class?

13. Cicero, *On the Commonwealth*   (54 B.C.)

During his illustrious public career in Rome, Marcus Tullius Cicero (106–43 B.C.) was a lawyer, states-man, author, and orator. In each role, he displayed his keen intelligence, fierce patriotism, and high moral standards. This excerpt is from the last chapter of his treatise On the Commonwealth *(54–51 B.C.), written at a time when Rome was rife with political and social conflicts. Here Cicero uses an imaginary conversation between two military heroes from the Punic Wars—Publius Cornelius Scipio Africanus (236–183 B.C.) and his adopted grandson, Publius Cornelius Scipio Aemilianus Africanus the Younger (185–129 B.C.)—to highlight the moral values and sense of destiny that he considered to be at the heart of the republic's greatness. Set in 129 B.C., the story begins with Scipio Africanus speaking to Publius Scipio the Younger in a dream twenty years earlier.*

Take courage, my Scipio, be not afraid, and carefully remember what I shall say to you.

XI. Do you see that city Carthage, which, though brought under the Roman yoke by me, is now renewing former wars, and cannot live in peace? (and he pointed to Carthage from a lofty spot, full of stars, and brilliant, and glittering;) to attack which city you are this day arrived in a station not much superior to that of a private soldier. Before two years, however, are elapsed, you

---

[17]If not derived from a primitive tribal taboo (for certainly vestals, whether chaste or unchaste, were buried in Rome), inhumation on a large scale and in a crowded community not only was unsanitary but also took too much space. Cremation could involve hazards from fire (see Cicero, Leg. 2, 23, 58).

From *The Treatises of M. T. Cicero,* trans. C. D. Yonge (London: Henry G. Bohn, 1853), 381–88.

shall be consul, and complete its overthrow; and you shall obtain, by your own merit, the surname of Africanus, which, as yet, belongs to you no otherwise than as derived from me. And when you have destroyed Carthage, and received the honour of a triumph, and been made censor, and, in quality of ambassador, visited Egypt, Syria, Asia, and Greece, you shall be elected a second time consul in your absence, and, by utterly destroying Numantia, put an end to a most dangerous war.

But when you have entered the Capitol in your triumphal car, you shall find the Roman commonwealth all in a ferment, through the intrigues of my grandson Tiberius Gracchus.

XII. It is on this occasion, my dear Africanus, that you show your country the greatness of your understanding, capacity, and prudence. But I see that the destiny, however, of that time is, as it were, uncertain; for when your age shall have accomplished seven times eight revolutions of the sun, and your fatal hours shall be marked out by the natural product of these two numbers, each of which is esteemed a perfect one, but for different reasons,—then shall the whole city have recourse to you alone, and place its hopes in your auspicious name. On you the senate, all good citizens, the allies, the people of Latium, shall cast their eyes; on you the preservation of the state shall entirely depend. In a word, *if you escape the impious machinations of your relatives,* you will, in quality of dictator, establish order and tranquillity in the commonwealth. . . .

XIII. Now, in order to encourage you, my dear Africanus, continued the shade of my ancestor, to defend the state with the greater cheerfulness, be assured that for all those who have in any way conduced to the preservation, defence, and enlargement of their native country, there is a certain place in heaven, where they shall enjoy an eternity of happiness. For nothing on earth is more agreeable to God, the Supreme Governor of the universe, than the assemblies and societies of men united together by laws, which are called States. It is from heaven their rulers and preservers came, and thither they return.

XIV. Though at these words I was extremely troubled, not so much at the fear of death, as at the perfidy of my own relations; yet I recollected myself enough to inquire, whether he himself, my father Paulus, and others whom we look upon as dead, were really living.

Yes, truly, replied he, they all enjoy life who have escaped from the chains of the body as from a prison. But as to what you call life on earth, that is no more than one form of death. But see, here comes your father Paulus towards you! And as soon as I observed him, my eyes burst out into a flood of tears; but he took me in his arms, embraced me, and bade me not weep.

XV. When my first transports subsided, and I regained the liberty of speech, I addressed my father thus:—Thou best and most venerable of parents, since this, as I am informed by Africanus, is the only substantial life, why do I linger on earth, and not rather haste to come hither where you are?

That, replied he, is impossible; unless that God, whose temple is all that vast expanse you behold, shall free you from the fetters of the body, you can have no admission into this place. Mankind have received their being on this very condition, that they should labour for the preservation of that globe, which is situated, as you see, in the midst of this temple, and is called earth.

Men are likewise endowed with a soul, which is a portion of the eternal fires, which you call stars and constellations; and which, being round spherical bodies, animated by divine intelligences, perform their cycles and revolutions with amazing rapidity. It is your duty, therefore, my Publius, and that of all who have any veneration for the Gods, to preserve this wonderful union of soul and body; nor without the express command of him who gave you a soul, should the least thought be entertained of quitting human life, lest you seem to desert the post assigned you by God himself.

But rather follow the examples of your grandfather here, and of me, your father, in paying a strict regard to justice and piety; which is due in a great degree to parents and relations, but most of all to our country. Such a life as this is the true way to heaven, and to the company of those, who, after having lived on earth and escaped from the body, inhabit the place which you now behold.

XVI. This was the shining circle, or zone, whose remarkable brightness distinguishes it among the constellations, and which, after the Greeks, you call the Milky Way.

From thence, as I took a view of the universe, everything appeared beautiful and admirable; for there, those stars are to be seen that are never visible from our globe, and everything appears of such magnitude as we could not have imagined. The least of all the stars, was that removed furthest from heaven, and situated next to the earth; I mean our moon, which shines with a borrowed light. Now the globes of the stars far surpass the magnitude of our earth, which at that distance appeared so exceedingly small, that I could not but be sensibly affected on seeing our whole empire no larger than if we touched the earth as it were at a single point. . . .

While I was busied in admiring the scene of wonders, I could not help casting my eyes every now and then on the earth.

XIX. On which Africanus said—I perceive that you are still employed in contemplating the seat and residence of mankind. But if it appears to you so small, as in fact it really is, despise its vanities, and fix your attention for ever on these heavenly objects. Is it possible that you should attain any human applause or glory that is worth the contending for? The earth, you see, is peopled but in a very few places, and those too of small extent; and they appear like so many little spots of green scattered through vast uncultivated deserts. And those who inhabit the earth are not only so remote from each other as to be cut off from all mutual correspondence, but their situation being in oblique or contrary parts of the globe, or perhaps in those diametrically opposite to yours, all expectation of universal fame must fall to the ground. . . .

If, then, you wish to elevate your views to the contemplation of this eternal seat of splendour, you will not be satisfied with the praises of your fellow-mortals, nor with any human rewards that your exploits can obtain; but Virtue herself must point out to you the true and only object worthy of your pursuit. Leave to others to speak of you as they may, for speak they will. Their discourses will be confined to the narrow limits of the countries you see, nor will their duration be very extensive, for they will perish like those who utter them, and will be no more remembered by their posterity.

XXIV. When he had ceased to speak in this manner, I said—Oh, Africanus, if indeed the door of heaven is open to those who have deserved well of their country, although, indeed, from my childhood, I have always followed yours and my father's steps, and have not neglected to imitate your glory, still I will from henceforth strive to follow them more closely.

Follow them, then, said he, and consider your body only, not yourself, as mortal. For it is not your outward form which constitutes your being, but your mind; not that substance which is palpable to the senses, but your spiritual nature. *Know, then, that you are a god*—for a god it must be which flourishes, and feels, and recollects, and foresees, and governs, regulates and moves the body over which it is set, as the Supreme Ruler does the world which is subject to him. For as that Eternal Being moves whatever is mortal in this world, so the immortal mind of man moves the frail body with which it is connected.

XXV. For whatever is always moving must be eternal, but that which derives its motion from a power which is foreign to itself, when that motion ceases must itself lose its animation.

That alone, then, which moves itself can never cease to be moved, because it can never desert itself. Moreover, it must be the source, and origin, and principle of motion in all the rest. There can be nothing prior to a principle, for all things must originate from it, and it cannot itself derive its existence from any other source, for if it did it would no longer be a principle. And if it had no beginning it can have no end, for a beginning that is put an end to will neither be renewed by any other cause, nor will it produce anything else of itself. All things, therefore, must originate from one source. Thus it follows, that motion must have its source in something which is moved by itself, and which can neither have a beginning nor an end. Otherwise all the heavens and all nature must perish, for it is impossible that they can of themselves acquire any power of producing motion in themselves.

XXVI. As, therefore, it is plain that what is moved by itself must be eternal, who will deny that this is the general condition and nature of minds? For, as everything is inanimate which is moved by an impulse exterior to itself, so what is animated is moved by an interior impulse of its own; for this is the peculiar nature and power of mind. And if that alone has the power of self-motion, it can neither have had a beginning, nor can it have an end.

Do you, therefore, exercise this mind of yours in the best pursuits. And the best pursuits are those which consist in promoting the good of your country. Such employments will speed the flight of your mind to this its proper abode; and its flight will be still more rapid, if, even while it is enclosed in the body, it will look abroad, and disengage itself as much as possible from its bodily dwelling, by the contemplation of things which are external to itself.

This it should do to the utmost of its power. For the minds of those who have given themselves up to the pleasures of the body, paying as it were a servile obedience to their lustful impulses, have violated the laws of God and man; and therefore, when they are separated from their bodies, flutter continually round the earth on which they lived, and are not allowed to return to this celestial region, till they have been purified by the revolution of many ages.

Thus saying he vanished, and I awoke from my dream.

■ Discussion Questions

1. Given this excerpt, what social and political values did Cicero consider essential to leading a good life on earth and gaining eternal life in the hereafter?
2. According to Cicero, how were these values being undermined, and with what consequences?
3. What does this story suggest about the Romans' view of the world and their place in it?

CHAPTER 5

The Roman Empire, c. 44 B.C.–A.D. 284

The civil wars sparked by the assassination of Julius Caesar in 44 B.C. may have marked the death of the Roman republic, but they also signaled the birth of the Roman Empire. Through masterful political and military maneuvering, Caesar's heir Octavian (63 B.C.–A.D. 14) emerged from the wars as Rome's undisputed leader. In recognition of this fact, in 27 B.C. the Senate granted him special powers and an honorary name, *Augustus* ("divinely favored"). He thereupon forged a new system of government that laid the foundations for two hundred years of peace and prosperity. The documents in this chapter bring the empire to life in the words of its emperor and those of the people living under imperial rule, from an official carrying out imperial orders to a prostitute advertising her services.

14. Augustus, *The Accomplishments of Augustus* (A.D. 14)

When Augustus assumed power in 27 B.C., he cast himself not as an innovator but rather as a guardian of tradition. In fact, over the next four decades, he used republican customs to cloak his true intent: the creation of a monarchical government in which he would reign supreme. In this document, Augustus describes how he achieved this goal and thereby transformed the republic into an empire. He composed the text to describe the course of his rule, and he ordered it to be engraved on bronze tablets upon his death and erected outside his mausoleum in Rome. That copy did not survive, but an almost complete one did, inscribed on the walls of a temple in modern-day Ankara, Turkey. Here Augustus commemorates the offices and honors bestowed upon him, his expenditures, and his triumphs in war and peace.

At the age of nineteen, on my own initiative and at my own expense, I raised an army by means of which I liberated the Republic, which was oppressed by the tyranny of a faction.[1] For which reason the senate, with honorific decrees, made me a member of its order in the consulship of Gaius Pansa and Aulus Hirtius [43 B.C.], giving me at the same time consular rank in voting, and granted me the *imperium*.[2] It ordered me as propraetor, together with the consuls, to see to it

---

[1]Antony and his adherents are meant. The period referred to is late 44 to early 43 B.C., when Octavian (as Augustus was then known) was in coalition with the Senate against Antony.

[2]**Imperium** was the supreme administrative right or power to command (in military, religious, and judicial matters), held first by Roman kings and in the republic by chief officials. [ED.]

From *Roman Civilization: Selected Readings,* ed. Naphtali Lewis and Meyer Reinhold, 3d ed., vol. 1 (New York: Columbia University Press, 1990), 561–72.

that the state suffered no harm.[3] Moreover, in the same year, when both consuls had fallen in the war, the people elected me consul and a triumvir for the settlement of the commonwealth.

Those who assassinated my father[4] I drove into exile, avenging their crime by due process of law; and afterwards when they waged war against the state, I conquered them twice on the battlefield [the two battles of Phillippi (42 B.C.)].

I waged many wars throughout the whole world by land and by sea, both civil and foreign, and when victorious I spared all citizens who sought pardon. Foreign peoples who could safely be pardoned I preferred to spare rather than to extirpate. About 500,000 Roman citizens were under military oath to me. Of these, when their terms of service were ended, I settled in colonies or sent back to their own municipalities a little more than 300,000, and to all of these I allotted lands or granted money as rewards for military service. I captured 600 ships, exclusive of those which were of smaller class than triremes.[5] . . .

The dictatorship offered to me in the consulship of Marcus Marcellus and Lucius Arruntius [22 B.C.] by the people and by the senate, both in my absence and in my presence, I refused to accept. In the midst of a critical scarcity of grain I did not decline the supervision of the grain supply, which I so administered that within a few days I freed the whole people from imminent panic and danger by my expenditures and efforts.[6] The consulship, too, which was offered to me at that time as an annual office for life, I refused to accept.

In the consulship of Marcus Vinicius and Quintus Lucretius, and again in that of Publius Lentulus and Gnaeus Lentulus, and a third time in that of Paullus Fabius Maximus and Quintus Tubero [in 19, 18, and 11 B.C.], though the Roman senate and people unitedly agreed that I should be elected sole guardian of the laws and morals with supreme authority, I refused to accept any office offered me which was contrary to the traditions of our ancestors.[7] The measures which the senate desired at that time to be taken by me I carried out by virtue of the tribunician power.[8] In this power I five times voluntarily requested and was given a colleague by the senate.[9] . . .

I built the following structures:[10] the senate house and the Chalcidicum adjoining it; the temple of Apollo on the Palatine with its porticoes; the temple of the deified Julius; the Lupercal; the portico at the Circus Flaminius, which I allowed to be called Octavia after the name of the man who had built an earlier portico on the same site; the state box at the Circus Maximus; the temples of Jupiter the Smiter and Jupiter the Thunderer on the Capitoline; the temple of Quirinus; the temples of Minerva and Queen Juno and of Jupiter Freedom on the Aventine; the temple of the Lares at the head of the Sacred Way; the temple of the Penates on the Velia; the temple of Youth and the temple of the Great Mother on the Palatine.

I repaired the Capitol and the theater of Pompey with enormous expenditures on both works, without having my name inscribed on them. I repaired the conduits of the aqueducts which were

---

[3]The formula for the "ultimate decree of the Senate." Augustus refers here to the war against Antony, which culminated in the two battles at Mutina in April of 43 B.C.

[4]Julius Caesar, his adoptive father. Yet in general Augustus sought to distance himself from the image and policies of Julius Caesar.

[5]The naval victories over Sextus Pompey (at Mylae and Naulochus) and over Antony and Cleopatra (at Actium) are meant. *Triremes* were the standard Greek war galley used until the Hellenistic period.

[6]This marks the beginning of the assumption by the Roman emperors of the *cura annonae* ("administration of the grain supply") of Rome as a permanent function of the imperial administration.

[7]In effect, Augustus was thus offered permanent dictatorship in a new guise.

[8]Augustus here refers to his moral and social legislation, the first installments of which were issued in 18 B.C.

[9]Marcus Agrippa, twice; Tiberius, three times.

[10]To identify for the reader each of the public works listed in this and the two following paragraphs would require a series of footnotes longer than the text.

falling into ruin in many places because of age, and I doubled the capacity of the aqueduct called Marcia by admitting a new spring into its conduit. I completed the Julian Forum and the basilica which was between the temple of Castor and the temple of Saturn, works begun and far advanced by my father, and when the same basilica was destroyed by fire, I enlarged its site and began rebuilding the structure, which is to be inscribed with the names of my sons; and in case it should not be completed while I am still alive, I left instructions that the work be completed by my heirs. In my sixth consulship [28 B.C.] I repaired eighty-two temples of the gods in the city, in accordance with a resolution of the senate, neglecting none which at that time required repair. In my seventh consulship [27 B.C.] I reconstructed the Flaminian Way from the city as far as Ariminum, and also all the bridges except the Mulvian and the Minucian.

On my own private land I built the temple of Mars Ultor and the Augustan Forum from spoils of war. On ground bought for the most part from private owners I built the theater adjoining the temple of Apollo which was to be inscribed with the name of my son-in-law Marcus Marcellus. In the Capitol, in the temple of the deified Julius, in the temple of Apollo, in the temple of Vesta, and in the temple of Mars Ultor I consecrated gifts from spoils of war which cost me about 100,000,000 sesterces.[11] In my fifth consulship [29 B.C.] I remitted to the municipalities and colonies of Italy 35,000 pounds of crown gold which they were collecting in honor of my triumphs; and afterwards, whenever I was acclaimed *imperator,* I did not accept the crown gold, though the municipalities and colonies decreed it with the same enthusiasm as before.

I gave a gladiatorial show three times in my own name, and five times in the names of my sons or grandsons; at these shows about 10,000 fought. Twice I presented to the people in my own name an exhibition of athletes invited from all parts of the world, and a third time in the name of my grandson. I presented games in my own name four times, and in addition twenty-three times in the place of other magistrates.[12] On behalf of the college of fifteen, as master of that college, with Marcus Agrippa as my colleague, I celebrated the Secular Games in the consulship of Gaius Furnius and Gaius Silanus. In my thirteenth consulship [2 B.C.] I was the first to celebrate the Games of Mars, which subsequently the consuls, in accordance with a decree of the senate and a law, have regularly celebrated in the succeeding years. Twenty-six times I provided for the people, in my own name or in the names of my sons or grandsons, hunting spectacles of African wild beasts in the circus or in the Forum or in the amphitheaters; in these exhibitions about 3,500 animals were killed. . . .

I brought peace to the sea by suppressing the pirates.[13] In that war I turned over to their masters for punishment nearly 30,000 slaves who had run away from their owners and taken up arms against the state. The whole of Italy voluntarily took an oath of allegiance to me and demanded me as its leader in the war in which I was victorious at Actium.[14] The same oath was taken by the provinces of the Gauls, the Spains, Africa, Sicily, and Sardinia. More than 700 senators served at that time under my standards; of that number eighty-three attained the consulship and about 170 obtained priesthoods, either before that date or subsequently, up to the day on which this document was written.

I extended the frontiers of all the provinces of the Roman people on whose boundaries were peoples not subject to our empire.[15] I restored peace to the Gallic and Spanish provinces and

---

[11]A **sesterce** is a Roman silver coin. [ED.]   [12]These were games in the theatrical and circus shows.
[13]The naval war with Sextus Pompey that ended in 36 B.C.
[14]The war against Antony and Cleopatra, who were defeated at Actium in 31 B.C.
[15]The emphasis is on the frontier policy in the west. The eastern provinces were hardly as well stabilized under Augustus.

likewise to Germany, that is to the entire region bounded by the Ocean from Gades to the mouth of the Elbe River. I caused peace to be restored in the Alps, from the region nearest to the Adriatic Sea as far as the Tuscan Sea, without undeservedly making war against any people. My fleet sailed the Ocean from the mouth of the Rhine eastward as far as the territory of the Cimbrians, to which no Roman previously had penetrated either by land or by sea. The Cimbrians, the Charydes, the Semnones, and other German peoples of the same region through their envoys sought my friendship and that of the Roman people.[16] At my command and under my auspices two armies were led almost at the same time into Ethiopia and into Arabia which is called Felix; and very large forces of the enemy belonging to both peoples were killed in battle, and many towns were captured. In Ethiopia a penetration was made as far as the town of Napata, which is next to Meroe; in Arabia the army advanced into the territory of the Sabaeans to the town of Mariba.[17]

I added Egypt to the empire of the Roman people.[18] . . .

I established colonies of soldiers in Africa, Sicily, Macedonia, in both Spanish provinces, in Achaea, Asia, Syria, Narbonese Gaul, and Pisidia. Italy, moreover, has twenty-eight colonies established by me, which in my lifetime have grown to be famous and populous.

A number of military standards lost by other generals I recovered, after conquering the enemy, from Spain, Gaul, and the Dalmatians. The Parthians I compelled to restore to me the spoils and standards of three Roman armies and to seek the friendship of the Roman people as suppliants.[19] The standards, moreover, I deposited in the inner shrine of the temple of Mars Ultor.

Through Tiberius Nero, who was then my stepson and legate, I conquered and subjected to the empire of the Roman people the Pannonian tribes, to which before my principate no army of the Roman people had ever penetrated; and I extended the frontier of Illyricum to the bank of the Danube River. An army of the Dacians which had crossed to our side of the river was conquered and destroyed under my auspices, and later on, my army crossed the Danube and compelled the Dacian tribes to submit to the orders of the Roman people. . . .

In my sixth and seventh consulships,[20] after I had put an end to the civil wars, having attained supreme power by universal consent, I transferred the state from my own power to the control of the Roman senate and the people. For this service of mine I received the title of Augustus by decree of the senate, and the doorposts of my house were publicly decked with laurels, the civic crown was affixed over my doorway, and a golden shield was set up in the Julian senate house, which, as the inscription on this shield testifies, the Roman senate and people gave me in recognition of my valor, clemency, justice, and devotion. After that time I excelled all in authority, but I possessed no more power than the others who were my colleagues in each magistracy.

When I held my thirteenth consulship, the senate, the equestrian order, and the entire Roman people gave me the title of "father of the country" and decreed that this title should be inscribed in the vestibule of my house, in the Julian senate house, and in the Augustan Forum on the pedestal of the chariot which was set up in my honor by decree of the senate. At the time I wrote this document I was in my seventy-sixth year.

---

[16]The reference is to the campaign of A.D. 5, when Tiberius penetrated Germany as far as the Elbe River.

[17]This is the disastrous expedition of Aelius Gallus in 25–24 B.C. against Arabia Felix (Yemen); the punitive Ethiopian expedition under Gaius Petronius in 24–22 B.C. achieved greater success.

[18]On the death of Cleopatra in 30 B.C.

[19]These were the standards lost by Crassus at the battle of Carrhae in 53 B.C. and in Mark Antony's disastrous operations against the Parthians in 36 B.C. They were restored as the result of diplomatic negotiations; Augustus's version is calculated to salve Roman pride.

[20]28 and 27 B.C. The reorganization of 28–27 B.C. put an end to the unlimited powers exercised by Augustus without legal title from the expiration of the triumvirate in 33 B.C. to that date. Augustus justifies his extralegal position by affirming that he held it "by universal consent."

■ **Discussion Questions**

1. What does this document reveal about the ways in which Augustus used tradition to effect political change?
2. Upon what foundation does Augustus's power and success as a ruler seem to rest?
3. What do you think Augustus's primary goal was in composing this account of his political career?

15. *Notices and Graffiti from Pompeii* (First Century A.D.)

Among the remarkable features of the Roman Empire was not simply its immense expanse but the many cities, both new and old, that dotted its landscape. The following messages, graffiti, and election notices from the Roman municipality of Pompeii illuminate the hustle and bustle of urban life in the first century of the empire. Located at the foot of Mount Vesuvius in southern Italy, Pompeii at the time was a thriving commercial city, with a fashionable resort nearby. In A.D. 79, Mount Vesuvius erupted, burying the city in cinders and ash. Although the local population was destroyed or fled, remarkably the city's buildings were preserved, as were hundreds of announcements painted in red on whitewashed walls, along with the scribbles of passersby. Here we see many facets of people's daily lives within the empire, from political appeals to lovesick lamentations.

In the Arrius Pollio block owned by Gnaeus Alleius Nigidius Maius, to lease from the fifteenth of next July, shops with their stalls, high-class second-story apartments, and a house. Prospective lessees may apply to Primus, slave of Gnaeus Alleius Nigidius Maius.

On the property owned by Julia Felix, daughter of Spurius, to lease from the thirteenth of next August to the thirteenth of the sixth August hence, or five consecutive years, the élite Venus Baths, shops, stalls, and second-story apartments. Interested parties may apply to the lessor in the matter.

The fruit dealers together with Helvius Vestalis unanimously urge the election of Marcus Holconius Priscus as duovir[1] with judicial power.

The goldsmiths unanimously urge the election of Gaius Cuspius Pansa as aedile.[2]

I ask you to elect Gaius Julius Polybius aedile. He gets good bread [for us].

The muleteers urge the election of Gaius Julius Polybius as duovir.

The worshippers of Isis unaminously urge the election of Gnaeus Helvius Sabinus as aedile.

Proculus, make Sabinus aedile and he will do as much for you.

His neighbors urge you to elect Lucius Statius Receptus duovir with judicial power; he is worthy. Aemilius Celer, a neighbor, wrote this. May you take sick if you maliciously erase this!

---

[1]A **duovir** was one of two chief magistrates of Roman municipalities. [ED.]
[2]An **aedile** was a municipal administrator. [ED.]

From *Roman Civilization: Selected Readings*, ed. Naphtali Lewis and Meyer Reinhold, 3d ed., vol. 2 (New York: Columbia University Press, 1990), 126–27, 237–38, 276–78.

Satia and Petronia support and ask you to elect Marcus Casellius and Lucius Albucius aediles. May we always have such citizens in our colony!

I ask you to elect Epidius Sabinus duovir with judicial power. He is worthy, a defender of the colony, and in the opinion of the respected judge Suedius Clemens and by agreement of the council, because of his services and uprightness, worthy of the municipality. Elect him!

If upright living is considered any recommendation, Lucretius Fronto is well worthy of the office.

Genialis urges the election of Bruttius Balbus as duovir. He will protect the treasury.

I ask you to elect Marcus Cerrinius Vatia to the aedileship. All the late drinkers support him. Florus and Fructus wrote this.

The petty thieves support Vatia for the aedileship.

I ask you to elect Aulus Vettius Firmus aedile. He is worthy of the municipality. I ask you to elect him, ballplayers. Elect him!

I wonder, O wall, that you have not fallen in ruins from supporting the stupidities of so many scribblers.[3]

Twenty pairs of gladiators of Decimus Lucretius Satrius Valens, life-time flamen[4] of Nero son of Caesar Augustus, and ten pairs of gladiators of Decimus Lucretius Valens, his son, will fight at Pompeii on April 8, 9, 10, 11, 12. There will be a full card of wild beast combats, and awnings [for the spectators]. Aemilius Celer [painted this sign], all alone in the moonlight.

Market days: Saturday in Pompeii, Sunday in Nuceria, Monday in Atella, Tuesday in Nola, Wednesday in Cumae, Thursday in Puteoli, Friday in Rome.

> 6th: cheese 1, bread 8, oil 3, wine 3[5]
> 7th: bread 8, oil 5, onions 5, bowl 1, bread for the slave[?] 2, wine 2
> 8th: bread 8, bread for the slave[?] 4, grits 3
> 9th: wine for the winner 1 *denarius,* bread 8, wine 2, cheese 2
> 10th: . . . 1 *denarius,* bread 2, for women 8, wheat 1 *denarius,* cucumber 1, dates 1, incense 1, cheese 2, sausage 1, soft cheese 4, oil 7

Pleasure says: "You can get a drink here for an *as,* a better drink for two, Falernian[6] for four.

A copper pot is missing from this shop. 65 sesterces reward if anybody brings it back, 20 sesterces if he reveals the thief so we can get our property back.

The weaver Successus loves the innkeeper's slave girl, Iris by name. She doesn't care for him, but he begs her to take pity on him. Written by his rival. So long.

---

[3]Unlike the others, this inscription is a *graffito,* scratched on the wall.

[4]A **flamen** was a priest. [ED.]

[5]The initial number is the day of the month, the numbers following the items of food indicate expenditures in *asses,* except where *denarii* are specified. A *denarius* was a Roman silver coin originally valued at ten, and later sixteen, asses. It was the equivalent of the Greek drachma. [ED.]

[6]One of the prized wines of the Italian countryside (named after a district in Campania), best known from the poems of Horace that sing its praises.

[Answer by the rival:] Just because you're bursting with envy, don't pick on a handsomer man, a lady-killer and a gallant.

[Answer by the first writer:] There's nothing more to say or write. You love Iris, who doesn't care for you.

Take your lewd looks and flirting eyes off another man's wife, and show some decency on your face!

Anybody in love, come here. I want to break Venus's ribs with a club and cripple the goddess's loins. If she can pierce my tender breast, why can't I break her head with a club?

> I write at Love's dictation and Cupid's instruction;
> But damn it! I don't want to be a god without you.

[A prostitute's sign:] I am yours for 2 *asses* cash.

■ Discussion Questions

1. Given these messages and notices, how would you describe life in Pompeii? What did people do for a living? What did the city look like?
2. What do the election announcements reveal about the residents' political expectations and their role in local politics?
3. Did any of these messages surprise you? Where might you find similar messages today?

16. Pliny the Younger, *Letters*   (A.D. 111–113)

Although Augustus describes his rise to power and ensuing glories in vivid detail, he provides little insight into the mechanics of running a vast and diverse empire. These letters help fill this gap. Pliny the Younger (A.D. 61/62–c. 114) wrote them while serving as governor of Bithynia, a Roman province in modern-day Turkey. A lawyer by training, Pliny had enjoyed a distinguished public career in Rome. Emperor Trajan (r. A.D. 98–117) appointed him to the provincial governorship in A.D. 111 to combat local fiscal mismanagement. Such internal disorder undermined not only the stability of the empire but also the glory of the emperor. More than one hundred pieces of Pliny's official correspondence regarding Bithynia are extant, including his letters to the emperor and the emperor's replies.

Gaius Pliny to the Emperor Trajan: . . . I entered Bithynia some days later than I had hoped, on the 17th of September. Still, I can't complain about the delay, since I did have the auspicious opportunity of celebrating your birthday in the province. Now I am examining the disbursements, revenues, and debtor lists of the municipality of Prusa. The closer my involvement becomes, the more I realize how necessary it is. In a number of cases, funds are being detained by private individuals for various reasons, and besides that, money is being paid out for expenses that are by no means legitimate. That is what I have to tell you, Sir, fresh upon my arrival. (10.17a)

Gaius Pliny to the Emperor Trajan: Sir, the citizens of Prusa have a public bath. It is dingy and old. Naturally they set a high priority on building a new one, and I think you can acquiesce in their aim. There will be the money to do it—first of all, those sums in private hands which I have

From *Rome: Late Republic and Principate,* ed. Walter Emile Kaegi Jr. and Peter White, vol. 2, *University of Chicago Readings in Western Civilization* (Chicago: University of Chicago Press, 1986), 178–82.

begun to call in and collect. And second, the townspeople are prepared to apply toward construction the money which has always gone to subsidize the dole of olive oil. But money aside, the prestige of the town and the magnificence of your reign are tied up in this project. (10.23)

Trajan to Pliny: If the construction of a new bath will not overtax the resources of Prusa, then we can acquiesce in their aim—provided that no assessment is levied for it, and that it does not force them to curtail basic operations later on. (10.24)

Gaius Pliny to the Emperor Trajan: While I was touring the other end of the province, a tremendous fire at Nicomedia destroyed many private homes and two public buildings on opposite sides of the same street, the temple of Isis and the civic boosters' center. The fire spread as far as it did thanks both to a high wind and to the shiftlessness of bystanders who chose to stand stock-still contemplating the disaster. But apart from that, the town had no pumps or buckets, or any kind of fire-fighting apparatus at all. Well, the equipment will be procured: I have already given instructions on that score. But please consider, Sir, whether you think a corps of professionals should be formed, limited to 150 persons. (10.33)

Trajan to Pliny: Your idea that a corps of firemen could be formed at Nicomedia has many precedents in its favor. But we need to keep in mind that your province and particularly the cities in that area have had trouble with just such outfits. Whatever name, for whatever purpose, we give to people who band together, they will turn into political groups in no time at all. Therefore it is better to provide equipment which will be of use in fighting fires, and to put property owners on notice that they should take action themselves, and call on the services of bystanders if circumstances require. (10.34)

Gaius Pliny to the Emperor Trajan: Sir, the citizens of Nicomedia have spent 3,318,000 sesterces on an aqueduct which was halted before it was finished, and finally torn down. They then committed 200,000 sesterces to a second aqueduct, but since this one was also abandoned, they face further expense on top of all the money they have already thrown away, if they are to have any water. I have personally inspected the spring, which is crystal-clear. I think the water should be carried by elevated conduit, according to the original plan, so that the supply will reach more than just the lower levels of the town. A few arches are still in place; some new ones could be built with dressed stone taken from the second project, and I think a fair stretch should be constructed of brick, which is cheaper and more convenient. But it is critically important that you send out a hydraulic engineer or an architect so that past experience here does not repeat itself. I can only assure you that in terms of utility and beauty, this project is fully worthy of your reign. (10.37)

Trajan to Pliny: Arrangements should be made to supply water to the town of Nicomedia. I have every confidence that you will set to work with the diligence that is called for. But, good lord, part of that diligence should be to find out whose fault it was that the Nicomedians wasted so much money up till now. We don't want them just scratching each other's backs with this starting and stopping of aqueducts. Therefore bring to my attention whatever you find out. (10.38)

Gaius Pliny to the Emperor Trajan: Sir, at Nicaea a theater which is well into the construction phase but not finished has already cost more than 10,000,000 sesterces (at any rate, that is what I am told; I have not gone over the books). All wasted, I am afraid. The structure has settled and developed huge cracks, possibly because it was built on soft, wet ground, or because the stone used was weak and porous. The question is to decide whether to continue work, or to stop, or even to demolish the building—the foundations and lower tiers that support the rest look a lot more grandiose than solid to me. With the interruption of work on the main part, some complementary structures which were promised by private citizens (halls outside, and a colonnade around the top of the auditorium) are now in limbo.

Before I arrived here, the citizens of Nicaea also began to restore their gymnasium, which had been destroyed by fire. The plans called for a more spacious complex with more buildings than before. They have already invested a fair amount, but to no practical purpose I fear: the layout is poorly designed and the buildings are too far apart. Furthermore an architect (admittedly a rival of the man who began the job) tells me that though the walls are twenty-two feet thick, they will not take the weight put on them: that is because the core consists of loose stone, and there is no outer girdle of brick.

At Claudiopolis, too, building is underway (if it should not be called excavation) for an enormous public bath sited in a hollow at the foot of a mountain. The funds in this case come from entrance fees which have either been paid already by the new members you graciously added to the town council, or which will be paid when I move to collect.

I am very anxious that good use be made of the public funds at Nicaea, and of your kind involvement (more precious than money) at Claudiopolis. And so I feel obliged to ask that you send out an architect to have a look at the baths as well as the theater. We need to know whether it makes more sense, after all the money that has been spent, to finish the projects as best we can according to plan, or whether to rebuild what needs rebuilding or move what needs moving so that we do not throw good money after bad. (10.39)

Trajan to Pliny: Since you are on the spot, you are in the best position to resolve what should be done about the theater under construction at Nicaea. I will be content to have some note of your decision. Wait till the theater is finished before pressing members of the community to follow through on projects meant to accompany it. These Greeks are in love with gymnasiums, which is probably why the Nicaeans were too ambitious when they started building. They should be content with something that meets their needs. Decide for yourself what to tell the citizens of Claudiopolis about their ill-located bath. It is not possible that you have no architects; there are men with experience and talent in every province. At least you shouldn't imagine that it saves time to have them sent from Rome, as we usually get them from Greece ourselves. (10.40)

Gaius Pliny to the Emperor Trajan: That day on which you saved the realm by taking it under your care, Sir, we commemorated with all the joy the thought inspires in us. We prayed that the gods would bless and protect you for the good of all mankind, because our security is linked to your well-being. I administered the oath of allegiance to the soldiers at the traditional ceremony, and the people of the province manifested their devotion by chiming in. (10.52)

Trajan to Pliny: My dear Pliny, I am grateful for your letter about the fealty and joy which soldiers and civilians alike showed during the ceremonies you organized on the anniversary of my accession. (10.53)

■ Discussion Questions

1. What aspects of the local administration within Bithynia do Pliny and Trajan regard as problematic, and why?
2. What challenges did Pliny face in his efforts to correct these problems?
3. What do these letters reveal about the relationship between central and local authority in the Roman Empire?

CHAPTER 6

The Transformation of the Roman Empire, A.D. 284–C. 600

The Roman Empire had faced many challenges since its formation at the end of the first century B.C., but by the fourth century A.D., the forces of change proved too powerful to resist, as the documents in this chapter attest. Christianity was spreading far and wide, even gaining the allegiance of the emperor Constantine in 312. Although polytheism persisted, over the course of the fourth century Christianity gained the upper hand, and its success permanently transformed Roman culture and society. At the same time, Germanic peoples crossed the empire's borders and migrated westward, eventually establishing kingdoms that replaced imperial government. These new regimes became the heirs of Roman civilization in the west, setting the stage for the development of medieval Europe, while in the east the Roman imperial legacy lived on in the Byzantine Empire.

17. St. Jerome, *Letter 107*   (A.D. 403)

The Christianization of the Roman Empire extended beyond public debates into family life. Biblical scholar and monk St. Jerome (A.D. c. 345–420) wrote this letter in A.D. 403 to Laeta, a Christian woman in Rome, regarding how best to educate her daughter, Paula. For Jerome, the answer was simple: send her to a monastery, where she would be trained to be a temple of God, shielded from the world's evils. Jerome's advice reveals the growing appeal of monasticism and its underlying ascetic ideals, which elevated virginity and sexual renunciation as the highest of Christian virtues. Monasticism thus offered women an identity outside the confines of their traditional roles as wives and mothers. Laeta heeded Jerome's advice, and Paula eventually became the head of a female monastery in Bethlehem, where Jerome himself lived and worked.

From *Select Letters of St. Jerome*, trans. F. A. Wright (Cambridge, Mass.: Harvard University Press, 1963), 338–47, 351, 359, 363–67.

LETTER CVII
TO LAETA[1]
A GIRL'S EDUCATION
WRITTEN A.D. 403

The blessed apostle Paul, writing to the Corinthians and instructing Christ's novice church in the ways of sacred discipline, among his other precepts laid down also the following rule: "The woman that hath an husband that believeth not, and if he be pleased to dwell with her, let her not leave him. For the unbelieving husband is sanctified by the believing wife, and the unbelieving wife is sanctified by the believing husband; else were your children unclean, but now they are holy."[2] . . . You yourself are the child of a mixed marriage; but now you and my dear Toxotius are Paula's parents. Who would ever have believed that the granddaughter of the Roman pontiff Albinus would be born in answer to a mother's vows; that the grandfather would stand by and rejoice while the baby's yet stammering tongue cried "Alleluia"; and that even the old man would nurse in his arms one of Christ's own virgins? . . . Christians are not born but made. The gilded Capitol to-day looks dingy, all the temples in Rome are covered with soot and cobwebs, the city is shaken to its foundations, and the people hurry past the ruined shrines and pour out to visit the martyrs' graves. . . .

Even in Rome now heathenism [polytheism] languishes in solitude. Those who once were the gods of the Gentiles are left beneath their deserted pinnacles to the company of owls and night-birds. The army standards bear the emblem of the cross. The purple robes of kings and the jewels that sparkle on their diadems are adorned with the gibbet sign that has brought to us salvation. To-day even the Egyptian Serapis[3] has become a Christian: Marnas[4] mourns in his prison at Gaza, and fears continually that his temple will be overthrown. From India, from Persia and from Ethiopia we welcome crowds of monks every hour. The Armenians have laid aside their quivers, the Huns are learning the psalter, the frosts of Scythia are warmed by the fire of faith. The ruddy, flaxen-haired Getae carry tent-churches about with their armies; and perhaps the reason why they fight with us on equal terms is that they believe in the same religion. . . .

It was my intention, in answer to your prayers and those of the saintly Marcella, to direct my discourse to a mother, that is, to you, and to show you how to bring up our little Paula, who was consecrated to Christ before she was born, the child of prayers before the hour of conception. In our own days we have seen something such as we read of in the prophets: Hannah exchanged her barrenness for fruitful motherhood, you have exchanged a fertility bound up with sorrow for children who will live for ever. I tell you confidently that you who have given your first-born to the Lord will receive sons at His hand. The first-born are the offerings due under the Law. . . .

Thus must a soul be trained which is to be a temple of God. It must learn to hear nothing and to say nothing save what pertains to the fear of the Lord. It must have no comprehension of foul words, no knowledge of worldly songs, and its childish tongue must be imbued with the

---

[1] Laeta, to whom this letter was sent in A.D. 403, married Toxotius, son of Paula and Toxotius, "in whose veins ran the noble blood of Aeneas" (Letter CVIII, 4). She herself was the daughter of a pagan, the pontiff Albinus, and had written to Jerome concerning the education of her child, Paula. The advice given in this letter—that the little girl should be sent to Bethlehem to be educated by her grandmother Paula and her aunt Eustochium—was accepted, and she eventually succeeded Eustochium as head of the nunnery there.

[2] 1 Corinthians, vii. 13.

[3] In A.D. 389, the temple of Serapis at Alexandria was pulled down, and a Christian church was built on the site.

[4] The chief Syrian god in Gaza.

sweet music of the psalms. Let boys with their wanton frolics be kept far from Paula: let even her maids and attendants hold aloof from association with the worldly, lest they render their evil knowledge worse by teaching it to her. Have a set of letters made for her, of boxwood or of ivory, and tell her their names. Let her play with them, making play a road to learning, and let her not only grasp the right order of the letters and remember their names in a simple song, but also frequently upset their order and mix the last letters with the middle ones, the middle with the first. Thus she will know them all by sight as well as by sound. When she begins with uncertain hand to use the pen, either let another hand be put over hers to guide her baby fingers, or else have the letters marked on the tablet so that her writing may follow their outlines and keep to their limits without straying away. Offer her prizes for spelling, tempting her with such trifling gifts as please young children. Let her have companions too in her lessons, so that she may seek to rival them and be stimulated by any praise they win. You must not scold her if she is somewhat slow; praise is the best sharpener of wits. . . .

Her very dress and outward appearance should remind her of Him to whom she is promised. Do not pierce her ears, or paint with white lead and rouge the cheeks that are consecrated to Christ. Do not load her neck with pearls and gold, do not weigh down her head with jewels, do not dye her hair red and thereby presage for her the fires of hell. . . .

Let her every day repeat to you a portion of the Scriptures as her fixed task. A good number of lines she should learn by heart in the Greek, but knowledge of the Latin should follow close after. If the tender lips are not trained from the beginning, the language is spoiled by a foreign accent and our native tongue debased by alien faults. You must be her teacher, to you her childish ignorance must look for a model. Let her never see anything in you or her father which she would do wrong to imitate. Remember that you are a virgin's parents and that you can teach her better by example than by words. Flowers quickly fade; violets, lilies, and saffron are soon withered by a baleful breeze. Let her never appear in public without you, let her never visit the churches and the martyrs' shrines except in your company. Let no youth or curled dandy ogle her. Let our little virgin never stir a finger's breadth from her mother when she attends a vigil or an all-night service. I would not let her have a favourite maid into whose ear she might frequently whisper: what she says to one, all ought to know. . . .

If ever you visit the country, do not leave your daughter behind at Rome. She should have neither the knowledge nor the power to live without you, and should tremble to be alone. Let her not converse with worldlings [worldly people], nor associate with virgins who neglect their vows. Let her not be present at slaves' weddings, nor take part in noisy household games. I know that some people have laid down the rule that a Christian virgin should not bathe along with eunuchs or with married women, inasmuch as eunuchs are still men at heart, and women big with child are a revolting sight. For myself I disapprove altogether of baths in the case of a full-grown virgin. She ought to blush at herself and be unable to look at her own nakedness. If she mortifies and enslaves her body by vigils and fasting, if she desires to quench the flame of lust and to check the hot desires of youth by a cold chastity, if she hastens to spoil her natural beauty by a deliberate squalor, why should she rouse a sleeping fire by the incentive of baths?[5] . . .

You will answer: "How shall I, a woman of the world living in crowded Rome, be able to keep all these injunctions?" Do not then take up a burden which you cannot bear. . . . Let her be reared in a monastery amid bands of virgins, where she will learn never to take an oath, and to regard a lie as sacrilege. Let her know nothing of the world, but live like the angels; let her be in the flesh and without the flesh, thinking all mankind to be like herself.

---

[5]That is, the Roman, or as we call them "Turkish," baths.

■ **Discussion Questions**

1. At the time Jerome wrote this letter, Christianity had been the official religion of the empire for more than a decade. What explicit signs of Christianity's triumph does Jerome describe?
2. How does Jerome think Paula should be raised, and why?
3. What do Jerome's views on Paula's education suggest about Christianity's attitudes toward women in general and female sexuality in particular?

18. *The Burgundian Code* (c. 475–525)

The migration of Germanic tribes into the West changed imperial politics and society just as profoundly as Christianity did. These newcomers gradually formed independent kingdoms based on a mixture of their own and Roman traditions, which soon superseded Roman provincial government. Law codes that were established by Germanic leaders from the fifth century on were a crucial component of their state-building efforts. Rome provided a powerful precedent in this regard, with its emphasis on written law as both the basis of social order and a manifestation of state authority. These excerpts are drawn from one of the most comprehensive early Germanic law codes, the Burgundian Code, compiled by the kings of the Burgundians, an East Germanic tribe, in the late fifth and early sixth centuries. At this time, they ruled over a large kingdom encompassing much of the Roman province of Gaul.

First Constitution

In the name of God in the second year of the reign of our lord the most glorious king Gundobad, this book concerning laws past and present, and to be preserved throughout all future time, has been issued on the fourth day before the Kalends of April (March 29) at Lyons. . . .

For the love of justice, through which God is pleased and the power of earthly kingdoms acquired, we have obtained the consent of our counts (*comites*) and leaders (*proceres*), and have desired to establish such laws that the integrity and equity of those judging may exclude all rewards and corruptions from themselves.

Therefore all administrators (*administrantes*) and judges must judge from the present time on between Burgundians and Romans according to our laws which have been set forth and corrected by a common method, to the end that no one may hope or presume to receive anything by way of reward or emolument from any party as the result of the suits or decisions; but let him whose case is deserving obtain justice and let the integrity of the judge alone suffice to accomplish this. . . .

Therefore let all nobles (*optimates*), counsellors (*consiliarii*), bailiffs (*domestici*), mayors of our palace (*maiores domus nostrae*), chancellors (*cancellarii*), counts (*comites*) of the cities or villages, Burgundian as well as Roman, and all appointed judges and military judges (*judices militantes*) know that nothing can be accepted in connection with those suits which have been acted upon or decided, and that nothing can be sought in the name of promise or reward from those litigating; nor can the parties (to the suit) be compelled by the judge to make a payment in order that they may receive anything (from their suit). . . .

Indeed if any judge, barbarian as well as Roman, shall not render decisions according to those provisions which the laws contain because he has been prevented by ignorance or negligence,

From *The Burgundian Code,* trans. Katherine Fischer Drew (Philadelphia: University of Pennsylvania Press, 1972), 17–24, 30–33, 40–47.

and he has been diverted from justice for this reason, let him know that he must pay thirty solidi[1] and that the case must be judged again on behalf of the aggrieved parties. . . .

OF MURDERS

If anyone presumes with boldness or rashness bent on injury to kill a native freeman of our people of any nation or a servant of the king, in any case a man of barbarian tribe, let him make restitution for the committed crime not otherwise than by the shedding of his own blood.

We decree that this rule be added to the law by a reasonable provision, that if violence shall have been done by anyone to any person, so that he is injured by blows of lashes or by wounds, and if he pursues his persecutor and overcome by grief and indignation kills him, proof of the deed shall be afforded by the act itself or by suitable witnesses who can be believed. Then the guilty party shall be compelled to pay to the relatives of the person killed half his wergeld according to the status of the person: that is, if he shall have killed a noble of the highest class (*optimas nobilis*), we decree that the payment be set at one hundred fifty solidi, i.e., half his wergeld; if a person of middle class (*mediocris*), one hundred solidi; if a person of the lowest class (*minor persona*), seventy-five solidi.

If a slave unknown to his master presumes to kill a native freeman, let the slave be handed over to death, and let the master not be made liable for damages.

If the master knows of the deed, let both be handed over to death.

If the slave himself flees (*defuerit*) after the deed, let his master be compelled to pay thirty solidi to the relatives of the man killed for the value (wergeld) of the slave.

Similarly in the case of royal slaves, in accordance with the status of such persons, let the same condition about murderers be observed.

In such cases let all know this must be observed carefully, that the relatives of the man killed must recognize that no one can be pursued except the killer; because just as we have ordered the criminals to be destroyed, so we will suffer the innocent to sustain no injury. . . .

LET BURGUNDIANS AND ROMANS BE HELD UNDER THE SAME CONDITION IN THE MATTER OF KILLING SLAVES

If anyone kills a slave, barbarian by birth, a trained (select) house servant or messenger, let him compensate sixty solidi; moreover, let the amount of the fine be twelve solidi. If anyone kills another's slave, Roman or barbarian, either ploughman or swineherd, let him pay thirty solidi.

Whoever kills a skilled goldsmith, let him pay two hundred solidi.

Whoever kills a silversmith, let him pay one hundred solidi.

Whoever kills a blacksmith, let him pay fifty solidi.

Whoever kills a carpenter, let him pay forty solidi. . . .

OF THE STEALING OF GIRLS

If anyone shall steal a girl, let him be compelled to pay the price set for such a girl ninefold, and let him pay a fine to the amount of twelve solidi.

If a girl who has been seized returns uncorrupted to her parents, let the abductor compensate six times the wergeld of the girl; moreover, let the fine be set at twelve solidi.

But if the abductor does not have the means to make the above-mentioned payment, let him be given over to the parents of the girl that they may have the power of doing to him whatever they choose.

---

[1]A **solidus** (pl. solidi) was a gold coin. [ED.]

If indeed, the girl seeks the man of her own will and comes to his house, and he has intercourse with her, let him pay her marriage price threefold; if moreover, she returns uncorrupted to her home, let her return with all blame removed from him.

If indeed a Roman girl, without the consent or knowledge of her parents, unites in marriage with a Burgundian, let her know she will have none of the property of her parents. . . .

Of Succession

Among Burgundians we wish it to be observed that if anyone does not leave a son, let a daughter succeed to the inheritance of the father and mother in place of the son.

If by chance the dead leave neither son nor daughter, let the inheritance go to the sisters or nearest relatives.

It is pleasing that it be contained in the present law that if a woman having a husband dies without children, the husband of the dead wife may not demand back the marriage price (*pretium*) which had been given for her.

Likewise, let neither the woman nor the relatives of the woman seek back that which a woman pays when she comes to her husband if the husband dies without children.

Concerning those women who are vowed to God and remain in chastity, we order that if they have two brothers they receive a third portion of the inheritance of the father, that is, of that land which the father, possessing by the right of *sors* (allotment), left at the time of his death. Likewise, if she has four or five brothers, let her receive the portion due to her.

If moreover she has but one brother, let not a half, but a third part go to her on the condition that, after the death of her who is a woman and a nun, whatever she possesses in usufruct from her father's property shall go to the nearest relatives, and she will have no power of transferring anything therefrom, unless perhaps from her mother's goods, that is, from her clothing or things of the cell (*rescellulae*), or what she has acquired by her own labor.

We decree that this should be observed only by those whose fathers have not given them portions; but if they shall have received from their father a place where they can live, let them have full freedom of disposing of it at their will. . . .

Of Burgundian Women Entering a Second or Third Marriage

If any Burgundian woman, as is the custom, enters a second or third marriage after the death of her husband, and she has children by each husband, let her possess the marriage gift (*donatio nuptialis*) in usufruct while she lives; after her death, let what his father gave her be given to each son, with the further provision that the mother has the power neither of giving, selling, or transferring any of the things which she received in the marriage gift.

If by chance the woman has no children, after her death let her relatives receive half of whatever has come to her by way of marriage gift, and let the relatives of the dead husband who was the donor receive half.

But if perchance children shall have been born and they shall have died after the death of their father, we command that the inheritance of the husband or children belong wholly to the mother. Moreover, after the death of the mother, we decree that what she holds in usufruct by inheritance from her children shall belong to the legal heirs of her children. Also we command that she protect the property of her children dying intestate.

If any son has given his mother something by will or by gift, let the mother have the power of doing whatever she wishes therewith; if she dies intestate, let the relatives of the woman claim the inheritance as their possession.

If any Burgundian has sons (children?) to whom he has given their portions, let him have the power of giving or selling that which he has reserved for himself to whomever he wishes. . . .

Of Knocking Out Teeth

If anyone by chance strikes out the teeth of a Burgundian of the highest class, or of a Roman noble, let him be compelled to pay fifteen solidi.

For middle-class freeborn people, either Burgundian or Roman, if a tooth is knocked out, let composition be made in the sum of ten solidi.

For persons of the lowest class, five solidi.

If a slave voluntarily strikes out the tooth of a native freeman, let him be condemned to have a hand cut off; if the loss which has been set forth above has been committed by accident, let him pay the price for the tooth according to the status of the person.

If any native freeman strikes out the tooth of a freedman, let him pay him three solidi. If he strikes out the tooth of another's slave, let him pay two solidi to him to whom the slave belongs. . . .

Of Injuries Which Are Suffered by Women

If any native freewoman has her hair cut off and is humiliated without cause (when innocent) by any native freeman in her home or on the road, and this can be proved with witnesses, let the doer of the deed pay her twelve solidi, and let the amount of the fine be twelve solidi.

If this was done to a freedwoman, let him pay her six solidi.

If this was done to a maidservant, let him pay her three solidi, and let the amount of the fine be three solidi.

If this injury (shame, disgrace) is inflicted by a slave on a native freewoman, let him receive two hundred blows; if a freedwoman, let him receive a hundred blows; if a maidservant, let him receive seventy-five blows.

If indeed the woman whose injury we have ordered to be punished in this manner commits fornication voluntarily (i.e., if she yields), let nothing be sought for the injury suffered.

Of Divorces

If any woman leaves (puts aside) her husband to whom she is legally married, let her be smothered in mire.

If anyone wishes to put away his wife without cause, let him give her another payment such as he gave for her marriage price, and let the amount of the fine be twelve solidi.

If by chance a man wishes to put away his wife, and is able to prove one of these three crimes against her, that is, adultery, witchcraft, or violation of graves, let him have full right to put her away: and let the judge pronounce the sentence of the law against her, just as should be done against criminals.

But if she admits none of these three crimes, let no man be permitted to put away his wife for any other crime. But if he chooses, he may go away from the home, leaving all household property behind, and his wife with their children may possess the property of her husband.

Of the Punishment of Slaves Who Commit a Criminal Assault on Freeborn Women

If any slave does violence to a native freewoman, and if she complains and is clearly able to prove this, let the slave be killed for the crime committed.

If indeed a native free girl unites voluntarily with a slave, we order both to be killed.

But if the relatives of the girl do not wish to punish their own relative, let the girl be deprived of her free status and delivered into servitude to the king.

■ **Discussion Questions**

1. What do these laws reveal about the social and political structure of the Burgundian kingdom? For example, did the king act alone in establishing the laws? Do the laws place the same value on all social groups?
2. What does the code reveal about Burgundian women and family life?
3. Historians regard the interaction between Germanic and Roman peoples as a key component of the process by which Germanic kingdoms replaced imperial government in western Europe. What evidence of such interaction can you find in this document?

19. Procopius, *Buildings* (c. 553–554)

The emperors of the eastern Roman provinces successfully resisted the tides of change that engulfed the West. In the process, they forged a new empire, Byzantium. Its roots extended back to 293, when Diocletian reorganized imperial territory into four districts—two in the east and two in the west. In 395, the empire was basically divided into eastern and western halves. Emperor Justinian (r. 527–565) played a pivotal role in shaping Byzantium's emerging identity as a bastion of Roman imperial glory and civilization. Here is a contemporary account of one of Justinian's most famous achievements, the reconstruction of the Church of the Holy Wisdom (Hagia Sophia) in the Byzantine capital, Constantinople. A courtier from Palestine, Procopius (d. after 562?), included the description in his book Buildings, *which he wrote to honor Justinian's architectural projects. Procopius sets the rebuilding of Hagia Sophia against the backdrop of the emperor's accomplishments as a whole, portraying the church as the embodiment of his power and divine favor.*

In our own age there has been born the Emperor Justinian, who, taking over the State when it was harassed by disorder, has not only made it greater in extent, but also much more illustrious, by expelling from it those barbarians who had from of old pressed hard upon it, . . . witness the way he has already added to the Roman domain many states which in his own times had belonged to others, and has created countless cities which did not exist before. And finding that the belief in God was, before his time, straying into errors and being forced to go in many directions, he completely destroyed all the paths leading to such errors, and brought it about that it stood on the firm foundation of a single faith. Moreover, finding the laws obscure because they had become far more numerous than they should be, and in obvious confusion because they disagreed with each other, he preserved them by cleansing them of the mass of their verbal trickery, and by controlling their discrepancies with the greatest firmness; as for those who plotted against him, he of his own volition dismissed the charges against them, and causing those who were in want to have a surfeit of wealth, and crushing the spiteful fortune that oppressed them, he wedded the whole State to a life of prosperity. Furthermore, he strengthened the Roman domain, which everywhere lay exposed to the barbarians, by a multitude of soldiers, and by constructing strongholds he built a wall along all its remote frontiers.

However, most of the Emperor's other achievements have been described by me in my other writings, so that the subject of the present work will be the benefits which he wrought as a builder. They do indeed say that the best king of whom we know by tradition was the Persian Cyrus, and

From *Procopius,* trans. H. B. Dewing, vol. 7 (Cambridge, Mass.: Harvard University Press, 1961), 5–17, 27.

that he was chiefly responsible for the founding of the kingdom of Persia for the people of his race. . . . But in the case of the king of our times, Justinian (whom one would rightly, I think, call a king by nature as well as by inheritance, since he is, as Homer says, "as gentle as a father"), if one should examine his reign with care, he will regard the rule of Cyrus as a sort of child's play. The proof of this will be that the Roman Empire, as I have just said, has become more than doubled both in area and in power generally. . . .

But now we must proceed, as I have said, to the subject of the buildings of this Emperor, so that it may not come to pass in the future that those who see them refuse, by reason of their great number and magnitude, to believe that they are in truth the works of one man. For already many works of men of former times which are not vouched for by a written record have aroused incredulity because of their surpassing merit. And with good reason the buildings in Byzantium, beyond all the rest, will serve as a foundation for my narrative. For "o'er a work's beginnings," as the old saying has it, "we needs must set a front that shines afar."

Some men of the common herd, all the rubbish of the city, once rose up against the Emperor Justinian in Byzantium, when they brought about the rising called the Nika Insurrection. . . . And by way of showing that it was not against the Emperor alone that they had taken up arms, but no less against God himself, unholy wretches that they were, they had the hardihood to fire the Church of the Christians, which the people of Byzantium call "Sophia," an epithet which they have most appropriately invented for God, by which they call His temple; and God permitted them to accomplish this impiety, foreseeing into what an object of beauty this shrine was destined to be transformed. So the whole church at that time lay a charred mass of ruins. But the Emperor Justinian built not long afterwards a church so finely shaped, that if anyone had enquired of the Christians before the burning if it would be their wish that the church should be destroyed and one like this should take its place, showing them some sort of model of the building we now see, it seems to me that they would have prayed that they might see their church destroyed forthwith, in order that the building might be converted into its present form. At any rate the Emperor, disregarding all questions of expense, eagerly pressed on to begin the work of construction, and began to gather all the artisans from the whole world. . . . Indeed this also was an indication of the honour in which God held the Emperor, that He had already provided the men who would be most serviceable to him in the tasks which were waiting to be carried out. And one might with good reason marvel at the discernment of the Emperor himself, in that out of the whole world he was able to select the men who were most suitable for the most important of his enterprises.

So the church has become a spectacle of marvellous beauty, overwhelming to those who see it, but to those who know it by hearsay altogether incredible. For it soars to a height to match the sky, and as if surging up from amongst the other buildings it stands on high and looks down upon the remainder of the city, adorning it, because it is a part of it, but glorying in its own beauty, because, though a part of the city and dominating it, it at the same time towers above it to such a height that the whole city is viewed from there as from a watch-tower. Both its breadth and its length have been so carefully proportioned, that it may not improperly be said to be exceedingly long and at the same time unusually broad. And it exults in an indescribable beauty. For it proudly reveals its mass and the harmony of its proportions, having neither any excess nor deficiency, since it is both more pretentious than the buildings to which we are accustomed, and considerably more noble than those which are merely huge, and it abounds exceedingly in sunlight and in the reflection of the sun's rays from the marble. Indeed one might say that its interior is not illuminated from without by the sun, but that the radiance comes into being within it, such an abundance of light bathes this shrine. . . . And whenever anyone enters this church to pray, he understands at once that it is not by any human power or skill, but by the influence of God, that this work has been so finely tuned. And so his mind is lifted up toward God and exalted, feeling that He cannot be far away, but must especially love to dwell in this place which He has chosen. And this does not happen only to one who sees the church for the first time, but the same experience comes to him on each successive occasion, as though the sight were new each time. Of this spectacle no one has ever had a surfeit, but when present in the church men rejoice in what they see, and when they leave it they take proud delight in conversing about it.

■ Discussion Questions

1. As described by Procopius, what were Justinian's most significant accomplishments?
2. What links does Procopius see between these accomplishments and Justinian's relationship with God?
3. What do you think Procopius's goals were in writing this account?

CHAPTER 7

The Heirs of the Roman Empire, 600–750

The seventh and eighth centuries marked the beginning of a new era in Western civilization—the Middle Ages. By this period, the Roman Empire had fragmented into three different worlds: Byzantine, Muslim, and western European. These heirs of the Roman Empire shared a common Roman heritage that they modified to suit their particular interests and circumstances. The documents for this chapter reveal various dimensions of this process, beginning in the first selection with the newly founded Muslim state, which conquered vast expanses of imperial territory by 730. This document indicates how the Muslim military conquests brought both change and continuity. The second set of documents illuminates the development of the western European kingdoms, where various barbarian peoples built new societies and cultures on the foundation of the Roman Empire.

20. *Islamic Terms of Peace*   (633–643)

The remarkable rise of Islam in the seventh century had far-reaching consequences. Muhammad (c. 570–632), a merchant-turned-holy man from the Arabian city of Mecca, founded the new faith, and his teachings soon gained widespread adherence across the Arabian peninsula. Together his converts formed a community united by the worship of God, expressed not only in individual prayer but also in the collective duty to "strive" (jihad) against unbelievers, often in war. By the eighth century, Islamic warriors had conquered all of Persia and much of the Byzantine Empire. These letters dictate the terms of peace to conquered communities and illuminate the Muslims' method of conquest and rule in the decade following Muhammad's death. In exchange for the payment of a special tax (jizya), non-Muslim subjects were allowed to live much as they had before. Consequently, Islam became not the destroyer of Hellenistic and Roman traditions but rather one of their heirs.

BĀNQIYĀ AND BASMĀ (633)

In the name of God, the Merciful and the Compassionate.

This is a letter from Khālid ibn al-Walīd to Ṣalūba ibn Nasṭūnā and his people.

I have made a pact with you for *jizya* and defense for every fit man, for both Bānqiyā and Basmā, for 10,000 dinars, excluding coins with holes punched in them, the wealthy according to the measure of his wealth, the poor according to the measure of his poverty, payable annually. You have been made head of your people and your people are content with you. I, therefore, and the Muslims who are with me, accept you, and I [? you] and your people are content. You have protection [*dhimma*] and defense. If we defend you, the *jizya* is due to us; if we do not, it is not, until we do defend you.

From *Islam: From the Prophet Muhammad to the Capture of Constantinople,* ed. Bernard Lewis, vol. 1 (New York: Walker & Co., 1974), 234–36, 238–40.

Witnessed by Hishām ibn al-Walīd, al-Qa'qā' ibn 'Amr, Jarīr ibn 'Abdallāh al-Ḥimyarī and Hanzala ibn al-Rabī'.

Written in the year 12, in Safar [April–May 633].

JERUSALEM (636)

In the name of God the Merciful and the Compassionate.

This is the safe-conduct accorded by the servant of God 'Umar, the Commander of the Faithful, to the people of Aelia [Jerusalem].

He accords them safe-conduct for their persons, their property, their churches, their crosses, their sound and their sick, and the rest of their worship.

Their churches shall neither be used as dwellings nor destroyed. They shall not suffer any impairment, nor shall their dependencies, their crosses, nor any of their property.

No constraint shall be exercised against them in religion nor shall any harm be done to any among them.

No Jew shall live with them in Aelia.

The people of Aelia must pay the *jizya* in the same way as the people of other cities.

They must expel the Romans and the brigands [?] from the city. Those who leave shall have safe-conduct for their persons and property until they reach safety. Those who stay shall have safe-conduct and must pay the *jizya* like the people of Aelia.

Those of the people of Aelia who wish to remove their persons and effects and depart with the Romans and abandon their churches and their crosses shall have safe-conduct for their persons, their churches, and their crosses, until they reach safety.

The country people who were already in the city before the killing of so-and-so may, as they wish, remain and pay the *jizya* the same way as the people of Aelia or leave with the Romans or return to their families. Nothing shall be taken from them until they have gathered their harvest.

This document is placed under the surety of God and the protection [*dhimma*] of the Prophet, the Caliphs and the believers, on condition that the inhabitants of Aelia pay the *jizya* that is due from them.

Witnessed by Khālid ibn al-Walīd, 'Amr ibn al-'Āṣ, 'Abd al-Raḥmān ibn 'Awf, Mu'āwiya ibn Abī Sufyān, the last of whom wrote this document in the year 15 [636].

JURJĀN (639)

In the name of God, the Merciful and the Compassionate.

This is a letter from Suwayd ibn Muqarrin to Ruzbān Sūl ibn Ruzbān, the inhabitants of Dihistān, and the rest of the inhabitants of Jurjān.

You have protection and we must enforce it on the condition that you pay the *jizya* every year, according to your capacity, for every adult male. If we seek help from any of you, the help counts as his *jizya* in place of the payment. They have safe-conduct for themselves, their property, their religions, and their laws. There will be no change in what is due to them as long as they pay and guide the wayfarer and show good will and lodge the Muslims and do not spy or betray. Whoever stays with them shall have the same terms as they have, and whoever goes forth has safe-conduct until he reaches a place of safety, provided that if anyone insults a Muslim he is severely punished, and if he strikes a Muslim, his blood is lawful.

Witnessed by Sawād ibn Qutba, Hind ibn 'Amr, Simāk ibn Makhrama, and 'Utayba ibn al-Nahhās.

Written in the year 18 [639].

ISFAHĀN (642)

In the name of God, the Merciful and the Compassionate.

A letter from 'Abdallāh to the Fādhūsafān and the inhabitants of Iṣfahān and its surroundings.

You are safe as long as you discharge your obligations, which are: to pay the *jizya*, which you must pay according to your capacity every year, paying it to whoever is the governor of your country, for every adult male; you must also guide the Muslim [traveler], keep his road in repair, lodge him for a day and a night, and provide the walker with a mount for one stage.

Do not assert your authority over any Muslim. What you owe to the Muslims is your goodwill and the payment of your dues; you have safe-conduct (*amān*) as long as you comply. But if you change anything, or if anyone among you changes anything and you do not hand him over, then you have no safe-conduct. If anyone insults a Muslim, he will be severely punished for it. If he strikes a Muslim, we shall kill him.

Written and witnessed by 'Abdallāh ibn Qays, 'Abdallāh ibn Warqā', and 'Isma ibn 'Abdallāh.

RAYY (642–643)

In the name of God, the Merciful and the Compassionate.

This is what Nu'aym ibn Muqarrin gave to al-Zaynabī ibn Qūla. He gave him safe-conduct (*amān*) for the inhabitants of Rayy and others who were with them, on condition of the annual payment of the *jizya*, according to capacity, for every adult male and on condition that they show goodwill and guide travelers, that they neither spy nor betray, that they lodge the Muslims for a day and a night, that they show deference to the Muslims. Anyone who insults or belittles a Muslim will receive crushing punishment; anyone who strikes a Muslim will be killed. If anyone changes this and his dead body is not handed over, then he will have changed the status of your whole community.

Written and witnessed.

TIFLĪS (642–643)

In the name of God, the Merciful and the Compassionate.

This is a letter from Ḥabīb ibn Maslama for the inhabitants of Tiflīs, in the land of Hurmuz, giving safe-conduct to you, your children, your families, your convents, your churches, your religions, and your prayers, on condition that you accept the humiliation [?] of the *jizya* at the rate of a full dinar for every household. You must not join separate households together in order to reduce the *jizya* which you pay, nor may we separate what is joined in order to increase the *jizya* which we receive.

You owe us your goodwill and your help, as far as you can, against the enemies of God and His Prophet and of those who believe; lodging for the Muslim wayfarer for a night, with food and drink such as are lawful for the people of the book; and guidance on the road, as far as this causes no harm to you. If one of the Muslims is stranded among you, you must deliver him to the nearest group of believers and Muslims, unless some obstacle intervenes. If you repent, perform the prayer, and pay the *zakāt*, then you are our brothers in religion [and our *mawālī*]. But he who turns away from the faith, Islam, and the *jizya* is the enemy of God and His Prophet and of those who believe. We seek help from God against him.

If something happens which distracts the Muslims from helping you and your enemy overcomes you, this is not held against them [? you] and does not invalidate the pact with you after you return to the side of the believers and Muslims. This is what is due from you and what is due to you.

Witnessed by God and His Angels and His Prophets and those who believe, and God is sufficient witness.

■ Discussion Questions

1. Aside from the payment of a poll tax (*jizya*), what were some of the obligations Muslims imposed on their non-Muslim subjects?
2. What did conquered peoples receive in exchange for the fulfillment of these obligations?
3. What does this system of quid pro quo suggest about Muslim attitudes toward nonbelievers?

21 The Life of Lady Balthild, Queen of the Franks (Late Seventh Century)

With the collapse of imperial government in the West in the fifth and sixth centuries, the kings from the Frankish royal dynasty, the Merovingians, came to dominate Roman Gaul. Their queens also wielded power, as The Life of Lady Balthild *demonstrates. Balthild (d. c. 680) was an Anglo-Saxon captive sold as a slave to the mayor of the palace in the Frankish kingdom of Neustria. He eventually offered her in marriage to King Clovis II (r. 638–657), which suggests she was from an important family with which the king sought political ties. On the king's death in 657, Balthild acted as regent until her eldest son came of age in 663 or 664. She thereupon retired from court to a monastery. The author of her* Life *is unknown, but his or her intent is clear: to hold her up as a model of Christian piety. Religious motives aside, the book illuminates women's place in court life as well as the growing influence of Christianity in Merovingian culture. This excerpt begins with Balthild's rise in station to queen.*

And in this station divine dispensation decided to honour her so that . . . she might obtain union with the king and, from her, royal progeny might come forth. And this has now come to pass, as it is obvious to everyone that the royal offspring reigning now is hers.

But as she had the grace of prudence conferred upon her by God, with watchful eagerness she obeyed the king as her lord, and to the princes she showed herself a mother, to the priests as a daughter, and to the young and the adolescents as the best possible nurse. And she was friendly to all, loving the priests as fathers, the monks as brothers, the poor as a faithful nurse does, and giving to each generous alms. She preserved the honour of the princes and kept their fitting counsel, always exhorting the young to religious studies and humbly and steadfastly petitioning the king for the churches and the poor. While still in secular dress, she desired to serve Christ; she prayed daily, tearfully commending herself to Christ, the heavenly king. And the pious king [Clovis], taking care of her faith and devotion, gave his faithful servant, Abbot Genesius, to her as support, and through his hands she served the priests and the poor, fed the hungry, clothed the naked with garments, and conscientiously arranged the burial of the dead. Through him she sent most generous alms of gold and silver to the monasteries of men and women. . . .

From *Late Merovingian France: History and Hagiography, 640–720,* ed. Paul Fouracre and Richard A. Gerberding (Manchester and New York: Manchester University Press, 1996), 121–23, 127, 131–32.

What more is there to say? At God's command, her husband, King Clovis, went forth from his body, leaving a lineage of sons with their mother. In his place after him, his son, the late King Clothar, took the throne of the Franks and then also with the excellent princes, Chrodbert, bishop of Paris, Lord Audoin, and Ebroin, mayor of the palace, along with the other great magnates and very many of the rest. And, indeed, the kingdom of the Franks was maintained in peace. Then indeed, a little while ago, the Austrasians peacefully received her son Childeric as king in Austrasia by the arrangement of Lady Balthild and, indeed, through the advice of the great magnates. But the Burgundians and the Neustrians were united. And we believe that, with God guiding, and in accordance with the great faith of Lady Balthild, these three kingdoms kept the harmony of peace among themselves.

At that time it happened that the heresy of simony stained the Church of God with its depraved practice in which they received the rank of bishop by paying a price for it. By the will of God [acting] through her, and at the urging of the good priests, the above-mentioned Lady Balthild stopped this impious evil so that no one would set a price on the taking of holy orders. Through her, the Lord also arranged for another very evil and impious practice to cease, one in which many men were more eager to kill their offspring than to provide for them in order to avoid the royal exactions which were inflicted upon them by custom, and from which they incurred a very heavy loss of property. This the lady prohibited for her own salvation so that no one presumed to do it. Because of this deed, truly a great reward awaits her.

Who, then, is able to say how many and how great were the sources of income, the entire farms and the large forests she gave up by donating them to the establishments of religious men in order to construct cells or monasteries? And she also built as God's own and private houses a huge nunnery for women consecrated by God at Chelles, near Paris where she placed the religious handmaiden of God, the girl Bertila, in the position of the first mother. And in this place the venerable Lady Balthild in turn decided to dwell under the pure rule of religion and to rest in peace. And in truth she fulfilled this with a devoted will. . . .

Indeed, with a most pious affection she loved her sisters as her own daughters, she obeyed their holy abbess as her mother, and rendered service to them as the lowest of handmaidens out of holy desire, just as [she had done] when she still ruled the royal palace and often visited her holy monastery. So strongly did she exhibit the example of great humility that she even served her sisters in the kitchen, and the lowest acts of cleaning, even the latrines, she herself did. All this she undertook with joy and a cheerful heart, in such humble service for Christ. For who would believe that the height of such power would serve in such lowly things if her most abundant and great love of Christ had not demanded it of her in every way? . . .

Indeed, we recall that other queens in the kingdom of the Franks have been noble and worshippers of God: Clothild, queen of the late King Clovis of old and niece of King Gundobad, who, by her holy exhortations, led both her very brave and pagan husband and many of the Frankish nobles to Christianity and brought them to the Catholic faith. She also was the first to construct the churches in honour of St Peter at Paris and St George in the little monastery for virgins at Chelles, and she founded many others in honour of the saints in order to store up her reward, and she enriched them with many gifts. The same is said of Ultrogoda, queen of the most Christian King Childebert, because she was a comforter of the poor and a helper of the servants of God and of monks. And [it is said] also of Queen Radegund, truly a most faithful handmaiden of God, queen of the late elder King Clothar, whom the grace of the Holy Spirit had so inflamed that she left her husband while he was still alive and consecrated herself to the Lord Christ under the holy veil, and, with Christ as her spouse, accomplished many good things. These things are read in her Acts.

But it is pleasing, nevertheless, to consider this about her whom it here concerns: the Lady Balthild. Her many good deeds were accomplished in our times, and that these things were done by her herself we have learned in the best manner. Concerning these things, we have here commemorated a few out of the many, and we do not think her to be the inferior in merits of those earlier [queens]; rather we know her to have outdone them in holy striving.

■ **Discussion Questions**

1. Why does the author think that Lady Balthild's life is exemplary?
2. To whom do you think the author directed his or her message, and why?
3. What does this source suggest about women's role in Merovingian politics and the relationship between this role and Christian values?

22. Pope Gregory the Great, *Letters* (598–601)

Although Britain stood on the periphery of the empire, it, too, could not escape the turmoil of the late imperial period. After the Roman army was recalled to Italy, the pagan Anglo-Saxons slowly took over the part that we now call England, while Wales and Cornwall remained Christian. Christianity was reintroduced into England from a variety of directions, of which Rome was among the most important. From here, Pope Gregory I (r. 590–604) dispatched two groups of missionaries to establish Roman-style Christianity in England. The first group, sent in 596–597, was led by Augustine and the second, sent in 601, by Mellitus; both were monks from Rome. In these letters, Gregory describes the mission's initial progress and then offers strategies for furthering its success. His letters point not only to the pope's growing influence in the West but also to the interaction between Roman and non-Roman customs.

To EULOGIUS, BISHOP OF ALEXANDRIA

Gregory to Eulogius, &c.

Our common son, the bearer of these presents, when he brought the letters of your Holiness found me sick, and has left me sick; whence it has ensued that the scanty water of my brief epistle has been hardly able to exude to the large fountain of your Blessedness. But it was a heavenly boon that, while in a state of bodily pain, I received the letter of your Holiness to lift me up with joy for the instruction of the heretics of the city of Alexandria, and the concord of the faithful, to such an extent that the very joy of my mind moderated the severity of my suffering. And indeed we rejoice with new exultation to hear of your good doings, though at the same time we by no means suppose that it is a new thing for you to act thus perfectly. For that the people of holy Church increases, that spiritual crops of corn for the heavenly garner are multiplied, we never doubted that this was from the grace of Almighty God which flowed largely to you, most blessed ones. . . .

But, since in the good things you do I know that you also rejoice with others, I make you a return for your favour, and announce things not unlike yours; for while the nation of the Angli, placed in a corner of the world, remained up to this time misbelieving in the worship of stocks and stones, I determined, through the aid of your prayers for me, to send to it, God granting it, a monk of my monastery for the purpose of preaching. And he, having with my leave been made bishop by the bishops of Germany, proceeded, with their aid also, to the end of the world to the

From *A Select Library of Nicene and Post-Nicene Fathers of the Christian Church,* 2d ser., vols. 12 and 13 (New York: Christian Literature Co., 1895 and 1898), 12:240, 13:84–85.

aforesaid nation; and already letters have reached us telling us of his safety and his work; to the effect that he and those that have been sent with him are resplendent with such great miracles in the said nation that they seem to imitate the powers of the apostles in the signs which they display. Moreover, at the solemnity of the Lord's Nativity which occurred in this first indiction, more than ten thousand Angli are reported to have been baptized by the same our brother and fellow-bishop. This have I told you, that you may know what you are effecting among the people of Alexandria by speaking, and what in the ends of the world by praying. For your prayers are in the place where you are not, while your holy operations are shewn in the place where you are.

To Mellitus, Abbot

Gregory to Mellitus, Abbot in France.[1]

Since the departure of our congregation, which is with thee, we have been in a state of great suspense from having heard nothing of the success of your journey. But when Almighty God shall have brought you to our most reverend brother the bishop Augustine, tell him that I have long been considering with myself about the case of the Angli; to wit, that the temples of idols in that nation should not be destroyed, but that the idols themselves that are in them should be. Let blessed water be prepared, and sprinkled in these temples, and altars constructed, and relics deposited, since, if these same temples are well built, it is needful that they should be transferred from the worship of idols to the service of the true God; that, when the people themselves see that these temples are not destroyed, they may put away error from their heart, and, knowing and adoring the true God, may have recourse with the more familiarity to the places they have been accustomed to. And, since they are wont to kill many oxen in sacrifice to demons, they should have also some solemnity of this kind in a changed form, so that on the day of dedication, or on the anniversaries of the holy martyrs whose relics are deposited there, they may make for themselves tents of the branches of trees around these temples that have been changed into churches, and celebrate the solemnity with religious feasts. Nor let them any longer sacrifice animals to the devil, but slay animals to the praise of God for their own eating, and return thanks to the Giver of all for their fulness, so that, while some joys are reserved to them outwardly, they may be able the more easily to incline their minds to inward joys. For it is undoubtedly impossible to cut away everything at once from hard hearts, since one who strives to ascend to the highest place must needs rise by steps or paces, and not by leaps. Thus to the people of Israel in Egypt the Lord did indeed make Himself known; but still He reserved to them in His own worship the use of the sacrifices which they were accustomed to offer to the devil, enjoining them to immolate animals in sacrifice to Himself; to the end that, their hearts being changed, they should omit some things in the sacrifice and retain others, so that, though the animals were the same as what they had been accustomed to offer, nevertheless, as they immolated them to God and not to idols, they should be no longer the same sacrifices. This then it is necessary for thy Love to say to our aforesaid brother, that he, being now in that country, may consider well how he should arrange all things.

---

[1]This letter was sent after the departure of Mellitus with the band of new missionaries from Rome to Britain, being intended to reach him while still in France.

■ **Discussion Questions**

1. Earlier in his papacy, Gregory had advised the destruction of pagan temples. How does Gregory reverse this decision in his letter to Mellitus, and why?

2. What does Gregory's change of approach suggest about the ways in which Latin Christianity adapted to non-Roman cultures?

3. Historians often refer to Gregory I as the "father of the medieval papacy" because of the role he played in transforming the papacy into the moral and spiritual head of the West. What evidence can you find in these letters to support this view?

CHAPTER 8

Unity and Diversity in Three Societies, 750–1050

The following documents illuminate the forces of unity and fragmentation driving the development of Byzantium, the Islamic world, and western Europe between 750 and 1050. By this time, the Byzantine emperors had regained much of their lost luster, and as the first document reveals, they considered themselves to be the rightful successors of Rome. Against this backdrop, the Islamic world continued to forge a unified sense of identity even as it fragmented into smaller political units (Document 24). In western Europe, the Carolingian king Charlemagne (r. 768–814) created a vast kingdom, the scope of which had not been seen since Roman times. As the third document illustrates, his success was based not simply on military victory but also on his ability to administer effectively the diverse regions under his rule.

23. *Digenis Akritas*   (Tenth or Eleventh Century)

Byzantium not only remained a unified state in the ninth and tenth centuries but also extended its power. Byzantine troops stemmed the Muslim advance and regained territory, to the benefit of the emperor's prestige and coffers. Victory came at a price, however, as the military aristocracy charged with defending the empire increased its control in the countryside. Written in the tenth or eleventh century, the Byzantine epic poem Digenis Akritas *("two-blood border lord") celebrates the legendary exploits of Digenis, a member of the military elite born of an Arab mother and a Greek father (hence his name). According to the legend, Digenis grew to be a fierce warrior who successfully battled against the Arabs on Byzantium's eastern frontier. In this selection, Digenis meets the Byzantine emperor (whose identity is uncertain), for whom he has both praise and advice.*

On hearing of these deeds, the Emperor
Who at that time was governing the Romans,
Basil the Bléssed, the great trophy winner,
Whose imperial fame was buried with him,
Chanced to be on campaign against the Persians
In those same places where the boy [Digenis] was living,
And when he heard about it was amazed.
So wishing greatly he might see the youth,
He sent a letter to him with these words:

From *Digenis Akritas: The Two-Blood Border Lord*, trans. Denison B. Hull (Athens: Ohio University Press, 1972), 59–61.

"We've learned the stories of your many exploits,
My son, and we have much rejoiced in them,
And offered thanks to God who works with you.
Our purpose is to see you with our own eyes,
And give requital worthy of your deeds.
Come to us gladly, without hesitation,
And don't suspect you'll suffer hurt from us."
When he received this, he returned an answer:
"I am your majesty's most abject slave;
Indeed, I have no right to your good things.
Master, what deed of mine do you admire,
Who am so humble, base, and quite undaring?
Still, he who trusts in God can do all things.
Therefore, since you desire to see your servant,
Be by the Euphrates after a little while.
You'll see me all you wish, my sacred master.
Don't think that I refuse to come before you,
But you have certain inexperienced soldiers,
And if perhaps they say something they shouldn't,
I certainly would deprive you of such men,
For such things, master, happen to the young."
    The Emperor read his letter word by word,
Admired the humbleness of the boy's statement,
And understood with pleasure his high courage.
    Since he wished strongly to behold the youth,
He took along with him a hundred soldiers,
Some spearmen too, and went to the Euphrates,
Ordering all on no account to utter
A word offensive to the Border Lord.
Those posted to keep watch on his account
Shortly announced the Emperor's arrival
To the marvelous Two-Blood Border Lord.
The Two-Blood came out all alone to meet him,
And bowed his head down to the ground, and said,
"Hail, you who take imperial power from God,
And rule us all because of the heathen's sins.
Why has it happened that the whole world's master
Comes before me, who am of no account?"
The Emperor, astonished when he saw him,
Forgot the burden of his majesty,
Advanced a little from his throne, embraced him,
Joyfully kissed him, and admired his stature,
And the great promise of his well-formed beauty.
"My son," he said, "you've proof of all your deeds;
The way you're put together shows your courage.
Would that Romania [Byzantium] had four such men!
So speak, my son, freely and openly,
And then take anything you wish from us."
"Keep everything, my lord," the boy replied,
"Because your love alone is enough for me.

It's not more blesséd to receive than give;
You have immense expenses in your army.
So I beseech your glorious majesty:
Love him who is obedient, pity the poor,
Deliver the oppressed from malefactors,
Forgive those who unwittingly make blunders,
And heed no slanders, nor accept injustice,
Sweep heretics out, confirm the orthodox.
These, master, are the arms of righteousness
With which you can prevail over all foes.
To rule and reign are not part of that power
Which God and His right hand alone can give.
Vile as I am, I grant your majesty
To take what you once gave Iconium
As tribute, and as much again, from them.
Master, I'll make you carefree about this
Until my soul shakes off this mortal coil."
      The Emperor was delighted at these words.
"O marvelous and excellent young man,"
He said, "we name you a patrician now,
And grant you all your grandfather's estates;
We give to you the power to rule the borders,
And will confirm this with a golden bull,
And furnish you with rich imperial raiment."

■ Discussion Questions

1. What does Digenis's conversation with the emperor reveal about the basis of imperial authority and prestige?
2. What advice does Digenis offer the emperor on the proper method of rule? What do his words
   suggest about the characteristics of an ideal emperor?
3. In this passage, it is the emperor, not Digenis, who arranges their meeting, at which the emperor pays homage to him. What does this imply about the status of warriors like Digenis in
   Byzantine society and the emperor's relationship to them?

24. Ahmad al-Ya'qūbī, *Kitāb al-buldān* (Ninth Century)

*While the Byzantine emperors were consolidating their empire, Islamic leaders were strengthening
their own. In 750, a new dynasty of caliphs, the Abbasids, seized control of the Islamic state, which
they brought to new heights of power and influence. The foundation of a new capital city, Baghdad,
in 762 by the Abbasids physically embodied the revolutionary nature of their rule. In the first fifty
years of their reign, they transformed Baghdad into the hub of the Islamic state. An early historian
of Islam and descendant of the Abbasid family, Ahmad al-Ya'qūbī (d. 897), experienced the
dynamism of the city firsthand during his travels as a young man, and he later included his*

From *Islam: From the Prophet Muhammad to the Capture of Constantinople*, vol. 2, ed. Bernard Lewis (New
York: Walker & Co., 1974), 69–73.

observations in a geographical work, Kitāb al-buldān, *which he wrote near the end of his life. Although composed after economic problems had begun to tarnish the Abbasids' luster,* Kitāb al-buldān *elucidates the cultural and economic forces binding the Islamic world together even at a time when the caliphate was fragmenting into separate political units.*

I begin with Iraq only because it is the center of this world, the navel of the earth, and I mention Baghdad first because it is the center of Iraq, the greatest city, which has no peer in the east or the west of the world in extent, size, prosperity, abundance of water, or health of climate, and because it is inhabited by all kinds of people, town-dwellers and country-dwellers. To it they come from all countries, far and near, and people from every side have preferred Baghdad to their own homelands. There is no country, the peoples of which have not their own quarter and their own trading and financial arrangements. In it there is gathered that which does not exist in any other city in the world. On its flanks flow two great rivers, the Tigris and the Euphrates, and thus goods and foodstuffs come to it by land and by water with the greatest ease, so that every kind of merchandise is completely available, from east and west, from Muslim and non-Muslim lands. Goods are brought from India, Sind, China, Tibet, the lands of the Turks, the Daylam, the Khazars, the Ethiopians, and others to such an extent that the products of the countries are more plentiful in Baghdad than in the countries from which they come. They can be procured so readily and so certainly that it is as if all the good things of the world are sent there, all the treasures of the earth assembled there, and all the blessings of creation perfected there.

Furthermore, Baghdad is the city of the Hashimites, the home of their reign, the seat of their sovereignty, where no one appeared before them and no kings but they have dwelt. Also, my own forbears have lived there, and one of them was governor of the city.

Its name is famous, and its fame widespread. Iraq is indeed the center of the world, for in accordance with the consensus of the astronomers recorded in the writings of ancient scholars, it is in the fourth climate, which is the middle climate where the temperature is regular at all times and seasons. It is very hot in the summer, very cold in the winter, and temperate in autumn and in spring. The passage from autumn to winter and from spring to summer is gradual and imperceptible, and the succession of the seasons is regular. So, the weather is temperate, the soil is rich, the water is sweet, the trees are thriving, the fruit luscious, the seeds are fertile, good things are abundant, and springs are easily found. Because of the temperate weather and rich soil and sweet water, the character of the inhabitants is good, their faces bright, and their minds untrammeled. The people excel in knowledge, understanding, letters, manners, insight, discernment, skill in commerce and crafts, cleverness in every argument, proficiency in every calling, and mastery of every craft. There is none more learned than their scholars, better informed than their traditionists, more cogent than their theologians, more perspicuous than their grammarians, more accurate than their readers, more skillful than their physicians, more melodious than their singers, more delicate than their craftsmen, more literate than their scribes, more lucid than their logicians, more devoted than their worshippers, more pious than their ascetics, more juridical than their judges, more eloquent than their preachers, more poetic than their poets, and more reckless than their rakes.

In ancient days, that is to say in the time of the Chosroes and the Persians, Baghdad was not a city, but only a village in the district of Bādūrayā. The city in Iraq which the Chosroes had chosen for their capital was al-Madā'in, seven parasangs from Baghdad. The audience chamber of Chosroes Anushirvan is still there. At that time there was nothing in Baghdad but a convent situated at a place called Qarn al-Ṣarāt, at the confluence of the Ṣarāt and the Tigris. This convent is called al-Dayr al-'Atīq [the ancient convent] and is still standing at the present time. It is the residence of the Catholicos, the head of the Nestorian Christians.

Nor does Baghdad figure in the wars of the Arabs at the time of the advent of Islam, since the Arabs founded Basra and Kūfa. Kūfa was founded in the year 17 [638] by Saʿd ibn Abī Waqqās al-Zuhrī, one of ʿUmar ibn al-Khaṭṭāb's governors. Basra, too, was founded in the year 17 by ʿUtba ibn Ghazwān al-Māzinī of the tribe of Māzin of Qays, also a governor of ʿUmar ibn al-Khaṭṭāb at that time. The Arabs settled down in these two places, but the important people, the notables, and the rich merchants moved to Baghdad.

The Umayyads lived in Syria and did not stay in Iraq. Muʿāwiya ibn Abī Sufyān, who had been governor of Syria in the name of ʿUmar ibn al-Khaṭṭāb and then of ʿUthmān ibn ʿAffān for twenty years, lived in Damascus with his family. When he seized power and sovereignty passed to him, he kept his residence and capital in Damascus, where he had his authority, his supporters, and his faction. The Umayyad kings after Muʿāwiya stayed in Damascus, since they were born there and knew no other place, and its people were their sole supporters.

Then the Caliphate came to the descendants of the paternal uncle of the Apostle of God, may God bless and save him and also his family, the line of ʿAbbās ibn ʿAbd al-Muṭṭalib. Thanks to clear discernment, sound intelligence, and perfect judgment, they saw the merits of Iraq, its magnificence, spaciousness, and central situation. They saw that it was not like Syria, with its pestilential air, narrow houses, rugged soil, constant diseases, and uncouth people; nor was it like Egypt, with changeable weather and many plagues, situated between a damp and fetid river, full of unhealthy mists that engender disease and spoil food, and the dry, bare mountains, so dry and salty and bad that no plant can grow nor any spring appear; nor like Ifrīqiya, far from the peninsula of Islam and from the holy house of God, with uncouth people and many foes; nor like Armenia, remote, cold and icy, barren, and surrounded by enemies; nor like the districts of the Jabal, harsh, rough, and snow-covered, the abode of the hard-hearted Kurds; nor like the land of Khurāsān, stretching to the east, surrounded on every side by rabid and war-like enemies; nor like the Ḥijāz where life is hard and means are few and the people's food comes from elsewhere, as Almighty God warned us in His book, through His friend Ibrāhīm, who said, "O Lord, I have given to my descendants as dwelling a valley without tillage" [Qurʾan]; nor like Tibet, where, because of the foul air and food, the people are discolored, with stunted bodies and tufty hair.

When they understood that Iraq was the best of countries, the ʿAbbasids decided to settle there. In the first instance the Commander of the Faithful, Abuʾl-ʿAbbās, that is ʿAbdallāh ibn Muḥammad ibn ʿAlī ibn ʿAbdallāh ibn ʿAbbās ibn ʿAbd al-Muṭṭalib, stayed in Kūfa. Then he moved to Anbar and built a city on the banks of the Euphrates which he called Hāshimiyya. Abuʾl-ʿAbbās, may God be pleased with him, died before the building of this city was completed.

Then, when Abū Jaʿfar al-Manṣūr succeeded to the Caliphate, he founded a new city between Kūfa and Ḥīra, which he also called Hāshimiyya. He stayed there for a while, until the time when he decided to send his son, Muḥammad al-Mahdī, to fight the Slavs in the year 140 [757–758]. He then came to Baghdad and stopped there, and asked, "What is the name of this place?" They answered, "Baghdad." "By God," said the Caliph, "this is indeed the city which my father Muḥammad ibn ʿAlī told me I must build, in which I must live, and in which my descendants after me will live. Kings were unaware of it before and since Islam, until God's plans for me and orders to me are accomplished. Thus, the traditions will be verified and the signs and proofs be manifest. Indeed, this island between the Tigris in the east and the Euphrates in the west is a marketplace for the world. All the ships that come up the Tigris from Wāsiṭ, Basra, Ubulla, Ahwāz, Fārs, ʿUmān, Yamāma, Baḥrayn, and beyond will anchor here; wares brought on ships down the Tigris from Mosul, Diyār-Rabīʿa, Ādharbayjān, and Armenia, and along the Euphrates from Diyār-Muḍar, Raqqa, Syria, the border marches, Egypt, and North Africa, will be brought and unloaded here. It will be the highway for the people of the Jabal, Iṣfahān, and the districts of Khurāsān. Praise be to God who preserved it for me and caused all those who came before me to neglect it. By God, I shall build it. Then I shall dwell in it as long as I live, and my descendants shall dwell in it after me. It will surely be the most flourishing city in the world.

■ Discussion Questions

1. Considering his family connections, do you think that we can accept Ahmad al-Yaʿqūbī's view of Baghdad at face value? Why or why not?
2. His potential biases aside, what does Ahmad al-Yaʿqūbī reveal about the geographical breadth and ethnic diversity of the Islamic Empire?
3. As described here, how did trade help unify the Islamic Empire when it was beginning to fragment politically?

25. *General Capitulary for the* Missi   (802)

*Although the Merovingians forged a powerful political polity on the demise of Roman provincial government, their success paled in comparison to that of the Carolingians, who deposed them in 751. By the 790s, Charlemagne had created an empire across Europe, using imperial Rome as a model. He was crowned emperor in 800 by Pope Leo III, which further exalted his power. To centralize his rule, Charlemagne dispatched officials—*missi dominici—*annually to every part of the empire to review local affairs and enforce royal legislation. This document, known as a capitulary, provided basic guidelines for these annual visits. Consisting of regulatory articles (*capitula *in Latin), capitularies were compiled at general assemblies convened by Charlemagne to discuss important issues with his magnates. These excerpts illuminate the forces binding the empire together as well as those that ultimately broke it apart.*

First chapter. Concerning the embassy sent out by the lord emperor. Therefore, the most serene and most Christian lord emperor Charles has chosen from his nobles the wisest and most prudent men, both archbishops and some of the other bishops also, and venerable abbots and pious laymen, and has sent them throughout his whole kingdom, and through them by all the following chapters has allowed men to live in accordance with the correct law. Moreover, where anything which is not right and just has been enacted in the law, he has ordered them to inquire into this most diligently and to inform him of it; he desires, God granting, to reform it. And let no one, through his cleverness or astuteness, dare to oppose or thwart the written law, as many are wont to do, or the judicial sentence passed upon him, or to do injury to the churches of God or the poor or the widows or the wards or any Christian. But all shall live entirely in accordance with God's precept, justly and under a just rule, and each one shall be admonished to live in harmony with his fellows in his business or profession; the canonical clergy ought to observe in every respect a canonical life without heeding base gain, nuns ought to keep diligent watch over their lives, laymen and the secular clergy ought rightly to observe their laws without malicious fraud, and all ought to live in mutual charity and perfect peace. And let the *missi* themselves make a diligent investigation whenever any man claims that an injustice has been done to him by any one, just as they desire to deserve the grace of omnipotent God and to keep their fidelity promised to Him, so that entirely in all cases everywhere, in accordance with the will and fear of God, they shall administer the law fully and justly in the case of the holy churches of God and of the poor, of wards and widows and of the whole people. And if there shall be anything of such a nature that they, together with the provincial counts, are not able of themselves to correct it and to do justice concerning it, they shall, without any ambiguity, refer this, together with their reports, to the judgment of the emperor; and the straight path of justice shall not be impeded by any one

From *Translations and Reprints from the Original Sources of European History,* vol. 6, ed. Dana Carleton Munro (Philadelphia: University of Pennsylvania Press, 1898), 16–19, 23–24, 26–27.

on account of flattery or gifts from any one, or on account of any relationship, or from fear of the powerful.

Concerning the fidelity to be promised to the lord emperor. And he commanded that every man in his whole kingdom, whether ecclesiastic or layman, and each one according to his vow and occupation, should now promise to him as emperor the fidelity which he had previously promised to him as king; and all of those who had not yet made that promise should do likewise, down to those who were twelve years old. And that it shall be announced to all in public, so that each one might know, how great and how many things are comprehended in that oath; not merely, as many have thought hitherto, fidelity to the lord emperor as regards his life, and not introducing any enemy into his kingdom out of enmity, and not consenting to or concealing another's faithlessness to him; but that all may know that this oath contains in itself this meaning:

First, that each one voluntarily shall strive, in accordance with his knowledge and ability, to live wholly in the holy service of God in accordance with the precept of God and in accordance with his own promise, because the lord emperor is unable to give to all individually the necessary care and discipline.

Secondly, that no man, either through perjury or any other wile or fraud, on account of the flattery or gift of any one, shall refuse to give back or dare to abstract or conceal a serf of the lord emperor or a district or land or anything that belongs to him; and that no one shall presume, through perjury or other wile, to conceal or abstract his fugitive fiscaline serfs who unjustly and fraudulently say that they are free.

That no one shall presume to rob or do any injury fraudulently to the churches of God or widows or orphans or pilgrims; for the lord emperor himself, after God and His saints, has constituted himself their protector and defender.

That no one shall dare to lay waste a benefice of the lord emperor, or to make it his own property.

That no one shall presume to neglect a summons to war from the lord emperor; and that no one of the counts shall be so presumptuous as to dare to dismiss thence any one of those who owe military service, either on account of relationship or flattery or gifts from any one.

That no one shall presume to impede at all in any way a ban or command of the lord emperor, or to dally with his work or to impede or to lessen or in any way to act contrary to his will or commands. And that no one shall dare to neglect to pay his dues or tax.

That no one, for any reason, shall make a practice in court of defending another unjustly, either from any desire of gain when the cause is weak, or by impeding a just judgment by his skill in reasoning, or by a desire of oppressing when the cause is weak. But each one shall answer for his own cause or tax or debt unless any one is infirm or ignorant of pleading; for these the *missi* or the chiefs who are in the court or the judge who knows the case in question shall plead before the court; or if it is necessary, such a person may be allowed as is acceptable to all and knows the case well; but this shall be done wholly according to the convenience of the chiefs or *missi* who are present. But in every case it shall be done in accordance with justice and the law; and that no one shall have the power to impede justice by a gift, reward, or any kind of evil flattery or from any hindrance of relationship. And that no one shall unjustly consent to another in anything, but that with all zeal and goodwill all shall be prepared to carry out justice.

For all the above mentioned ought to be observed by the imperial oath.

That bishops and priests shall live according to the canons and shall teach others to do the same.

That bishops, abbots, abbesses, who are in charge of others, with the greatest veneration shall strive to surpass their subjects in this diligence and shall not oppress their subjects with a harsh rule or tyranny, but with sincere love shall carefully guard the flock committed to them with mercy and charity or by the examples of good works. . . .

That bishops, abbots and abbesses, and counts shall be mutually in accord, following the law in order to render a just judgment with all charity and unity of peace, and that they shall live faithfully in accordance with the will of God, so that always everywhere through them and among them a just judgment shall be rendered. The poor, widows, orphans and pilgrims shall have consolation and defence from them; so that we, through their good-will, may deserve the reward of eternal life rather than punishment. . . .

That counts and *centenarii*[1] shall compel all to do justice in every respect, and shall have such assistants in their ministries as they can securely confide in, who will observe law and justice faithfully, who will oppress the poor in no manner, who will not dare under any pretext, on account of flattery or reward, to conceal thieves, robbers, murderers, adulterers, magicians, wizards or witches, and all sacrilegious men, but instead will give them up that they may be punished and chastised in accordance with the law, so that, God granting it, all of these evils may be removed from the Christian people.

That judges shall judge justly in accordance with the written law, and not according to their own will.

And we command that no one in our whole kingdom shall dare to deny hospitality to rich or poor or pilgrims, that is, no one shall deny shelter and fire and water to pilgrims traversing our country in God's name, or to anyone travelling for the love of God or for the safety of his own soul. . . .

Concerning embassies coming from the lord emperor. That the counts and *centenarii* shall provide most carefully, as they desire the grace of the lord emperor, for the *missi* who are sent out, so that they may go through their departments without any delay; and he commands to all everywhere that they ought to see to it that no delay is encountered anywhere, but they shall cause them to go on their way in all haste and shall provide for them in such a manner as our *missi* may direct. . . .

And against those who announce the justice of the lord emperor, let no one presume to plot any injury or damage, or to stir up any enmity. But if any one shall have presumed, let him pay the imperial ban or, if he deserves a heavier punishment, it is commanded that he shall be brought to the emperor's presence. . . .

That all shall be fully and well prepared, whenever our order or proclamation shall come. But if any one shall then say that he was unprepared and shall have neglected our command, he shall be brought to the palace; and not only he, but also all who dare to transgress our ban or command. . . .

And that all shall be entirely of one mind with our *missi* in performing justice in every respect. And that they shall not permit the use of perjury at all, for it is necessary that this most evil crime shall be removed from the Christian people. But if any one after this shall have been proved a perjurer, let him know that he shall lose his right hand; and they shall be deprived of their property until we shall render our decision. . . .

Lastly, therefore, we desire all our decrees to be known in our whole kingdom through our *missi* now sent out, either among the men of the church, bishops, abbots, priests, deacons, canons, all monks or nuns, so that each one in his ministry or profession may keep our ban or decree, or where it may be fitting to thank the citizens for their good will, or to furnish aid, or where there may be need still of correcting anything. Likewise also to the laymen and in all places everywhere, whether they concern the guardianship of the holy churches or of widows and orphans and the weaker; or the robbing of them; or the arrangements for the assembling of the army; or any other matters; how they are to be obedient to our precept and will, or how they observe our

---

[1] A *centenarius* is the ruler of a *centena;* the latter is a subdivision of province or county.

ban, or how each one strives in all things to keep himself in the holy service of God; so that all these good things may be well done to the praise of omnipotent God, and we may return thanks where it is fitting. But where we believe there is anything unpunished, we shall so strive to correct it with all our zeal and will that with God's aid we may bring it to correction, both for our own eternal glory and that of all our faithful. Likewise we desire all the above to be fruitfully known by our counts or *centenarii,* our ministerials.

■ Discussion Questions

1. What does this document reveal about Charlemagne's vision of himself and his empire? In what ways were his Christian beliefs central to both?
2. Why do you think Charlemagne considered it necessary for all freemen to swear an oath of fidelity to him as emperor? How was the notion of fidelity crucial to the success of his government?
3. What do the oath and the other articles suggest about the means by which Charlemagne sought to unify his empire?

CHAPTER 9

Renewal and Reform, 1050–1200

In the late eleventh and twelfth centuries, trade and agricultural production were on the rise, promoting the development of a new, cash-based economy. A greater prevalence of wealth prompted a range of responses at all levels of medieval society. The first document set elucidates how economic growth transformed Europe as new municipalities were established and old ones enlarged. With the economy booming, many ecclesiastical leaders feared that the church was becoming too entangled in its web. The second document suggests how this fear helped spark a religious reform movement that elevated the papacy to new heights of power. The final documents unveil the social and cultural manifestations of these currents of renewal and reform.

26. *Urban Charters of Jaca, Spain* (c. 1077) and *Lorris, France* (1155)

Cities were common in the Roman Empire but featured less prominently in early medieval Europe. In that period, wealth and power were derived largely from land. Then, in the eleventh century, agricultural and commercial growth resulted in new cities and towns springing up across Europe as places where people congregated to live and work. These two charters attest to the rise of medieval urbanism and its economic and social implications. The first is a charter of laws and freedoms (fuero) bestowed on the community of Jaca in Christian Spain by Sancho I (r. 1063–1094), king of Aragon, around 1077. The second charter was granted by King Louis VII of France (r. 1137–1180) in 1155; it regulated the governance of the town of Lorris.

[CHARTER FOR JACA, SPAIN]

[Emblem of Christ] In the name of our Lord Jesus Christ and of the undivided Trinity, Father and Son and Holy Spirit, amen. This is a charter of authority and confirmation which I Sancho, by the grace of God king of the Aragonese and Pamplonese, make to you.

Notice to all men who are even in the east and west and north and south that I wish to establish a city [*civitatem*] in my village [*villa*][1] which is called "Jaca."

---

[1]The word *villa* does not always mean "village" in medieval Latin, but it does often refer to unwalled settlements in Mediterranean Europe.

From *Medieval Iberia*, ed. Olivia Remie Constable (Philadelphia: University of Pennsylvania Press, 1997), 123–25; and *A Source Book of Mediaeval History*, Frederic Austin Ogg (New York: American Book Co., 1907), 328–30.

First, I remit to you all bad *fueros* which you had until this day that I established Jaca to be a city; and so, because I wish it to be well settled, I concede and confirm to you and to all who settle in my city Jaca all the good *fueros* which you have asked of me in order that my city be well settled.

And each one may enclose his part as he can.

And if it happen that anyone of you comes to dispute and will strike anyone before me or in my palace when I am standing there, let him fine for 1000 s. or lose the fight.

And if anyone, whether knight or burgher or peasant, should strike another, and not in my presence nor in my palace although I be in Jaca, let him not pay the fine [*calonia*] except according to the *fuero* you have when I am not in the town.

And if it happen that someone be found killed in a robbery in Jaca or its district, you are not obligated to pay homicide.[2]

I give and concede to you and your successors with good will that you not go in the army [*hoste*] unless with bread for three days. And this should be in the name of battle in the field [*de lite campale*] or where I or my successors are surrounded by our enemies. And if the lord of the house does not wish to go there, let him substitute one armed footman.

And wherever you can buy anything in Jaca or outside of Jaca, or acquire any man's inheritance, you may have it free and unencumbered without any bad cut [*malo cisso*].[3]

And after you hold it undisturbed for a year and a day, anyone wishing to disturb them or take it away from you shall give me 60 s., and shall confirm your inheritance.

And as far as you can go and return in a day, everywhere, you may have pastures and woods, observing the boundaries of the men living there.

And that you should not have duel-war between you, unless agreeable to both; nor with men from elsewhere, unless with consent of the men of Jaca.

And that none of you should sit captive giving pledges of your foot [*de vestro pede*].[4]

And if any of you commits fornication with any willing woman, except a married one, you shall not pay calumny. And if it happens that he forces her, let him give her a husband or receive her as his wife. And if the raped woman appeals on the first or second day, let her prove by truthful witnesses of Jaca. If she wishes to appeal after three days, it shall avail her nothing.

And if any of you goes against his neighbor in anger and armed with lance, sword, club, or knife, let him fine for it 1000 s. or lose the fight.

And if anyone kills another let him pay 500 s.

And if one strikes another in conflict or grabs him by the hair, let him pay 25 s. for it.

And if he falls to the ground, let him pay 250 s.

And if anyone enters his neighbor's house in anger, or makes seizures there, let him pay 25 s. to the lord of the house.

And that my agent [*merinus*] not receive calumny[5] from any man of Jaca save with the approval of six better men [*vicinis*] of Jaca.

And none of all the men of Jaca should go to judgment anywhere but in Jaca.

And if anyone has false measure or weight, let him pay 60 s.

And that all men should go to mill in mills where they wish, except Jews and those who make bread for sale.

And you should not give or sell your honors to the church or to *infanzones*.[6]

---

[2]That is, the murder fine sometimes imposed by lords on communities.
[3]The "cut," like tallage elsewhere, was an arbitrary tax.
[4]Meaning unclear.
[5]*Calumny* was a payment exacted for slander.
[6]The *infanzones* were the lesser aristocracy of knights in Aragon.

And if any man is imprisoned for debt, let him who wishes to capture him do so with my agent; and let him put [him] in my palace, and let my jailer guard him; and after three days, he who took him should give him farthing's worth [*obolatam*]; and if he refuse to do [this], my jailer may release him.

And if any man seize as pledge the Saracen man or Saracen woman of his neighbor, let him put him in my palace; and the lord of the male and female Saracen shall give him bread and water, because he is a human being [*homo*] and should not starve like a beast.

And whoever wishes to disrupt this charter which I make to the settlers of Jaca, let him be excommunicated and anathematized for his cruelty and wholly separated from all God's faithful, whether he be of my stock or of another. Amen, amen, amen.

[CHARTER FOR LORRIS, FRANCE]

1. Every one who has a house in the parish of Lorris shall pay as *cens* sixpence only for his house, and for each acre of land that he possesses in the parish.[1]

2. No inhabitant of the parish of Lorris shall be required to pay a toll or any other tax on his provisions; and let him not be made to pay any measurage fee on the grain which he has raised by his own labor.[2]

3. No burgher shall go on an expedition, on foot or on horseback, from which he cannot return the same day to his home if he desires.[3]

4. No burgher shall pay toll on the road to Étampes, to Orléans, to Milly (which is in the Gâtinais), or to Melun.[4]

5. No one who has property in the parish of Lorris shall forfeit it for any offense whatsoever, unless the offense shall have been committed against us or any of our *hôtes.*[5]

6. No person while on his way to the fairs and markets of Lorris, or returning, shall be arrested or disturbed, unless he shall have committed an offense on the same day. . . .[6]

9. No one, neither we nor any other, shall exact from the burghers of Lorris any tallage, tax, or subsidy. . . .[7]

12. If a man shall have had a quarrel with another, but without breaking into a fortified house, and if the parties shall have reached an agreement without bringing a suit before the

---

[1]This trifling payment of sixpence a year was made in recognition of the lordship of the king, the grantor of the charter. Aside from it, the burgher had full rights over his land.

[2]The burghers, who were often engaged in agriculture as well as commerce, are to be exempt from tolls on commodities bought for their own sustenance and from the ordinary fees due the lord for each measure of grain harvested.

[3]The object of this provision is to restrict the amount of military service due the king. The burghers of small places like Lorris were farmers and traders who made poor soldiers and who were ordinarily exempted from service by their lords. The provision for Lorris practically amounted to an exemption, for such service as was permissible under Chapter 3 of the charter was not worth much.

[4]The Gâtinais was the region in which Lorris was situated. Étampes, Milly, and Melun all lay to the north of Lorris, in the direction of Paris. Orléans lay to the west. The king's object in granting the burghers the right to carry goods to the towns specified without payment of tolls was to encourage commercial intercourse.

[5]This protects the landed property of the burghers against the crown and crown officials. With two exceptions, fine or imprisonment, not confiscation of land, is to be the penalty for crime. *Hôtes* denotes persons receiving land from the king and under his direct protection.

[6]This provision is intended to attract merchants to Lorris by placing them under the king's protection and assuring them that they would not be molested on account of old offenses.

[7]This chapter safeguards the personal property of the burghers, as Chapter 5 safeguards their land. Arbitrary imposts are forbidden and any of the inhabitants who as serfs had been paying arbitrary tallage are relieved of the burden. The nominal *cens* (Chapter 1) was to be the only regular payment due the king.

provost, no fine shall be due to us or our provost, no fine shall be due to us or our provost on account of the affair. . . .[8]

15. No inhabitant of Lorris is to render us the obligation of *corvée*, except twice a year, when our wine is to be carried to Orleans, and not elsewhere.[9]

16. No one shall be detained in prison if he can furnish surety that he will present himself for judgment.

17. Any burgher who wishes to sell his property shall have the privilege of doing so; and, having received the price of the sale, he shall have the right to go from the town freely and without molestation, if he so desires, unless he has committed some offense in it.

18. Any one who shall dwell a year and a day in the parish of Lorris, without any claim having pursued him there, and without having refused to lay his case before us or our provost, shall abide there freely and without molestation. . . .[10]

35. We ordain that every time there shall be a change of provosts in the town the new provost shall take an oath faithfully to observe these regulations; and the same thing shall be done by new sergeants[11] every time that they are installed.

■ Discussion Questions

1. What do these two documents reveal about the role of kings in promoting urban growth in medieval Europe?
2. What did Louis VII and Sancho I seek to gain in granting their respective charters? What similarities and differences do you see in each king's goals?
3. Based on these two charters, why do you think people decided to move to newly established cities and towns? What did city life have to offer?

27. Emperor Henry IV and Pope Gregory VII, *Letters of the Investiture Conflict* (1076)

The commercial revolution helped spark not only economic changes but also religious ones. Pope Gregory VII (r. 1073–1085) became the driving force behind a movement for church reform, which strove to liberate the church from secular influence and wealth. His zeal brought him head-to-head

---

[8]An agreement outside of court was allowable in all cases except when there was a serious breach of the public peace. The provost was the chief officer of the town. He was appointed by the crown and was charged chiefly with the administration of justice and the collection of revenues. All suits of the burghers were tried in his court. They had no active part in their own government, as was generally true of the franchise towns.

[9]Another part of the charter specifies that only those burghers who owned horses and carts were expected to render the king even this service.

[10]This clause, which is very common in the town charters of the twelfth century (especially in the case of towns on the royal domain) is intended to attract serfs from other regions and so to build up population. As a rule, the towns were places of refuge from seignorial oppression, and the present charter undertakes to limit the time within which the lord might recover his serf who had fled to Lorris to a year and a day—except in cases where the serf should refuse to recognize the jurisdiction of the provost's court in the matter of the lord's claim.

[11]The sergeants were deputies of the provost, somewhat on the order of town constables.

From *Imperial Lives and Letters of the Eleventh Century,* trans. Theodor E. Mommsen and Karl F. Morrison (New York: Columbia University Press, 1962), 150–51; and *The Correspondence of Pope Gregory VII,* trans. Ephraim Emerton (New York: Columbia University Press, 1932), 90–91.

with Emperor Henry IV (r. 1056–1106) who, claiming to be crowned by God, asserted the traditional right to oversee the church in his realm. These two letters illuminate each side of the debate. The first is a letter that Henry sent to Gregory in January 1076 after the pope had denounced him for not obeying papal mandates prohibiting (among other things) laymen from "investing" (that is, appointing) church leaders. In response, the pope excommunicated and deposed Henry. The lines of the conflict were thus drawn, pitting imperial and papal claims of authority against each other. Although the battle ended in 1122 with a compromise, the papacy emerged as a more powerful force than ever before.

[From the Emperor]

Henry, King not by usurpation, but by the pious ordination of God, to Hildebrand, now not Pope, but false monk:

You have deserved such a salution as this because of the confusion you have wrought; for you left untouched no order of the Church which you could make a sharer of confusion instead of honor, of malediction instead of benediction.

For to discuss a few outstanding points among many: Not only have you dared to touch the rectors of the holy Church—the archbishops, the bishops, and the priests, anointed of the Lord as they are—but you have trodden them under foot like slaves who know not what their lord may do. In crushing them you have gained for yourself acclaim from the mouth of the rabble. You have judged that all these know nothing, while you alone know everything. In any case, you have sedulously used this knowledge not for edification, but for destruction, so greatly that we may believe Saint Gregory, whose name you have arrogated to yourself, rightly made this prophesy of you when he said: "From the abundance of his subjects, the mind of the prelate is often exalted, and he thinks that he has more knowledge than anyone else, since he sees that he has more power than anyone else."

And we, indeed, bore with all these abuses, since we were eager to preserve the honor of the Apostolic See. But you construed our humility as fear, and so you were emboldened to rise up even against the royal power itself, granted to us by God. You dared to threaten to take the kingship away from us—as though we had received the kingship from you, as though kingship and empire were in your hand and not in the hand of God.

Our Lord, Jesus Christ, has called us to kingship, but has not called you to the priesthood. For you have risen by these steps: namely, by cunning, which the monastic profession abhors, to money; by money to favor; by favor to the sword. By the sword you have come to the throne of peace, and from the throne of peace you have destroyed the peace. You have armed subjects against their prelates; you who have not been called by God have taught that our bishops who have been called by God are to be spurned; you have usurped for laymen the bishops' ministry over priests, with the result that these laymen depose and condemn the very men whom the laymen themselves received as teachers from the hand of God, through the imposition of the hands of bishops.

You have also touched me, one who, though unworthy, has been anointed to kingship among the anointed. This wrong you have done to me, although as the tradition of the holy Fathers has taught, I am to be judged by God alone and am not to be deposed for any crime unless—may it never happen—I should deviate from the Faith. For the prudence of the holy bishops entrusted the judgment and the deposition even of Julian the Apostate not to themselves, but to God alone. The true pope Saint Peter also exclaims, "Fear God, honor the king." You, however, since you do not fear God, dishonor me, ordained of Him.

Wherefore, when Saint Paul gave no quarter to an angel from heaven if the angel should preach heterodoxy, he did not except you who are now teaching heterodoxy throughout the earth. For he says, "If anyone, either I or an angel from heaven, preach any other gospel unto you than that which we have preached unto you, let him be accursed." Descend, therefore, condemned by this anathema and by the common judgment of all our bishops and of ourself. Relinquish the

Apostolic See which you have arrogated. Let another mount the throne of Saint Peter, another who will not cloak violence with religion but who will teach the pure doctrine of Saint Peter.

I, Henry, King by the grace of God, together with all our bishops, say to you: Descend! Descend!

[FROM THE POPE]

O blessed Peter, prince of the Apostles, mercifully incline thine ear, we [*sic*] pray, and hear me, thy servant, whom thou hast cherished from infancy and hast delivered until now from the hand of the wicked who have hated and still hate me for my loyalty to thee. Thou art my witness, as are also my Lady, the Mother of God, and the blessed Paul, thy brother among all the saints, that thy Holy Roman Church forced me against my will to be its ruler. I had no thought of ascending thy throne as a robber, nay, rather would I have chosen to end my life as a pilgrim than to seize upon thy place for earthly glory and by devices of this world. Therefore, by thy favor, not by any works of mine, I believe that it is and has been thy will, that the Christian people especially committed to thee should render obedience to me, thy especially constituted representative. To me is given by thy grace the power of binding and loosing in Heaven and upon earth.

Wherefore, relying upon this commission, and for the honor and defense of thy Church, in the name of Almighty God, Father, Son and Holy Spirit, through thy power and authority, I deprive King Henry, son of the emperor Henry, who has rebelled against thy Church with unheard of audacity, of the government over the whole kingdom of Germany and Italy, and I release all Christian men from the allegiance which they have sworn or may swear to him, and I forbid anyone to serve him as king. For it is fitting that he who seeks to diminish the glory of thy Church should lose the glory which he seems to have.

And, since he has refused to obey as a Christian should or to return to the God whom he has abandoned by taking part with excommunicated persons, has spurned my warnings which I gave him for his soul's welfare, as thou knowest, and has separated himself from thy Church and tried to rend it asunder, I bind him in the bonds of anathema in thy stead and I bind him thus as commissioned by thee, that the nations may know and be convinced that thou art Peter and that upon thy rock the son of the living God has built his Church and the gates of hell shall not prevail against it.

■ **Discussion Questions**

1. What does Henry IV mean by denouncing the pope as a "false monk"?
2. What do the emperor's denunciations reveal about his conception of the source and scope of his power?
3. How did Henry's self-image conflict with Gregory's understanding of his own authority as reflected in his excommunication and deposition of the emperor?

28. Hildegard of Bingen, *Selected Writings* (Twelfth Century)

As Europe's political, economic, and physical landscape changed in the twelfth century, so, too, did its intellectual life. Though lacking a formal education, Hildegard of Bingen (1098–1179) was among the most creative scholars of her day. Born to a noble German family, Hildegard entered a Benedictine

From Hildegard of Bingen, *Symphonia*, trans. Barbara Newan, 2d ed. (Ithaca, N.Y.: Cornell University Press, 1998), 117; and *The Letters of Hildegard of Bingen*, vol. 1, trans. Joseph Baird and Radd Ehrman (New York and Oxford: Oxford University Press, 1994), 76–80.

convent as a young girl. Her life there was unremarkable until 1141, when a divine voice ordered her to "tell and write" about the visions she had had since her childhood. Thus began her extraordinary career as an author, preacher, and mystic. Here are two selections from her many writings. The first, "Antiphon for the Virgin," is a hymn from her collection of liturgical songs, Symphony of the Harmony of Heavenly Revelations *(c. 1158). The* Symphony *reveals Hildegard's passion for music, which lay at the heart of Benedictine monasticism. This fact helps explain why she found it so difficult to comply with an interdict, imposed on her convent by prelates in Mainz in 1178, that forbade the community to chant their prayers and songs. She responded to the prohibition in the second selection, a letter in which she describes the power of music to reveal God's majesty.*

ANTIPHON FOR THE VIRGIN

Because it was a woman
who built a house for death
a shining girl tore it down.
So now
when you ask for blessings
seek the supreme one
in the form of a woman
surpassing all that God made
since in her
(O tender! O blessed!)
he became one of us.

[LETTER TO THE PRELATES OF MAINZ]

By a vision, which was implanted in my soul by God the Great Artisan before I was born, I have been compelled to write these things because of the interdict by which our superiors have bound us, on account of a certain dead man buried at our monastery, a man buried without any objection, with his own priest officiating. Yet only a few days after his burial, these men ordered us to remove him from our cemetery. Seized by no small terror, as a result, I looked as usual to the True Light, and, with wakeful eyes, I saw in my spirit that if this man were disinterred in accordance with their commands, a terrible and lamentable danger would come upon us like a dark cloud before a threatening thunderstorm.

Therefore, we have not presumed to remove the body of the deceased inasmuch as he had confessed his sins, had received extreme unction and communion, and had been buried without objection. Furthermore, we have not yielded to those who advised or even commanded this course of action. Not, certainly, that we take the counsel of upright men or the orders of our superiors lightly, but we would not have it appear that, out of feminine harshness we did injustice to the sacraments of Christ, with which this man had been fortified while he was still alive. But so that we may not be totally disobedient we have, in accordance with their injunction, ceased from singing the divine praises and from participation in Mass, as has been our regular monthly custom.

As a result, my sisters and I have been greatly distressed and saddened. Weighed down by this burden, therefore, I heard these words in a vision: It is improper for you to obey human words ordering you to abandon the sacraments of the Garment of the Word of God, Who, born virginally of the Virgin Mary, is your salvation. Still, it is incumbent upon you to seek permission to participate in the sacraments from those prelates who laid the obligation of obedience upon you. For ever since Adam was driven from the bright region of paradise into the exile of this world on account of his disobedience, the conception of all people is justly tainted by that first transgression. Therefore, in accordance with God's inscrutable plan, it was necessary for a man free from all pollution to be born in human flesh, through whom all who are predestined to life might be cleansed from corruption and might be sanctified by the communion of his body so that he might remain in them and they in him for their fortification. That person, however, who is disobedient to the commands of God, as Adam was, and is completely forgetful of Him must be completely cut off from participation in the sacrament of His body, just as he himself has turned away from Him in disobedience. And he must remain so until, purged through penitence, he is permitted by the authorities to receive the communion of the Lord's body again. In contrast, however, a person who is aware that he has incurred such a restriction not as a result of anything that he has done, either consciously or deliberately, may be present at the service of the lifegiving sacrament, to be cleansed by the Lamb without sin, Who, in obedience to the Father, allowed Himself to be sacrificed on the altar of the cross that he might restore salvation to all.

In that same vision I also heard that I had erred in not going humbly and devoutly to my superiors for permission to participate in the communion, especially since we were not at fault in receiving that dead man into our cemetery. For, after all, he had been fortified by his own priest with proper Christian procedure, and, without objection from anyone, was buried in our cemetery, with all Bingen joining in the funeral procession. And so God has commanded me to report these things to you, our lords and prelates. Further, I saw in my vision also that by obeying you we have been celebrating the divine office incorrectly, for from the time of your restriction up to the present, we have ceased to sing the divine office, merely reading it instead. And I heard a voice coming from the Living Light concerning the various kinds of praises, about which David speaks in the psalm: "Praise Him with sound of trumpet: praise Him with psaltery and harp," and so forth up to this point: "Let every spirit praise the Lord" [Ps 150.3,6]. These words use outward, visible things to teach us about inward things. Thus the material composition and the quality of these instruments instruct us how we ought to give form to the praise of the Creator and turn all the convictions of our inner being to the same. When we consider these things carefully, we recall that man needed the voice of the living Spirit, but Adam lost this divine voice through disobedience. For while he was still innocent, before his transgression, his voice blended fully with the voices of the angels in their praise of God. Angels are called spirits from that Spirit which is God, and thus they have such voices by virtue of their spiritual nature. But Adam lost that angelic voice which he had in paradise, for he fell asleep to that knowledge which he possessed before his sin, just as a person on waking up only dimly remembers what he had seen in his dreams. And so when he was deceived by the trick of the devil and rejected the will of his Creator, he became wrapped up in the darkness of inward ignorance as the just result of his iniquity.

God, however, restores the souls of the elect to that pristine blessedness by infusing them with the light of truth. And in accordance with His eternal plan, He so devised it that whenever He renews the hearts of many with the pouring out of the prophetic spirit, they might, by means of His interior illumination, regain some of the knowledge which Adam had before he was punished for his sin.

And so the holy prophets, inspired by the Spirit which they had received, were called for this purpose: not only to compose psalms and canticles (by which the hearts of listeners would be inflamed) but also to construct various kinds of musical instruments to enhance these songs of praise with melodic strains. Thereby, both through the form and quality of the instruments, as well as through the meaning of the words which accompany them, those who hear might be taught, as we said above, about inward things, since they have been admonished and aroused by outward things. In such a way, these holy prophets get beyond the music of this exile and recall to mind that divine melody of praise which Adam, in company with the angels, enjoyed in God before his fall.

Men of zeal and wisdom have imitated the holy prophets and have themselves, with human skill, invented several kinds of musical instruments, so that they might be able to sing for the delight of their souls, and they accompanied their singing with instruments played with the flexing of the fingers, recalling, in this way, Adam, who was formed by God's finger, which is the Holy Spirit. . . .

But when the devil, man's great deceiver, learned that man had begun to sing through God's inspiration and, therefore, was being transformed to bring back the sweetness of the songs of heaven, mankind's homeland, he was so terrified at seeing his clever machinations go to ruin that he was greatly tormented. Therefore, he devotes himself continually to thinking up and working out all kinds of wicked contrivances. Thus he never ceases from confounding confession and the sweet beauty of both divine praise and spiritual hymns, eradicating them through wicked suggestions, impure thoughts, or various distractions from the heart of man and even from the mouth of the Church itself, wherever he can, through dissension, scandal, or unjust oppression.

Therefore, you and all prelates must exercise the greatest vigilance to clear the air by full and thorough discussion of the justification for such actions before your verdict closes the mouth of any church singing praises to God or suspends it from handling or receiving the divine sacraments. And you must be especially certain that you are drawn to this action out of zeal for God's justice, rather than out of indignation, unjust emotions or a desire for revenge, and you must always be on your guard not to be circumvented in your decisions by Satan, who drove man from celestial harmony and the delights of paradise.

Consider, too, that just as the body of Jesus Christ was born of the purity of the Virgin Mary through the operation of the Holy Spirit so, too, the canticle of praise, reflecting celestial harmony, is rooted in the Church through the Holy Spirit. The body is the vestment of the spirit, which has a living voice, and so it is proper for the body, in harmony with the soul, to use its voice to sing praises to God. Whence, in metaphor, the prophetic spirit commands us to praise God with clashing cymbals and cymbals of jubilation, as well as other musical instruments which men of wisdom and zeal have invented, because all arts pertaining to things useful and necessary for mankind have been created by the breath that God sent into man's body. For this reason it is proper that God be praised in all things. . . .

Therefore, those who, without just cause, impose silence on a church and prohibit the singing of God's praises and those who have on earth unjustly despoiled God of His honor and glory will lose their place among the chorus of angels, unless they have amended their lives through true penitence and humble restitution. Moreover, let those who hold the keys of heaven beware not to open those things which are to be kept closed nor to close those things which are to be kept open, for harsh judgment will fall upon those who rule, unless, as the apostle says, they rule with good judgment.

And I heard a voice saying thus: Who created heaven? God. Who opens heaven to the faithful? God. Who is like Him? No one. And so, O men of faith, let none of you resist Him or oppose Him, lest He fall on you in His might and you have no helper to protect you from His judgment. This time is a womanish time,[1] because the dispensation of God's justice is weak. But the strength of God's justice is exerting itself, a female warrior battling against injustice, so that it might fall defeated.

■ Discussion Questions

1. How does Hildegard justify her defiance of the prelates of Mainz? What does her defiance suggest about her self-image?
2. Why does Hildegard consider music to be essential to Christian worship?

---

[1]This is a frequent theme in the letters and the other works: the loss of the "virility" of the earlier Church. Hence a woman, paradoxically, has been called by God to help restore this lost virility.

3. Based on these two selections, in what ways does Hildegard express the heightened emphasis on the humanity of Christ and Mary that was a distinguishing feature of twelfth-century spirituality? Why do you think Mary in particular may have appealed to her?

29. Saints Francis and Clare of Assisi, *Selected Writings* (Thirteenth Century)

The church was very much entwined in the world of wealth, power, and splendor celebrated in the vernacular literature of the twelfth and early thirteenth centuries. A variety of new religious movements emerged in reaction against the church's perceived worldliness and neglect of its pastoral mission. St. Francis of Assisi (c. 1182–1226) founded what would become the most popular and largest of these movements in Europe, the Franciscans. The excerpts from his Rule, *written in 1223, illuminate the fundamental principles guiding the order. The Franciscans' message of poverty, humility, and penance prompted people from all walks of life to follow their path, including Clare of Assisi (1194–1253). Upon hearing Francis preach in 1212, she established a community of pious women modeled after his ideals, which became the Order of the Sisters of St. Francis. Although the sisters were eventually cloistered, the passages from Clare's* Testament *reveal not only how their ideals remained true to those of St. Francis but also how medieval women played an important role in cultivating new forms of piety.*

[EXCERPT FROM THE *RULE* OF ST. FRANCIS]

This is the rule and way of living of the minorite brothers: namely to observe the holy Gospel of our Lord Jesus Christ, living in obedience, without personal possessions, and in chastity. Brother Francis promises obedience and reverence to our lord pope Honorius, and to his successors who canonically enter upon their office, and to the Roman Church. And the other brothers shall be bound to obey brother Francis and his successors.

If any persons shall wish to adopt this form of living, and shall come to our brothers, they shall send them to their provincial ministers; to whom alone, and to no others, permission is given to receive brothers. But the ministers shall diligently examine them in the matter of the catholic faith and the ecclesiastical sacraments. And if they believe all these, and are willing to faithfully confess them and observe them steadfastly to the end; and if they have no wives, or if they have them and the wives have already entered a monastery, or if they shall have given them permission to do so . . . the ministers shall say unto them the word of the holy Gospel, to the effect that they shall go and sell all that they have and strive to give it to the poor. But if they shall not be able to do this, their good will is enough. And the brothers and their ministers shall be on their guard and not concern themselves for their temporal goods; so that they may freely do with those goods exactly as God inspires them. . . . Afterwards there shall be granted to them the garments of probation: namely two gowns without cowls and a belt, and hose and a cape down to the belt; unless to these same ministers something else may at some time seem to be preferable in the sight of God. But, when the year of probation is over, they shall be received into obedience; promising always to observe that manner of living, and this Rule. . . .

I firmly command all the brothers by no means to receive coin or money, of themselves or through an intervening person. But for the needs of the sick and for clothing the other brothers, the ministers alone and the guardians shall provide through spiritual friends, as it may seem to

From *Select Historical Documents of the Middle Ages,* ed. Ernest Henderson (London: G. Bell & Sons, 1921), 344–49; and *Francis and Clare: The Complete Works,* trans. Regis J. Armstrong and Ignatius C. Brady (New York: Paulist Press, 1982), 226–32.

them that necessity demands, according to time, place and cold temperature. This one thing being always regarded, that, as has been said, they receive neither coin nor money.

Those brothers to whom God has given the ability to labour, shall labour faithfully and devoutly; in such way that idleness, the enemy of the soul, being excluded, they may not extinguish the spirit of holy prayer and devotion; to which other temporal things should be subservient. As a reward, moreover, for their labour, they may receive for themselves and their brothers the necessaries of life, but not coin or money; and this humbly, as becomes the servants of God and the followers of most holy poverty.

The brothers shall appropriate nothing to themselves, neither a house, nor a place, nor anything; but as pilgrims and strangers in this world, in poverty and humility serving God, they shall confidently go seeking for alms. Nor need they be ashamed, for the Lord made Himself poor for us in this world. This is that height of most lofty poverty, which has constituted you my most beloved brothers heirs and kings of the kingdom of Heaven, has made you poor in possessions, has exalted you in virtues. . . .

All the brothers shall be bound always to have one of the brothers of that order as general minister and servant of the whole fraternity, and shall be firmly bound to obey him. . . .

The brothers may not preach in the bishopric of any bishop if they have been forbidden to by him. And no one of the brothers shall dare to preach at all to the people, unless he have been examined and approved by the general minister of this fraternity, and the office of preacher have been conceded to him. I also exhort those same brothers that, in the preaching which they do, their expressions shall be chaste and chosen, to the utility and edification of the people; announcing to them vices and virtues, punishment and glory, with briefness of discourse; for the words were brief which the Lord spoke upon earth.

The brothers who are the ministers and servants of the other brothers shall visit and admonish their brothers and humbly and lovingly correct them; not teaching them anything which is against their soul and against our Rule. But the brothers who are subjected to them shall remember that, before God, they have discarded their own wills. Wherefore I firmly command them that they obey their ministers in all things which they have promised God to observe, and which are not contrary to their souls and to our Rule. . . .

I firmly command all the brothers not to have suspicious intercourse or to take counsel with women. And, with the exception of those to whom special permission has been given by the Apostolic Chair, let them not enter nunneries. Neither may they become fellow god-parents with men or women, lest from this cause a scandal may arise among the brothers or concerning brothers.

Whoever of the brothers by divine inspiration may wish to go among the Saracens and other infidels, shall seek permission to do so from their provincial ministers. But to none shall the ministers give permission to go, save to those whom they shall see to be fit for the mission.

Furthermore, through their obedience I enjoin on the ministers that they demand from the lord pope one of the cardinals of the holy Roman Church, who shall be the governor, corrector and protector of that fraternity, so that, always subjected and lying at the feet of that same holy Church, steadfast in the catholic faith, we may observe poverty and humility, and the holy Gospel of our Lord Jesus Christ; as we have firmly promised.

[Excerpt from the *Testament* of St. Clare]

In the name of the Lord!

Among all the other gifts which we have received and continue to receive daily from our benefactor, *the Father of mercies* (2 Cor 1:3), and for which we must express the deepest thanks to our glorious God, our vocation is a great gift. Since it is the more perfect and greater, we should be so much more thankful to Him for it. For this reason the Apostle writes: "Acknowledge your calling" (1 Cor 1:26).

The Son of God became for us *the Way* which our Blessed Father Francis, His true lover and imitator, has shown and taught us by word and example.

Therefore, beloved Sisters, we must consider the immense gifts which God has bestowed on us, especially those which He has seen fit to work in us through His beloved servant, our blessed Father Francis, not only after our conversion but also while we were still [living among] the vanities of the world.

For, almost immediately after his conversion, while he had neither brothers nor companions, when he was building the Church of San Damiano in which he was totally filled with divine consolation, he was led to abandon the world completely. This holy man, in the great joy and enlightenment of the Holy Spirit, made a prophecy about us which the Lord fulfilled later. Climbing the wall of that church he shouted in French to some poor people who were standing nearby: "Come and help me build the monastery of San Damiano, because ladies will dwell here who will glorify our heavenly Father throughout His holy Church by their celebrated and holy manner of life."

In this, then, we can consider the abundant kindness of God toward us. Because of His mercy and love, He saw fit to speak these words about our vocation and selection through His saint. And our most blessed Father prophesied not only for us, but also for those who were to come to this [same] holy vocation to which the Lord has called us.

With what solicitude and fervor of mind and body, therefore, must we keep the commandments of our God and Father, so that, with the help of the Lord, we may return to Him an increase of His *talents*. For the Lord Himself not only has set us as an example and mirror for others, but also for our [own] sisters whom the Lord has called to our way of life, so that they in turn will be a mirror and example to those living in the world. . . .

After the most high heavenly Father saw fit in His mercy and grace to enlighten my heart to do penance according to the example and teaching of our most blessed Father Francis, shortly after his own conversion, I, together with the few sisters whom the Lord had given me soon after my conversion, voluntarily promised him obedience, since the Lord had given us the Light of His grace through his holy life and teaching.

But when the Blessed Francis saw that, although we were physically weak and frail, we did not shirk deprivation, poverty, hard work, distress, or the shame or contempt of the world— rather, as he and his brothers often saw for themselves, we considered [all such trials] as great delights after the example of the saints and their brothers—he rejoiced greatly in the Lord. And moved by compassion for us, he promised to have always, both through himself and through his Order, the same loving care and special solicitude for us as for his own brothers.

And thus, by the will of God and our most blessed Father Francis, we went to dwell at the Church of San Damiano. There, in a short time, the Lord increased our number by His mercy and grace so that what He had predicted through His saint might be fulfilled. We had stayed in another place [before this], but only for a little while.

Later on he wrote a form of life for us, [indicating] especially that we should persevere always in holy poverty. And while he was living, he was not content to encourage us by many words and examples to love and observe holy poverty; [in addition] he also gave us many writings so that, after his death, we should in no way turn away from it. [In a similar way] the Son of God never wished to abandon this holy poverty while He lived in the world, and our most blessed Father Francis, following His footprints, never departed, either in example or teaching, from this holy poverty which he had chosen for himself and for his brothers.

Therefore, I, Clare, the handmaid of Christ and of the Poor Sisters of the Monastery of San Damiano—although unworthy—and the little plant of the holy Father, consider together with my sisters our most high profession and the command of so great a father. [We also take note] in some [sisters] of the frailty which we feared in ourselves after the death of our holy Father Francis, [He] who was our pillar of strength and, after God, our one consolation and support.

[Thus] time and again, we bound ourselves to our Lady, most holy Poverty, so that, after my death, the Sisters present and to come would never abandon her.

And, as I have always been most zealous and solicitous to observe and to have the other sisters observe the holy poverty which we have promised the Lord and our holy Father Francis, so, too, the others who will succeed me in office should be bound always to observe it and have it observed by the other sisters. . . .

In the Lord Jesus Christ, I admonish and exhort all my sisters, both those present and those to come, to strive always to imitate the way of holy simplicity, humility, and poverty and [to preserve] the integrity of [our] holy manner of life, as we were taught by our blessed Father Francis from the beginning of our conversion to Christ. Thus may they always remain *in the fragrance* of a good name, both among those who are afar off and those who are near. [This will take place] not by our own merits but solely by the mercy and grace of our Benefactor, *the Father of mercies*. . . .

I also beg that sister who will have the office [of caring for] the sisters to strive to exceed others more by her virtues and holy life than by her office so that, encouraged by her example, the Sisters may obey her not so much out of duty but rather out of love. Let her also be prudent and attentive to her sisters just as a good mother is to her daughters; and especially, let her take care to provide for them according to the needs of each one from the things which the Lord shall give. Let her also be so kind and so available that all [of them] may reveal their needs with trust and have recourse to her at any hour with confidence as they see fit, both for her sake and that of her sisters.

But the sisters who are subjects should keep in mind that for the Lord's sake they have given up their own wills. Therefore I ask that they obey their mother as they have promised the Lord of their own free will so that, seeing the charity, humility, and unity they have toward one another, their mother might bear all the burdens of her office more lightly. Thus what is painful and bitter might be turned into sweetness for her because of their holy way of life. . . .

So that it may be observed better, I leave this writing for you, my dearest and most beloved Sisters, those present and those to come, as a sign of the blessing of the Lord and of our most blessed Father Francis and of my blessing—I who am your mother and servant.

▪ Discussion Questions

1. Based on his *Rule,* how would you characterize Francis's spirituality and sense of mission? Why do you think this appealed to so many people at the time?
2. How does Clare echo Francis's ideals in her *Testament?*
3. What goals did Francis and Clare share in composing the *Rule* and *Testament,* respectively?
4. What do both documents reveal about contemporary attitudes toward women?

CHAPTER 10

An Age of Confidence, 1200–1340

Powerful kings, pious women, rowdy students, and vernacular poets were just a few of the people who infused medieval government, culture, and religion with vitality and confidence in the thirteenth and early fourteenth centuries. During this period, many monarchies consolidated their power, new and representative institutions developed, and the church appeared to reach its pinnacle. With expansion came the search for harmony, order, and unity—a search obvious in almost every document of the period in the medieval West, from religious writings (Document 30) to university statutes (Document 31) to vernacular love poetry (Document 32).

30. Hadewijch of Brabant, *Letters and Poems of a Female Mystic* (1220–1240)

The body of work composed by medieval women writers is considerable and wide ranging—religious and mystical writings, poems, and courtly love literature, medical treatises, and songs. Often the line between the genres was blurred, especially in religious writing. Hadewijch of Brabant was one of many such women writers, and our knowledge of her comes primarily from her writings in her native Dutch, which include thirty-one letters, fourteen visions, forty-five stanzaic poems, and sixteen to twenty-nine other poems. Criticized by members of her own (probably Beguine) community (a community she may have led), Hadewijch nonetheless typifies many women writers in this period. She uses mystical and seemingly erotic language to describe a relationship with Christ. Although some Beguines bordered on the edge of unorthodoxy and even heresy, most works by female mystics fit harmoniously with the writings of such church leaders as Bernard of Clairvaux and Richard and Hugh of St. Victor.

May God let you know, dear child, who He is and how He uses His servants and His handmaidens in particular, and may He consume you in Him. In the depth of His wisdom he shall teach you what he is and how wondrously sweet the beloved dwells in the other beloved, and how thoroughly one dwells in the other, so that neither one nor the other knows themselves apart. But they possess and rejoice in each other mouth in mouth, heart in heart, body in body, soul in soul, and one sweet divine nature flows through them both, and both are one through themselves, yet remain themselves, and will always remain so. . . . Still, I could never endure, dear child, that someone before me loved God as dearly as I. I believe that many loved Him as fondly and dearly, yet I could hardly bear that someone would know Him with such passion.

From "The Brabant Mystic: Hadewijch," in *Medieval Women Writers*, ed. Katherina M. Wilson (Athens: University of Georgia Press, 1984), 193–95, 198–201.

From the age of ten I have been overwhelmed with such passionate love that I would have died during the first two years of this experience if God had not granted me a power unknown to common people and made me recover with His own being. For He soon granted me reason, sometimes enlightened with many wonderful revelations, and I received many wonderful gifts from Him, when he let me feel His presence and showed Himself to me. I was aware of many signs that were between Him and me, as with friends who are used to concealing little and revealing much when their feelings for each other have grown most intimate, when they taste, eat, and drink and consume each other wholly. Through these many signs God, my lover, showed to me early in life, He made me gain much confidence in Him, and I often thought that no one loved him as dearly as I. . . . I do no longer believe that my love for Him is the dearest, nor do I believe that there is one alive who loves God as dearly as I. Sometimes I am so enlightened with love that I realize my failure to give my beloved what He deserves; sometimes when I am blinded with love's sweetness, when I am tasting and feeling her, I realize she is enough for me; and sometimes when I am feeling so fulfilled in her presence, I secretly admit to her that she is enough for me. . . .

In the fifth unspeakable hour love seduces the heart and the soul, and the soul is driven out of herself and out of love's nature and back into love's nature. The soul has then ceased to wonder about the power and darkness of love's designs, and has forgotten the pains of love. Then the soul knows love only through love herself, which may seem lower but is not. For where knowledge is most intimate the beloved knows least.

In the sixth unspeakable hour love despises reason and all that lies within reason and above it and below. Whatever belongs to reason stands against the blessed state of love. . . .

Born is the new season as the old one that lasted so long is drawing to a close.

Those prepared to do love's service will receive her rewards: new comfort and new strength.

If they love her with the vigor of love, they will soon be one with love in love.

To be one with love is an awesome calling and those who long for it should spare no effort.

Beyond all reason they will give their all and go through all.

For love dwells so deep in the womb of the Father that her power will unfold only to those who serve her with utter devotion. . . .

Those who long to be one with love achieve great things, and shirk no effort.

They shall be strong and capable of any task that will win them the love of love, to help the sick or the healthy, the blind, the crippled, or the wounded.

For this is what the lover owes to love. . . .

Those who trust in love with all their being shall be given all they need.

For she brings comfort to the sad and guidance to those who cannot read.

Love will be pleased with the lover if he accepts no other comfort and trusts in her alone.

Those who desire to live in love alone with all their might and heart shall so dispose all things that they shall soon possess her all.

Like the noble season born to bring us flowers in the fields, so the noble ones are called to bear the yoke, the bonds of love.

Faith grows forever in their deeds, and noble flowers blossom and their fruits.

The world is fashioned with faith, and the lover dwells in highest love, one with her in everlasting friendship. . . .

And outside love their truth cannot be known: to those who do not dwell in love the burden is not light but heavy, and they suffer fears unknown to love.

For the servants' law is fear but love is the law of sons.

What is this burden light in love, this yoke so sweet?

It is that noble thrust inside, that touch of love in the beloved which makes him one with her, one will, one being, one beyond revoke.

And ever deeper digs desire and all that is dug up is drunk by love, for love's demands on love surpass the mind of man.

These things are beyond the mind of man: how the lover whom love has overwhelmed with love beholds the beloved so full of love.

For he rests not an hour, before he sails with love through all that is and looks upon her splendor with devotion.

For in love's face he reads the designs she has for him, and in truth in love's face he sees clear and undeceived so many pains so sweet.

This he clearly sees: the lover must love in truth alone. . . .

All their secret veins will run into that stream where love gives love away, where love's friends are made drunk with love and filled with wonder at her passion.

And all this remains concealed to strangers, but to the wise it stands revealed. . . .

[T]heir life is free and undisturbed, and well may they say, "I am all of love and love is all of me."

For what will harm them when they claim the sun, the moon, and all the stars?

Love be praised for the birds that rejoice now and were sad in winter, and soon the proud hearts will rejoice that dwelled in pain too long.

And in the fullness of her power she shall give them a reward that will surpass the mind of man. . . .

Burning desire is taught in the school of highest love.

She confounds the experienced, she brings happiness to the wretched, she makes them lords of all over which love holds sway.

Of this I am certain beyond all doubt.

To those who can serve love no more I give this good advice.

Let them still beg for her comfort if they falter and serve her with devotion according to her highest counsel.

Let them think how great love's power is, for only those near to death cannot be healed.

They have risen high that have received love's power, and in that power they shall read her judgment over them.

■ Discussion Questions

1. Examine closely the language in which Hadewijch expresses her feelings. How does she use gender imagery and language? Do you believe men and women envisioned their relationship with God in different terms?
2. How would you describe Hadewijch's relationship with God and God's relationship with her? Does it surprise you?
3. Why might some members of Hadewijch's community and some church authorities have been concerned with her writings, as well as those of other female mystics? How did her approach challenge some accepted ways of thinking?
4. How does Hadewijch reflect the religious and cultural change of her times?

31. *Medieval University Life* (Twelfth to Early Thirteenth Centuries)

The development of permanent centers of learning in the twelfth and thirteenth centuries in cities across Europe attests to the vitality of the age. Royal patronage and the formation of a sense of common identity among masters students were key to the rise of medieval universities as self-governing

From *Translations and Reprints from the Original Sources of European History,* vol. 2, no. 3, ed. Dana Carleton Munro (Philadelphia: University of Pennsylvania Press, 1898), 2–7; and *Wine, Women, and Song: Mediaeval Latin Students' Songs,* trans. John Addington Symonds (London: Chatto & Windus, 1907), 58–64.

institutions. The first two sections of this document consist of special privileges granted by King Frederick I (r. 1152–1190) of Germany in 1158 to all students within his domains and by King Philip II of France (r. 1180–1223) in 1200 to students at Paris. In this way, students were enveloped within both rulers' growing bureaucracies as each strove to increase his power. We hear the voices of students themselves in two anonymous poems describing the anxieties and pleasures of their way of life.

[EXCERPT FROM STUDENT PRIVILEGES GRANTED BY FREDERICK I]

After a careful consideration of this subject by the bishops, abbots, dukes, counts, judges, and other nobles of our sacred palace, we, from our piety, have granted this privilege to all scholars who travel for the sake of study, and especially, to the professors of divine and sacred laws, namely, that they may go in safety to the places in which the studies are carried on, both they themselves and their messengers, and may dwell there in security. For we think it fitting that, during good behavior, those should enjoy our praise and protection, by whose learning the world is enlightened to the obedience of God and of us, his ministers and the life of the subjects is moulded; and by a certain special love we defend them from all injuries.

For who does not pity those who exile themselves through love for learning, who wear themselves out in poverty in place of riches, who expose their lives to all perils and often suffer bodily injury from the vilest men—this must be endured with vexation. Therefore, we declare by this general and ever to be valid law, that in the future no one shall be so rash as to venture to inflict any injury on scholars, or to occasion any loss to them on account of a debt owed by an inhabitant of their province—a thing which we have learned is sometimes done by an evil custom. And let it be known to the violators of this constitution, and also to those who shall at the time be the rulers of the places, that a four-fold restitution of property shall be exacted from all and that, the mark of infamy being affixed to them by the law itself, they shall lose their office forever. . . .

We also order this law to be inserted among the imperial constitutions under the title, *ne filius pro patre, etc.*

Given at Roncaglia, in the year of our Lord 1158, in the month of November. . . .

[EXCERPT FROM STUDENT PRIVILEGES GRANTED BY PHILIP II]

In the Name of the sacred and indivisible Trinity, amen. Philip, by the grace of God, King of the French.

Concerning the safety of the students at Paris in the future, by the advice of our subjects we have ordained as follows: we will cause all the citizens of Paris to swear that if any one sees an injury done to any student by any layman, he will testify truthfully to this, nor will any one withdraw in order not to see [the act]. And if it shall happen that any one strikes a student, except in self-defense, especially if he strikes the student with a weapon, a club or a stone, all laymen who see [the act] shall in good faith seize the malefactor or malefactors and deliver them to our judge; nor shall they withdraw in order not to see the act, or seize the malefactor, or testify to the truth. Also, whether the malefactor is seized in open crime or not, we will make a legal and full examination through clerks or laymen or certain lawful persons; and our count and our judges shall do the same. And if by a full examination we or our judges are able to learn that he who is accused, is guilty of the crime, then we or our judges shall immediately inflict a penalty, according to the quality and nature of the crime; notwithstanding the fact that the criminal may deny the deed and say that he is ready to defend himself in single combat, or to purge himself by the ordeal by water.

Also, neither our provost nor our judges shall lay hands on a student for any offence whatever; nor shall they place him in our prison, unless such a crime has been committed by the student, that he ought to be arrested. And in that case, our judge shall arrest him on the spot, without striking him at all, unless he resists, and shall hand him over to the ecclesiastical judge, who ought to guard him in order to satisfy us and the one suffering the injury. And if a serious crime has been committed, our judge shall go or shall send to see what is done with the student. . . .

In order, moreover, that these [decrees] may be kept more carefully and may be established forever by a fixed law, we have decided that our present provost and the people of Paris shall affirm by an oath, in the presence of the scholars, that they will carry out in good faith all the above-mentioned. And always in the future, whosoever receives from us the office of provost in Paris, among the other initiatory acts of his office, namely, on the first or second Sunday, in one of the churches of Paris,—after he has been summoned for the purpose,—shall affirm by an oath, publicly in the presence of the scholars, that he will keep in good faith all the above-mentioned. And that these decrees may be valid forever, we have ordered this document to be confirmed by the authority of our seal and by the characters of the royal name, signed below.

A WANDERING STUDENT'S PETITION

I, a wandering scholar lad,
   Born for toil and sadness,
Oftentimes am driven by
   Poverty to madness.

Literature and knowledge I
   Fain would still be earning,
Were it not that want of pelf[1]
   Makes me cease from learning.

These torn clothes that cover me
   Are too thin and rotten;
Oft I have to suffer cold,
   By the warmth forgotten.

Scarce I can attend at church,
   Sing God's praises duly;
Mass and vespers both I miss,
   Though I love them truly.

Oh, thou pride of N——,
   By thy worth I pray thee
Give the suppliant help in need,
   Heaven will sure repay thee.

Take a mind unto thee now
   Like unto St. Martin;
Clothe the pilgrim's nakedness,
   Wish him well at parting.

So may God translate your soul
   Into peace eternal,
And the bliss of saints be yours
   In His realm supernal.

---

[1]**Pelf** means money. [ED.]

A Song of the Open Road

We in our wandering,
Blithesome and squandering,
    Tara, tantara, teino![2]

Eat to satiety,
Drink with propriety;
    Tara, tantara, teino!

Laugh till our sides we split,
Rags on our hides we fit;
    Tara, tantara, teino!

Jesting eternally,
Quaffing infernally:
    Tara, tantara, teino!

Craft's in the bone of us,
Fear 'tis unknown of us:
    Tara, tantara, teino!

When we're in neediness,
Thieve we with greediness:
    Tara, tantara, teino!

Brother catholical,
Man apostolical,
    Tara, tantara, teino!

Say what you will have done,
What you ask 'twill be done!
    Tara, tantara, teino!

Folk, fear the toss of the
Horns of philosophy!
    Tara, tantara, teino!

Here comes a quadruple
Spoiler and prodigal!
    Tara, tantara, teino!

License and vanity
Pamper insanity:
    Tara, tantara, teino!

As the Pope bade us do,
Brother to brother's true:
    Tara, tantara, teino!

---

[2]This refrain appears to be intended to imitate a bugle-call.

Brother, best friend, adieu!
Now, I must part from you!
    Tara, tantara, teino!

When will our meeting be?
Glad shall our greeting be!
    Tara, tantara, teino!

Vows valedictory
Now have the victory;
    Tara, tantara, teino!

Clasped on each other's breast,
Brother to brother pressed,
    Tara, tantara, teino!

▪ Discussion Questions

1. Why do you think Frederick I and Philip II were concerned for students' welfare? What benefits do you think they gained from guaranteeing students certain privileges?
2. What do both sets of privileges reveal about state building at the time? What role did official records such as these play in the process?
3. What picture of student life do the authors paint in the two poems? Do you see any similarities with your own experiences as a student?

32. Dante Alighieri, *Human and Divine Love* (Late Thirteenth to Early Fourteenth Centuries)

Like many Florentines, Dante Alighieri (1265–1321) was heavily involved in politics, serving in the city government, as envoy to Pope Boniface VIII, and eventually suffering exile from his beloved city. But Dante is most celebrated as one of the world's greatest poets. Some of his writings are political, but it is in his vernacular writings, especially the Divine Comedy *and* La Vita Nuova, *that his great genius lies. Dante, through his artistry, is widely credited as making Tuscan the language of Italy and spreading the use of the vernacular.* La Vita Nuova *("The New Life") (1292) is a celebration of human and divine love, written two years after the death of Beatrice, whom Dante tells us he met in 1274. Beatrice Portinari, married to a member of the rich and famous Bardi banking family, became in Dante's words his great love from the moment he first saw her when he was nine. His platonic/philosophical love for her—and what she represented—was in what some scholars call the courtly love tradition: love for the unattainable woman who teaches her "lover" about the mysteries of love. The* Divine Comedy, *consisting of the* Inferno, Purgatorio, *and* Paradiso, *was written between 1313 and 1321. Although Virgil is Dante's guide in the nether regions, Beatrice allows him to glimpse the wonders of paradise.*

From Dante Alighieri, *La Vita Nuova,* trans. Barbara Reynolds (New York: Penguin Books, 1980), 29, 31, 41, 46, 57; and Dante Alighieri, *The Comedy of Dante Alighieri the Florentine, Cantica III: Paradise,* trans. Dorothy L. Sayers and Barbara Reynolds (New York: Penguin Books, 1981), 53–56, 64, 73, 76, 84, 85, 90, 92, 93.

FROM LA VITA NUOVA

Nine times the heaven of the light had revolved in its own movement since my birth and had almost returned to the same point when the woman whom my mind beholds in glory first appeared before my eyes. She was called Beatrice by many who did not know what it meant to call her this. . . . When exactly nine years had passed since this gracious being appeared to me, as I have described, it happened that on the last day of this intervening period this marvel appeared before me again, dressed in purest white, walking between two other women of distinguished bearing, both older than herself. As they walked down the street she turned her eyes towards me where I stood in fear and trembling, and with her ineffable courtesy, which is now rewarded in eternal life, she greeted me; and such was the virtue of her greeting that I seemed to experience the height of bliss. It was exactly the ninth hour of day when she gave me her sweet greeting. As this was the first time she had ever spoken to me, I was filled with such joy that, my senses reeling, I had to withdraw from the sight of others. . . . Whenever and wherever she appeared, in the hope of receiving her miraculous salutation I felt I had not an enemy in the world. Indeed, I glowed with a flame of charity which moved me to forgive all who had ever injured me; and if at that moment someone had asked me a question, about anything, my only reply would have been: "Love." . . . And when this most gracious being actually bestowed the saving power of her salutation, I do not say that Love as an intermediary could dim for me such unendurable bliss. . . .

I became like a person who does not know which road to take on his journey, who wants to set out but does not know where to start. . . .

One imperfection only Heaven has:
The lack of her; so now for her it pleads
And every saint with clamour intercedes,
Only compassion is our advocate.
God understands to whom their prayers relate
And answers them: "My loved ones, bear in peace
That she, your hope, remain until I please
Where one knows he must lose her, soon or late,
And who will say in Hell, 'Souls unconfessed!
I have beheld the hope of Heaven's blessed.'"
My lady is desired in highest heaven.

FROM THE DIVINE COMEDY, PARADISO

O power divine, grant me in song to show
    The blest realm's image—shadow though it be—
    Stamped on my brain; thus far thyself bestow,

            . . .

When Beatrice, intent upon the sun,
    Turned leftward, and so stood and gazed before;
    No eagle e'er so fixed his eyes thereon.
And, as the second ray doth evermore
    Strike from the just and dart back up again,
    Just as the peregrine will stoop and soar,
So through her eyes, her gesture, pouring in
    On my mind's eye, shaped mine; I stared wide-eyed
    On the sun's face, beyond the wont of men.

            . . .

Beatrice stood, her eyes still riveted
    On the eternal wheels; and, constantly,
    Turning mine thence, I gazed on her instead.

    . . .

Whence she to whom my whole self open was
    As to myself, to calm my troubled fit
    Stayed not my question, but without pause
Opened her lips: "Thou dullest thine own wit
    With false imagination, nor perceivest
    That which thou wouldst perceive, being rid of it.
Thou art not still on earth, as thou believest;
    Lightning from its sphere falling never matched
    The speed which thou, returning there, achievest."
But I, my first bewilderment despatched
    By these few smiling words, was more perplexed
    Now, by a new one which I promptly hatched.
I said: "I rest content, no longer vexed
    By one great doubt; but how come I to fly
    Through these light spheres? This doubt assails me next."
She turned on me, after a pitying sigh,
    A look such as a mother's eyes let fall
    Upon her infant, babbling feverishly.
Then she began: "All beings great and small
    Are linked in order; and this orderliness
    Is form, which stamps God's likeness on the All.
Herein the higher creatures see the trace
    Of the Prime Excellence who is the end
    For which that form was framed in the first place."

    . . .

Beatrice gazed on heav'n and I on her;
    Then, while a quarrel might thud home, and wing,
    And from the mocking-point unloose, as 'twere,
I found I'd come where a most wondrous thing
    Enthralled my sight; whence she, being privy thus
    To my whole thought and secret questioning,
Turning to me, as blithe as beautëous:
    "Lift up to God," said she, "thy grateful sense,
    Who with the first star now uniteth us."
Meseemed a cloud enclosed us, lucid, dense,
    Solid, and smooth, like to the diamond stone
    Smitten upon the sun's radiance.
Into itself eternal union
    Received us both, as water doth receive
    A ray of light and still remains all one,

    . . .

The sun that warmed my bosom first with love
    Had brought the beauteous face of truth to light,
    Unveiling it by proof and counter-proof.
Corrected and convinced I must outright
    Confess me, and, the better to convey

These sentiments, I raised my head upright;
But what I saw so carried me away
    To gaze on it, that ere I could confess,
    I had forgotten what I meant to say.

. . .

Toward Beatrice's self I moved me, turning;
    But on mine eyes her light at first so blazed,
    They could not bear the beauty and the burning;
And I was slow to question, being amazed.

. . .

"O Loved," said I, "of the First Lover! O
    Most heavenly Lady, by whose words I live
    More and yet more, bathed in their quickening glow.
My love's whole store is too diminutive,
    Too poor in thanks to give back grace for grace;
    May he that sees, and has the power, so give!
That nothing save the light of truth allays
    Our intellect's disquiet I now see plain—
    God's truth, which holds all truth within its rays.

. . .

This thought invites and makes me more secure
    To ask you, Lady, with all reverence due,
    About a further truth I find obscure.
This would I know: can one atone to you
    For broken vows with other merchandise,
    Nor weigh too short upon your balance true?"
Beatrice looked at me, and lo! her eyes
    Grew so divine, with sparkling love alight,
    That I was lost in wonder and surprise,
My gaze downcast, my powers all put to flight.

. . .

"If in the fire of love I flame thus hot
    Upon thee, past all wont of mortal mood,
    Forcing thine eyes' surrender, marvel not.
This comes of perfect sight, with power endued
    To apprehend, and foot by foot to move
    Deeper into the apprehended good.
Full well I see thine intellect give off
    Splendours already of the eternal light
    Which once to look upon is aye to love;
And if aught else your wandering loves invite,
    Still it is nothing but some gleams of this
    Which there shine through, though not yet known aright.
Fain wouldst thou learn if any service is
    Enough to offset broken vows, and fend
    The soul against pursuit for damages."
Thus did Beatrice to my canto lend
    The prelude; nor paused there, but fluently
    Pursued her sacred theme unto the end.

. . .

Thus unto me, even in the words I write,
  Beatrice; and, all desire, she turned her glance
  Then to where most the world is quick with light.
Her silence and her altered countenance
  Restrained my busy wits from chattering,
  Primed as they were with questions in advance;
And, as the shaft smites home or e'er the string
  Has ceased vibrating, so we found us there,
  Shot to the second realm, untarrying;
And O! such joy I saw my Lady wear
  When to that shining heav'n she entered in
  The planet's self grew brighter yet with her.

▪ Discussion Questions

1. Some scholars question Beatrice Portinari's existence or her personal inspiration for *La Vita Nuova* and *Paradiso*. Does it matter? Why or why not?
2. How does Dante's writing fit into the courtly love tradition? How does it fit into that of the medieval cult of the Virgin Mary?
3. What, if anything, does it tell you about the status of women that Dante chose Beatrice as his guide to heaven? What does it mean when he says "she was called Beatrice by many who did not know what it meant to call her this"? How is this statement important?
4. Dante is often portrayed as a "medieval" rather than a "Renaissance" poet. Why? What connections do you see in his poetry with the intellectual culture of the time?

CHAPTER II

Crisis and Renaissance, 1340–1500

Pestilence, warfare, a church in crisis, rebellions, pogroms, famines, and floods—to people living in the fourteenth century, it must have appeared that the end of the world was at hand. Fourteenth-century men and women came up with explanations, yet with the historian's luxury of retrospect, we can see the interconnectedness of events—what French historians call a *conjuncture*. Overpopulation, soil depletion, and warfare had reduced the average life span even before plague struck. During the Black Death, scapegoats were often sought, even though many saw the plague as divine punishment. The documents in this chapter evince both a grim side to the Renaissance, particularly the horror of war and danger of politics, and man's potential to overcome his condition.

33. *The Black Death* (Fourteenth Century)

Few events have had such a shattering impact on every aspect of society as the plague, which reached Europe in 1347. The Black Death decimated a society already weakened by a demographic crisis, famines, and climatic disasters. It is estimated that one-third of Europe's population died in the first wave of plague, which was followed by repeated outbreaks. Some cities may have lost over half their people in 1347–1348 alone. The devastation was social, psychological, economic, political, and even artistic, yet many historians believe that it led to significant changes and even improvements in Western life. This set of documents describes the arrival of the plague in various places and responses to it, including searches for its cause and for people on whom to fix blame.

FROM GABRIELE DE' MUSSIS (D. 1356), A LAWYER IN PIACENZA

In 1346, in the countries of the East, countless numbers of Tartars and Saracens were struck down by a mysterious illness which brought sudden death. . . . An eastern settlement under the rule of the Tartars called Tana, which lay to the north of Constantinople and was much frequented by Italian merchants, was totally abandoned after an incident there which led to its being besieged and attacked by hordes of Tartars who gathered in a short space of time. The Christian merchants, who had been driven out by force, were so terrified of the power of the Tartars that, to save themselves and their belongings, they fled in an armed ship to Caffa, a settlement in the same part of the world which had been founded long ago by the Genoese.

Oh God! See how the heathen Tartar races, pouring together from all sides, suddenly invested the city of Caffa and besieged the trapped Christians there for almost three years. There, hemmed in by an immense army, they could hardly draw breath, although food could be shipped

From *The Black Death,* ed. and trans. Rosemary Horrox (Manchester: Manchester University Press, 1994), 16–21, 23, 207, 208, 219–22.

in, which offered them some hope. But behold, the whole army was affected by a disease which overran the Tartars and killed thousands upon thousands every day. It was as though arrows were raining down from heaven to strike and crush the Tartars' arrogance. All medical advice and attention was useless; the Tartars died as soon as the signs of disease appeared on their bodies: swellings in the armpit or groin caused by coagulating humours, followed by a putrid fever.

The dying Tartars, stunned and stupefied by the immensity of the disaster brought about by the disease, and realising that they had no hope of escape, lost interest in the siege. But they ordered corpses to be placed in catapults and lobbed into the city in the hope that the intolerable stench would kill everyone inside. What seemed like mountains of dead were thrown into the city, and the Christians could not hide or flee or escape from them, although they dumped as many of the bodies as they could in the sea. And soon the rotting corpses tainted the air and poisoned the water supply, and the stench was so overwhelming that hardly one in several thousand was in a position to flee the remains of the Tartar army. Moreover, one infected man could carry the poison to others, and infect people and places with the disease by look alone. No one knew, or could discover, a means of defence.

Thus almost everyone who had been in the East, or in the regions to the south and north, fell victim to sudden death after contracting this pestilential disease, as if struck by a lethal arrow which raised a tumour on their bodies. The scale of the mortality and the form which it took persuaded those who lived, weeping and lamenting, through the bitter events of 1346 to 1348—the Chinese, Indians, Persians, Medes, Kurds, Armenians, Cilicians, Georgians, Mesopotamians, Nubians, Ethiopians, Turks, Egyptians, Arabs, Saracens, and Greeks (for almost all the East has been affected) that the last judgement had come. . . .

As it happened, among those who escaped from Caffa by boat were a few sailors who had been infected with the poisonous disease. Some boats were bound for Genoa, others went to Venice and to other Christian areas. When the sailors reached these places and mixed with the people there, it was as if they had brought evil spirits with them: every city, every settlement, every place was poisoned by the contagious pestilence. . . .

Scarcely one in seven of the Genoese survived. In Venice, where an inquiry was held into the mortality, it was found that more than 70 percent of the people had died, and that within a short period 20 out of 24 excellent physicians had died. The rest of Italy, Sicily, and Apulia and the neighbouring regions maintain that they have been virtually emptied of inhabitants. The people of Florence, Pisa, and Lucca, finding themselves bereft of their fellow residents, emphasize their losses. The Roman Curia at Avignon, the provinces on both sides of the Rhône, Spain, France, and the Empire cry up their griefs and disasters—all of which makes it extraordinarily difficult for me to give an accurate picture.

By contrast, what befell the Saracens can be established from trustworthy accounts. In the city of Babylon alone (the heart of the Sultan's power), 480,000 of his subjects are said to have been carried off by the disease in less than three months in 1348—and this is known from the Sultan's register which records the names of the dead, because he receives a gold bezant for each person buried. . . .

I am overwhelmed, I can't go on. Everywhere one turns there is death and bitterness to be described. The hand of the Almighty strikes repeatedly, to greater and greater effect. The terrible judgement gains power as time goes by.

FROM HERMAN GIGAS, A FRANCISCAN FRIAR IN GERMANY, WHOSE ACCOUNT
GOES UNTIL 1349

In 1347 there was such a great pestilence and mortality throughout almost the whole world that in the opinion of well-informed men scarcely a tenth of mankind survived. The victims did not linger long, but died on the second or third day. . . . Some say that it was brought about by the corruption of the air; others that the Jews planned to wipe out all the Christians with poison and had poisoned wells and springs everywhere. And many Jews confessed as much under torture: that they had bred spiders and toads in pots and pans, and had obtained poison from overseas; and that not every Jew knew about this, only the more powerful ones, so that it would not be betrayed. . . . [M]en say that bags full of poison were found in many wells and springs.

FROM HEINRICH TRUCHESS, A FORMER PAPAL CHAPLAIN AND CANON OF CONSTANCE

The persecution of the Jews began in November 1348, and the first outbreak in Germany was at Sölden, where all the Jews were burnt on the strength of a rumour that they had poisoned wells and rivers, as was afterwards confirmed by their own confessions and also by the confessions of Christians whom they had corrupted. . . . Within the revolution of one year, that is from All Saints [1 November] 1348 until Michaelmas [29 September] 1349 all the Jews between Cologne and Austria were burnt and killed for this crime, young men and maidens and the old along with the rest. And blessed be God who confounded the ungodly who were plotting the extinction of his church.

FROM THE COUNCILLORS OF COLOGNE TO CONRAD VON WINTERTHUR TO THE BÜRGERMEISTER AND COUNCILLORS OF STRASSBURG ON 12 JANUARY 1349

Very dear friends, all sorts of rumours are now flying about against Judaism and the Jews prompted by this unexpected and unparalleled mortality of Christians, which, alas, has raged in various parts of the world and is still woefully active in several places. Throughout our city, as in yours, many-winged Fame clamours that this mortality was initially caused, and is still being spread, by the poisonings of springs and wells, and that the Jews must have dropped poisonous substances into them. When it came to our knowledge that serious charges had been made against the Jews in several small towns and villages on the basis of this mortality, we sent numerous letters to you and to other cities and towns to uncover the truth behind these rumours, and set a thorough investigation in train. . . .

If a massacre of the Jews were to be allowed in the major cities (something which we are determined to prevent in our city, if we can, as long as the Jews are found to be innocent of these or similar actions) it could lead to the sort of outrages and disturbances which would whip up a popular revolt among the common people—and such revolts have in the past brought cities to misery and desolation. In any case we are still of the opinion that this mortality and its attendant circumstances are caused by divine vengeance and nothing else. Accordingly we intend to forbid any harassment of the Jews in our city because of these flying rumours, but to defend them faithfully and keep them safe, as our predecessors did—and we are convinced that you ought to do the same.

PAPAL BULL *SICUT JUDEIS* OF CLEMENT VI ISSUED IN JULY 1348

Recently, however, it has been brought to our attention by public fame—or more accurately, infamy—that numerous Christians are blaming the plague with which God, provoked by their sins, has afflicted the Christian people, on poisonings carried out by the Jews at the instigation of the devil, and that out of their own hot-headedness they have impiously slain many Jews, making no exception for age or sex; and that the Jews have been falsely accused of such outrageous behaviour. . . . [I]t cannot be true that the Jews, by such a heinous crime, are the cause or occasion of the plague, because throughout many parts of the world the same plague, by the hidden judgment of God, has afflicted and afflicts the Jews themselves and many other races who have never lived alongside them.

We order you by apostolic writing that each of you upon whom this charge has been laid, should straitly command those subject to you, both clerical and lay ... not to dare (on their own authority or out of hot-headedness) to capture, strike, wound or kill any Jews or expel them from their service on these grounds; and you should demand obedience under pain of excommunication.

■ Discussion Questions

1. Examine the documents and try to determine their historical accuracy from internal evidence alone. What gives you clues about an author's objectivity (or lack thereof)?
2. What explanations are offered for the onset of plague? What (if any) is the understanding of the disease process?
3. Look at the account by Mussis and the bull of Pope Clement VI. What do they have in common? How did different groups of people react to the plague?
4. Why would some Christian authorities (the city councillors or the pope mentioned in these documents) attempt to protect the Jews? Why was such protection of no avail in many places? Why did some Jews confess? Discuss the attempt of societies (in some cases) to find scapegoats.

34. Christine de Pisan, *Lament on the Evils of the Civil War*   (1410)

Christine de Pisan (1364–c. 1430) is considered by some to be the first feminist. Born in Italy, she was raised in Paris after her father, a scholar and physician who gave her a superb education, was called to the court of Charles V. After his death, and then that of her husband in 1389, Christine turned to writing to support her children. She became the first professional female writer in Europe. Patronized by kings, queens, and dukes, Christine wrote numerous works of prose and poetry, including The Book of the City of Ladies, *a defense of women. The epistle quoted here was written in 1410, when France was at a low point in the Hundred Years' War. In this letter she urges the leaders of society to look at what their disunity has done to France and its people, and she urges them to come together instead of fighting one another.*

Alone, and suppressing with great difficulty the tears which blur my sight and pour down my face like a fountain, so much that I am surprised to have the time to write this weary lament, whose writing the pity for the coming disaster makes me erase with bitter tears, and I say in pain: Oh, how can it be that the human heart, as strange as Fortune is, can make man revert to the nature of a voracious and cruel beast? Where is the reason that gives him the name of a rational animal? How can Fortune have the power to transform a man so much, that he is changed into a serpent, the enemy of mankind? Oh, alas, here is the reason why, noble French princes. With deference to you, where is now the sweet natural blood among you which has been for a long time the true summit of kindness in the world? . . .

For God's sake! For God's sake! High Princes, let these facts open your eyes and may you see as already accomplished what the preparations for taking arms will do in their end; thus you will see ruined cities, towns and castles destroyed, and fortresses razed to the ground. And where?

From Christine de Pisan, *The Epistle of the Prison of Human Life with an Epistle to the Queen of France and Lament on the Evils of the Civil War,* ed. and trans. Josette A. Wisman (New York: Garland Publishing, 1984), 85, 87, 89, 91, 93, 95.

In the very heart of France! The noble knights and youth of France, all of one nature, one single soul and body, which used to defend the crown and the public good, are now gathered in a shameful battle one against another, father against son, brother against brother, relatives against one another, with deadly swords, covering the pitiful fields with blood, dead bodies, and limbs. Oh, dishonorable victory may be to the one who has it! What glory will Fame give to it? . . .

Oh you, knight who comes from such a battle, tell me, I pray you, what honor did you win there? . . . And what will follow, in God's name? Famine, because of the wasting and ruining of things that will ensue, and the lack of cultivation, from which will spring revolts by the people who have been too often robbed, deprived and oppressed, their food taken away and stolen here and there by soldiers, subversion in the towns because of outrageous taxes. . . . So cry, cry, beat your hands and cry—as once the sad Argia did in such a case, along with the ladies of Argos— you ladies, damsels, and women of the kingdom of France! Because the swords that will make you widows and deprive you of your children and kin have already been sharpened! . . .

Oh, crowned Queen of France, are you still sleeping? Who prevents you from restraining now this side of your kin and putting an end to this deadly enterprise? Do you not see the heritage of your noble children at stake? . . .

Come, all you wise men of this realm, come with your queen! What use are you if not for the royal council? Everyone should offer his hand. You used to concern yourselves even with small matters. How shall France be proud of so many wise men, if now they cannot see to her safety, and the fount of the clergy keep her from perishing? Where then are your plans and wise thoughts? . . . For you resemble Nineveh, which God condemned to perish, and which received his wrath because of the great sins which were many there, and because of this, the situation is very doubtful, unless the sentence is not revoked by the intercession of devout prayers.

People, be firm! And you, pious woman, cry mercy for this grievous storm! Ah, France, France, once a glorious kingdom! . . .

Oh, Duke of Berry, Noble Prince, excellent father and scion of royal children, son of a King of France, brother and uncle, father of all the antiquity of the lily! How is it possible that your tender heart can bear to see you, on a given day, assembled in deadly battle array to bear painful arms against your nephews? . . .

So, come, come, Noble Duke of Berry, Prince of High Excellence, and follow the divine law which orders peace! Take a strong hold of the bridle, and stop this dishonorable army, at least until you have talked to the parties. So come to Paris, to your father's city where you were born and which cries to you with tears and sighs, asking and begging for you to come. Come quickly to comfort this suffering city. . . . [A]lthough it is now discussed in various tongues on each side that hopes for victory in the battle and they all say: "We will win and work for it"—they are bragging foolishly. For it must not be ignored that the outcome of all battles is strange and unknown. For although man proposed it, Fortune disposes it. . . . Was the victory of the King of Athens, mortally wounded in battle, of any worth to him? Is a multitude of men an advantage in such a case? Was Xerxes not defeated, although he had so many men that all vales and hills were covered with them? Are a good reason and a just quarrel of any value? If it were so, the king Saint Louis, who obtained so many beautiful victories, would not have been defeated at Tunis by the infidels. . . . And above all, although war and battles are in all cases very dangerous and difficult to avoid, no doubt that among such close kin, tied by nature in one bond of love, they are perverse. . . . I believe the cost would be less, and that this army, by a common will and true unity, should be directed against those who are our natural enemies, and that the good and faithful French should take care of these people, and not kill one another. . . . Ah, Very Reverend Prince, Noble Duke of Berry, do hear this. . . . May the Blessed Holy Spirit, Author of all peace, give you the heart and the courage to achieve such a thing! Amen. And may he greet me, a poor voice crying in this kingdom, wanting peace and welfare for all, your servant Christine, moved by a very fair mind, the gift to see that day!

■ **Discussion Questions**

1. What, in Christine's view, are the costs of war, in human and dynastic terms?
2. How important is it that Christine refers in several instances to "the French" and "France"? To whom does Christine direct her admonitions? Why?
3. What kind of allusions does Christine use to convince her readers that they should not continue a civil war that is keeping them from fighting the "common enemy"? What does this tell you about her education?
4. Do you think this "poor voice crying in the kingdom" can be seen as a precursor to Joan of Arc? Why or why not?

35. Giovanni Pico della Mirandola, *Oration on the Dignity of Man* (1496)

The work of Giovanni Pico della Mirandola (1463–1494), a Neo-platonic thinker and Dominican friar, celebrates man's potential. The Oration on the Dignity of Man *was the preface to nine hundred theses written by Pico in his early twenties, for a public disputation that never in fact took place. Steeped in the Aristotelian and Platonic traditions, Pico knew Latin, Arabic, Greek, Hebrew, and Aramaic. He was deeply interested in Hebrew mysticism, pre-Socratic thought, and occult knowledge attributed at the time to Hermes Trismegistus. Not surprisingly, some of Pico's ideas were deemed heretical by a papal commission. Thereafter, he lived under the protection of Lorenzo de' Medici until he died at the age of thirty-one. The Oration explores the concept of free will—the human ability to choose, for good or ill.*

I have read in the ancient annals of the Arabians, most reverend Fathers, that when asked what on the world's stage could be considered most admirable, Abdala the Saracen answered that there is nothing more admirable to be seen than man. In agreement with this opinion is the saying of Hermes Trismegistus: "What a great miracle, O Asclepius, is man!"

When I had thought over the meaning of these maxims, the many reasons for the excellence of man advanced by many men failed to satisfy me. . . .

At last, it seems to me that I have understood why man is the most fortunate living thing worthy of all admiration and precisely what rank is his lot in the universal chain of being, a rank to be envied not only by the brutes but even by the stars and by minds beyond this world. It is a matter past faith and extraordinary! . . .

God the Father, the supreme Architect, had already built this cosmic home which we behold, this most majestic temple of divinity, in accordance with the laws of a mysterious wisdom. He had adorned the region above the heavens with intelligences, had quickened the celestial spheres with eternal souls and had filled the vile and filthy parts of the lower world with a multitude of animals of every kind. But when the work was completed, the Maker kept wishing that there were someone who could examine the plan of so great an enterprise, who could love its beauty, who could admire its vastness. On that account, when everything was completed, as Moses and Timaeus both testify, He finally took thought of creating man. However, not a single archetype remained from which he might fashion this new creature, not a single treasure remained which he might bestow upon this new son, and not a single seat remained in the whole world in

From *The Italian Renaissance Reader,* ed. Julia Conaway Bondanella and Mark Musa (New York: Meridian, 1987), 180–83.

which the contemplator of the universe might sit. All now was complete; all things had been assigned to the highest, the middle, and the lowest orders. But it was not in the nature of the Father's power to fail in this final creative effort, as though exhausted; nor was it in the nature of His wisdom to waver in such a crucial matter through lack of counsel; and it was not in the nature of His Beneficent Love that he who was destined to praise God's divine generosity in regard to others should be forced to condemn it in regard to himself. At last, the Supreme Artisan ordained that the creature to whom He could give nothing properly his own should share in whatever He had assigned individually to the other creatures. He therefore accepted man as a work of indeterminate nature, and placing him in the center of the world, addressed him thus:

"O Adam, we have given you neither a place nor a form nor any ability exclusively your own, so that according to your wishes and your judgment, you may have and possess whatever place, form, or abilities you desire. The nature of all other beings is limited and constrained in accordance with the laws prescribed by us. Constrained by no limits, in accordance with your own free will, in whose hands we have placed you, you shall independently determine the bounds of your own nature. We have placed you at the world's center, from where you may more easily observe whatever is in the world. We have made you neither celestial nor terrestrial, neither mortal nor immortal, so that with honor and freedom of choice, as though the maker and molder of yourself, you may fashion yourself in whatever form you prefer. You shall have the power to degenerate into the inferior forms of life which are brutish; you shall have the power, through your soul's judgment, to rise to the superior orders which are divine." . . .

In man alone, at the moment of his creation, the Father placed the seeds of all kinds and the germs of every way of life. Whatever seeds each man cultivates will mature and bear their own fruit in him; if vegetative, he will be like a plant; if sensitive, he will become a brute; if rational, he will become a celestial being; if intellectual, he will be an angel and the son of God. . . .

Who would not admire this our chameleon? Or who could admire any other being more greatly than man? Asclepius the Athenian justly says that man was symbolized in the mysteries by the figure of Proteus because of his ability to change his character and transform his nature. This is the origin of those metamorphoses or transformations celebrated among the Hebrews and the Pythagoreans. For the occult theology of the Hebrews sometimes transforms the holy Enoch into an angel of divinity and sometimes transforms other people into other divinities. The Pythagoreans transform impious men into beasts and, if Empedocles is to be believed, even into plants. Echoing this, Mohammed often had this saying on his lips: "He who deviates from divine law becomes a beast," and he was right in saying so. For it is not the bark that makes the beast of burden but its irrational and sensitive soul; neither is it the spherical form which makes the heavens, but their undeviating order; nor is it the freedom from a body which makes the angel but its spiritual intelligence. . . .

Are there any who will not admire man? In the sacred Mosaic and Christian writings, man, not without reason, is sometimes described by the name of "all flesh" and sometimes by that of "every creature," since man molds, fashions, and transforms himself according to the form of all flesh and the character of every creature. For this reason, the Persian Evantes, in describing Chaldean theology, writes that man does not have an inborn and fixed image of himself but many which are external and foreign to him; whence comes the Chaldean saying: "Man is a being of varied, manifold, and inconstant nature."

But why do we reiterate all these things? To the end that from the moment we are born we are born into the condition of being able to become whatever we choose.

■ Discussion Questions

1. Examine the words Pico uses to describe God and how God went about the process of creation. Why might these ideas have been considered dangerous?

2. What, according to Pico, are man's abilities? Why were these abilities and possibilities given to human beings?

3. What kinds of sources does Pico use to support his ideas? What is their importance as part of his philosophy?

4. What makes this document a "statement" of Renaissance thought?

36. Alessandra Strozzi, *Letters from a Widow and Matriarch of a Great Family*   (1450–1465)

Women in medieval and Renaissance Europe were usually under legal guardianship—typically that of a father or husband. Women of the lower classes may have enjoyed a semblance of freedom in work and marriage early in their lives. In contrast, their upper-class counterparts gained their greatest prestige and power through widowhood. Alessandra (1407–1471) married Matteo Strozzi, a wealthy merchant whose business had branches throughout Europe. When Matteo died of the effects of the plague while exiled for being in opposition to Cosimo de' Medici (1389–1464), Alessandra's financial situation became difficult, for she had sons and daughters to marry and a great household to maintain. She engaged in lengthy correspondence with her sons about political, marital, and economic conditions that affected the family. In these excerpts from letters to her son Filippo, we can glimpse the "other" side of the Renaissance—exile; political danger if one did not agree with the ruling faction; marriages that were contracted solely for reasons of politics, honor, and clientage; and slavery.

TO FILIPPO, 1450

Really, as long as there are young girls in the house, you do nothing but work for them, so when she leaves I will have no one to attend to but you three. And when I get the house in a little better shape I would love it if you would think about coming home. You would have no cause to be ashamed with what there is now, and you could do honor to any friend who dropped in to see you at home. But two or three years from now it will all be much better. And I would love to get you a wife; you're of an age now to know how to manage the help and to give me some comfort and consolation. I have none. . . .

You know that some time ago I bought Cateruccia, our slave, and for several years now, though I haven't laid a hand on her, she has behaved so badly toward me and the children that you wouldn't believe it if you hadn't seen it. Our Lorenzo could tell you all about it. . . . I've always suffered it because I can't chastise her, and besides I thought you would come once a month so that we could come to a decision together or she could be brought to better obedience. For several months now she has been saying and is still saying that she doesn't want to stay here, and she is so moody that no one can do a thing with her. If it weren't for love of Lesandra, I would have told you to sell her, but because of her malicious tongue, I want to see Lesandra safely out of the house first. But I don't know if I can hold out that long: mark my words, I'm going to get her out of my sight because I don't want this constant battle. She pays no more attention to me than if I were the slave and she were the mistress, and she threatens us all so that Lesandra and I are both afraid of her.

From *University of Chicago Readings in Western Civilization, 5: The Renaissance,* ed. Eric Cochrane and Julius Kirshner (Chicago: University of Chicago Press, 1986), 109, 113–17.

To Filippo, 1459

It grieves me, my son, that I'm not near you to take some of these troublesome things off your hands. You should have told me the first day Matteo fell sick so I could have jumped on a horse and been there in just a few days. But I know that you didn't do it for fear I would get sick or would be put to trouble. . . . I have been told that in the honors you arranged for the burial of my son you did honor to yourself as well as to him. You did all the better to pay him such honor there, since here they don't usually do anything for those who are in your condition [that is, in exile]. Thus I am pleased that you did so. Here these two girls, who are unconsolable over the death of their brother, and I have gone into mourning, and because I had not yet gotten the woolen cloth to make a mantle for myself, I have gotten it now and I will pay for it.

To Filippo, 1465

I told you in my other [letter] what happened about 60 [the daughter of Francesco Tanagli], and there's nothing new there. And you have been advised that there is no talk of 59 [a woman who belonged to the Adimari family] until we have placed the older girl. 13 [Marco Parenti] believes we should do nothing further until we can see our way clearly concerning these two and see what way they will go. Considering their age, this shouldn't take too long. It's true that my wish would be to see both of you with a companion, as I have told you many times before. That way when I die I would think you ready to take the step all mothers want—seeing their sons married—so your children could enjoy what you have acquired with enormous effort and stress over the long years. To that end, I have done my very best to keep up the little I have had, foregoing the things that I might have done for my soul's sake and for that of our ancestors. But for the hope I have that you will take a wife (in the aim of having children), I am happy to have done so. So what I would like would be what I told you. Since then I have heard what Lorenzo's wants are and how he was willing to take her to keep me happy, but that he would be just as glad to wait two years before binding himself to the lady. I have thought a good deal about the matter, and it seems to me that since nothing really advantageous to us is available, and since we have time to wait these two years, it would be a good idea to leave it at that unless something unexpected turns up. Otherwise, it doesn't seem to me something that requires immediate thought, particularly considering the stormy times we live in these days, when so many young men on this earth are happy to inhabit it without taking a wife. The world is in a sorry state, and never has so much expense been loaded on the backs of women as now. No dowry is so big that when the girl goes out she doesn't have the whole of it on her back, between silks and jewels. . . . If 60 works out well, we could sound out the possibility of the other girl for him. There's good forage there if they were to give her, and at any [other] time it would have been a commendable move. As things are going now, it seems to me better to wait and see a while for him. . . . This way something may come of it, and they will not offer a wife without money, as people are doing now, since it seems superfluous to those who are giving 50 to give her a dowry. 13 wrote you that 60's father touched on the matter with him in the way I wrote you about. He says that you should leave it to us to see to it and work it out. For my part, I've done my diligent best, and I can't think what more I could have done—for your consolation than my own. . . .

Niccolò has gone out of office, and although he did some good things, they weren't the ones I would have wanted. Little honor has been paid to him or to the other outgoing magistrates, either when they were in office, or now that they have stepped down. Our scrutineer was quite upset about it, as were we, but I feel that what was done will collapse, and it is thought they will start fresh. This Signoria has spent days in deliberation, and no one can find out anything about them. They have threatened to denounce whoever reveals anything as a rebel, so things are being done in total secrecy. I have heard that 58 [the Medici] is everything and 54 [the Pitti] doesn't stand a chance. For the moment, it looks to me as if they will get back to 56 [the Pucci] in the runoffs, if things continue to go as now. May God, who can do all, set this city right, for it is in a bad way. Niccolò went in proudly and then lost heart—as 14's [Soderini] brother said, "He went in a lion and he will go out a lamb," and that's just what happened to him. When he saw the votes were going against him, he began to humble himself. Now, since he left office, he goes about accompanied by five or six armed men for fear. . . . It would have been better for him if [he had never been elected], for he would never have made so many enemies. . . .

[T]hink about having Niccolò Strozzi touch on the matter with Giovanfrancesco for 45 [Lorenzo], if you think it appropriate. Although I doubt that she would deign [to marry] so low, still, it sometimes happens that you look in places that in other times you wouldn't have dreamed of, by the force of events—deaths or other misfortunes. So think about it.

■ Discussion Questions

1. What is Alessandra's role as matriarch of her family? What else can you tell about women during the Renaissance?
2. What is Alessandra's view of the politics of the city in her day? Why would Alessandra use numbers to designate people?
3. What is Alessandra's relation to her slave? How does the existence of slavery affect your view of Florence's vaunted "liberty for all"?
4. How were marriages formed among the middle and upper classes? What was required before one could marry?

CHAPTER 12
Struggles over Beliefs, 1500–1648

For kings, nobles, and ordinary folk alike, the sixteenth through mid-seventeenth centuries was a time of turmoil and change, as the following documents illustrate. These conflicts began with the Protestant Reformation, which shattered the Christian humanist ideal of peace and unity, and came to a head in the Thirty Years' War (1618–1648), which devastated central Europe and left many rulers bankrupt. The religious wars that galvanized much of Europe in this period were fueled by both ecclesiastical and lay leaders' attempts to maintain the commonly held idea that political and social stability depended on religious conformity. With the escalation of violence, however, some people argued successfully that peace would come only if state interests took precedence over religious ones. Europeans' views of the earth and the heavens also expanded because of the rise of new scientific methods and overseas exploration.

37. Argula von Grumbach and John Hooker,
Women's Actions in the Reformation (1520s–1530s)

Throughout the Middle Ages, laywomen were actively involved in their religion, through attendance at Mass, sermons, and pilgrimages, and their "greater piety" (than that of men) was remarked on by many churchmen. This trend continued in the early decades of the Reformation but assumed new forms, providing a particular window of opportunity for women to defend their faith when challenged through speech, print, or action. The first document is from the writings of Argula von Grumbach (1492–c. 1554), a Bavarian noblewoman who was by 1522 a follower of Martin Luther (1483–1546), whose challenges and writings initiated the Protestant Reformation. Called a silly bag, a shameless whore, and a female desperado, among other epithets, von Grumbach wrote prose and poetry beginning in 1523 in defense of Luther and Philipp Melanchthon (1497–1560), Luther's coworker and follower, and against the arrest of a Lutheran student at Ingolstadt. She also responded in kind to the sarcasm of another student. Tens of thousands of copies of her writings were in circulation within a few years. The second document is by the Englishman John Hooker, who was Exeter's city chamberlain during the dissolution of the monasteries, when the city's Catholic women took matters into their own hands on the arrival of Thomas Cromwell's visitors in 1535 or 1536.

From *http://home.infi.net/`ddisse/grumbach.html*; Argula von Grumbach, ". . . A Hundred Women Would Emerge to Write"; and Joyce Youings, *The Dissolution of the Monasteries* (London: Allen & Unwin; New York: Barnes & Noble, 1971), 164–65.

ARGULA VON GRUMBACH

To the Scholars of Ingolstadt

I find there is a text in Matthew 10 which runs: "Whosoever confesses me before another I too will confess before my heavenly Father." . . . Words like these, coming from the very mouth of God, are always before my eyes. For they exclude neither woman or man.

And this is why I am compelled as a Christian to write to you.

To Bavarian Princes

My heart goes out to our princes, whom you have seduced and betrayed so deplorably. For I realize that they are ill informed about divine Scripture. If they could spare the time from other business, I believe they, too, would discover the truth that no one has a right to exercise sovereignty over the word of God. . . . My heart goes out to them; for they have no one with enough integrity to tell them what is going on. And I realize very well that it is for their wealth, torn from them every day, that they are loved rather than for themselves. I am prepared to write to them in this vein, since, because of other business, they have no leisure to sit down and read for themselves.

To the Ingolstadt Scholars

I beseech you for the sake of God, and exhort you by God's judgment and righteousness, to tell me in writing which of the articles written by Martin or Melanchthon you consider heretical. In German not a single one seem heretical to me. And the fact is that a great deal has been published in German, and I've read it all. . . . I beseech and request a reply from you if you consider I am in error, though I am not aware of it. For Jerome was not ashamed of writing a great deal to women, to Blessilla, for example, to Paula, Eustochium, and so on. Yes, and Christ himself, he who is the only teacher of us all, was not ashamed to preach to Mary Magdalene, and to the young woman at the well.

I do not flinch from appearing before you, from listening to you, from discussing with you. For by the grace of God I, too, can ask questions, hear answers, and read in German. . . . I have no Latin, but you have German, being born and brought up in this tongue. What I have written to you is no woman's chit-chat, but the word of God, and as a member of the Christian Church, against which the gates of Hell cannot prevail.

In Response to a Verse Attack by an Ingolstadt Student

Now Judith when this she heard,
To the priests went straight away,
Gave them instruction manifold
How God their fathers led of old,
When, as now, in tribulation;
Gave ample scriptural demonstration.
She also took the rulers on:
Boldly said: "What have you done
To leave the people in such pain?"
Soon caused their hearts to lift again.

. . .

God therefore made her hand so strong
That Holofernes was undone.
She then lopped off his very head.
Who'd ever have believed this deed?
That him they called a mighty god
Should thus become a laughing stock.

. . .

More of the same in Judges is found,
You can read of there [*sic*], if you care.
There was a seer, Deborah by name,
Who was sent by God, much the same,
To lead the people of Israel
To judge and govern them as well.
Had you been living at that time,
Wise man, no doubt you'd have tried
To stop God carrying out his plan
By acting through a poor woman.
You'd surely could never have endured
God's victory through woman assured.

. . .

If you argue I'm too ignorant
Then share with me your wisdom grand!
But a spindle is all you offer,
In every teaching it's what you proffer.
But this fine Master of the Sentence
Would teach me my domestic duties!
These duties I carry out day by day
How could I ever forget them, pray?
Though Christ tells me—I hear his voice—
To hear his words is the very best choice.

JOHN HOOKER: POPULAR REACTIONS AT EXETER

The commissioners came to this city in the summertime to execute their commission, and beginning first with the priory of St. Nicholas, after that they [had] viewed the same they went thence to dinner and commanded [a man] in the time of their absence to pull down the rood loft in the church. In the meanwhile, and before they did return, certain women and wives in the city, namely Joan Reeve, Elizabeth Glandfield, Agnes Collaton, Alice Miller, Joan Reed and others, minding to stop the suppressing of that house, came in all haste to the said church, some with spikes, some with shovels, some with pikes, and some with such tools as they could get and, the church door being fast, they broke it open. And finding there the man pulling down the rood loft they all sought, [by] all the means they could, to take him and hurled stones unto him, in so much that for his safety he was driven to take to the tower for his refuge. And yet they pursued him so eagerly that he was enforced to leap out at a window and so to save himself, and very hardly he escaped the breaking of his neck, but yet he broke one of his ribs. John Blakealler, one of the aldermen of the city, being advertised thereof, he with all speed got him to the said monastery, he thinking what with fair words and what with foul words to have stayed and pacified the women. But how so ever he talked with them they were plain with him and the aforesaid Elizabeth Glandfield gave him a blow and set him packing. The Mayor [William Hurst], having understanding hereof and being very loathe the visitors should be advertised of any such disorders and troubles, he came down with his officers, before whose coming they [the women] had made fast the church doors and had bestowed themselves in places meet as they thought to stand to their defences. Notwithstanding, the Mayor broke in upon them and with much ado he apprehended and took them all and sent them to ward. The visitors being then made acquainted herewith, they gave thanks to the Mayor for his care and diligence . . . and so they proceeded to the suppressing of the house, and before their departure they intreated the Mayor for releasing of the women.

■ Discussion Questions

1. What can you tell of Argula von Grumbach's background and learning from her writings alone?
2. What main points does Argula von Grumbach make against the princes and, primarily, the Ingolstadt scholars?
3. Why did the Catholic women of Exeter attack the commissioners sent out to dissolve the monastery? Are you surprised by their behavior?
4. Despite their many differences, do you see anything in common between Argula von Grumbach and the women of Exeter?

38. Henry IV, *Edict of Nantes* (1598)

Henry IV's promulgation of the Edict of Nantes in 1598 marked the end of the French Wars of Religion by recognizing French Protestants as a legally protected religious minority. Drawing largely on earlier edicts of pacification, the Edict of Nantes comprised ninety-two general articles, fifty-six secret articles, and two royal warrants. The two series of articles represented the edict proper and were registered by the highest courts of law in the realm (parlements). *The following excerpts from the general articles reveal the triumph of political concerns over religious conformity on the one hand, and the limitations of religious tolerance in early modern France on the other.*

Henry, By the Grace of God, King of *France,* and *Navarre,* To all Present, and to Come, greeteth. Among the infinite Mercies that God hath pleased to bestow upon us, that most Signal and Remarkable is, his having given us Power and Strength not to yield to the dreadful Troubles, Confusions, and Disorders, which were found at our coming to this Kingdom, divided into so many Parties and Factions, that the most Legitimate was almost the least, enabling us with Constancy in such manner to oppose the Storm, as in the end to surmount it, reducing this Estate to Peace and Rest. . . . For the general difference among our good Subjects, and the particular evils of the soundest parts of the State, we judged might be easily cured, after the Principal cause (the continuation of the Civil Wars) was taken away, in which we have, by the blessing of God, well and happily succeeded, all Hostility and Wars through the Kingdom being now ceased, and we hope he will also prosper us in our other affairs, which remain to be composed, and that by this means we shall arrive at the establishment of a good Peace, with tranquility and rest. . . . Amongst our said affairs . . . one of the principal hath been, the many complaints we received from divers of our Provinces and Catholick Cities, for that the exercise of the Catholick Religion was not universally re-established, as is provided by Edicts or Statutes heretofore made for the Pacification of the Troubles arising from Religion; as also the Supplications and Remonstrances which have been made to us by our Subjects of the reformed Religion, as well upon the execution of what hath been granted by the said former Laws, as that they desire to have some addition for the exercise of their Religion, the liberty of their Consciences and the security of their Persons and Fortunes; presuming to have just reasons for desiring some enlargement of Articles, as not being without great apprehensions, because their Ruine hath been the principal pretext and original foundation of the late Wars, Troubles, and Commotions. Now not to burden us with too much

English text of "The Edict" as in Edmund Everard, *The Great Pressures and Grievances of the Protestants in France,* London, 1681. Appendix 4 in Roland Mousnier, *The Assassination of Henry IV,* trans. Joan Spencer (London: Faber and Faber, 1973), 316–47.

business at once, as also that the fury of War was not compatible with the establishment of Laws, how good soever they might be, we have hitherto deferred from time to time giving remedy herein. But now that it hath pleased God to give us a beginning of enjoying some Rest, we think we cannot imploy our self better, than to apply to that which may tend to the glory and service of his holy name, and to provide that he may be adored and prayed unto by all our Subjects: and if it hath not yet pleased him to permit it to be in one and the same form of Religion, that it may at the least be with one and the same intention, and with such rules that may prevent amongst them all troubles and tumults. . . . For this cause, we have upon the whole judged it necessary to give to all our said Subjects one general Law, Clear, Pure, and Absolute, by which they shall be regulated in all differences which have heretofore risen among them, or may hereafter rise, wherewith the one and other may be contented, being framed according as the time requires: and having had no other regard in this deliberation than solely the Zeal we have to the service of God, praying that he would henceforward render to all our subjects a durable and Established peace. . . . We have by this Edict or Statute perpetuall and irrevocable said, declared, and ordained, saying, declaring, and ordaining;

That the memory of all things passed on the one part and the other, since the beginning of the month of *March,* 1585. untill our coming to the Crown, and also during the other precedent troubles, and the occasion of the same, shall remain extinguished and suppressed, as things that had never been. . . .

We prohibit to all our Subjects of what State and Condition soever they be, to renew the memory thereof, to attaque, resent, injure, or provoke one the other by reproaches for what is past, under any pretext or cause whatsoever, by disputing, contesting, quarrelling, reviling, or offending by factious words; but to contain themselves, and live peaceably together as Brethren, Friends, and fellow-Citizens, upon penalty for acting to the contrary, to be punished for breakers of Peace, and disturbers of the publick quiet.

We ordain, that the Catholick Religion shall be restored and re-established in all places, and quarters of this Kingdom and Countrey under our obedience, and where the exercise of the same hath been intermitted, to be there again, peaceably and freely exercised without any trouble or impediment. . . .

And not to leave any occasion of trouble and difference among our Subjects, we have permitted and do permit to those of the Reformed Religion, to live and dwell in all the Cities and places of this our Kingdom and Countreys under our obedience, without being inquired after, vexed, molested, or compelled to do any thing in Religion, contrary to their Conscience. . . .

We permit also to those of the said Religion to hold, and continue the Exercise of the same in all the Cities and Places under our obedience, where it hath by them been Established and made publick by many and divers times, in the Year 1586, and in 1597, until the end of the Month of *August.* . . .

In like manner the said Exercise may be Established, and re-established in all the Cities and Places where it hath been established, or ought to be by the Statute of Pacification, made in the Year 1577. . . .

As also not to exercise the said Religion in our Court, nor in our Territories and Countries beyond the Mountains, nor in our City of *Paris,* nor within five Leagues of the said City. . . .

We prohibit all Preachers, Readers, and others who speak in public, to use any words, discourse, or propositions tending to excite the People to Sedition; and we enjoin them to contain and comport themselves modestly, and to say nothing which shall not be for the instruction and edification of the Auditors, and maintaining the peace and tranquillity established by us in our said Kingdom. . . .

They shall also be obliged to keep and observe the Festivals of the Catholick Church, and shall not on the same dayes work, sell, or keep open shop, nor likewise the Artisans shall not work out of their shops, in their chambers or houses privately on the said Festivals, and other dayes forbidden, of any trade, the noise whereof may be heard without by those that pass by, or by the Neighbours. . . .

We ordain, that there shall not be made any difference or distinction upon the account of the said Religion, in receiving Scholars to be instructed in the Universities, Colledges, or Schools, nor of the sick or poor into Hospitals, sick houses or publick Almshouses. . . .

We Will and Ordain, that all those of the Reformed Religion, and others who have followed their party, of what State, Quality or Condition soever they be, shall be obliged and constrained by all due and reasonable wayes, and under the penalties contained in the said Edict or Statute relating thereunto, to pay tythes to the Curates, and other Ecclesiasticks, and to all others to whom they shall appertain. . . .

To the end to re-unite so much the better the minds and good will of our Subjects, as is our intention, and to take away all complaints for the future; We declare all those who make or shall make profession of the said Reformed Religion, to be capable of holding and exercising all Estates, Dignities, Offices, and publick charges whatsoever. . . .

We declare all Sentences, Judgments, Procedures, Seisures, Sales, and Decrees made and given against those of the Reformed Religion, as well living as dead, from the death of the deceased King *Henry* the Second our most honoured Lord and Father in Law, upon the occasion of the said Religion, Tumults and Troubles since happening, as also the execution of the same Judgments and Decrees, from henceforward cancelled, revoked, and annulled. . . .

Those also of the said Religion shall depart and desist henceforward from all Practices, Negotiations, and Intelligences, as well within as without our Kingdom; and the said Assemblies and Councels established within the Provinces, shall readily separate, and also all the Leagues and Associations made or to be made under what pretext soever, to the prejudice of our present Edict, shall be cancelled and annulled, . . . prohibiting most expresly to all our Subjects to make henceforwards any Assesments or Leavy's of Money, Fortifications, Enrolments of men, Congregations and Assemblies of other than such as are permitted by our present Edict, and without Arms. . . .

We give in command to the People of our said Courts of Parliaments, Chambers of our Courts, and Courts of our Aids, Bayliffs, Chief-Justices, Provosts and other our Justices and Officers to whom it appertains, and to their Leivetenants, that they cause to be read, published, and Registred this present Edict and Ordinance in their Courts and Jurisdictions, and the same keep punctually, and the contents of the same to cause to be injoyned and used fully and peaceably to all those to whom it shall belong, ceasing and making to cease all troubles and obstructions to the contrary, for such is our pleasure: and in witness hereof we have signed these presents with our own hand; and to the end to make it a thing firm and stable for ever, we have caused to put and indorse our Seal to the same. Given at *Nantes* in the Month of *April* in the year of Grace 1598. and of our Reign the ninth.

Signed

HENRY

■ **Discussion Questions**

1. What are the edict's principal objectives?
2. In what ways does the edict balance the demands of French Catholics and Protestants?
3. What limits does the edict place on Protestants' religious rights?
4. Did Henry IV regard this edict as a permanent solution to the religious divisions in the realm?

39. Saint Ignatius of Loyola, *A New Kind of Catholicism* (1546, 1549, 1553)

The interests of Ignatius of Loyola (1491–1556), born of a Spanish noble family, centered more on chivalry and national glory than religion before his serious injury in battle. While recovering, he experienced a conversion when he began reading the only books available to him, The Golden Legend *(about saints' lives) and the* Life of Christ. *Entering a monastery, he started work on* The Spiritual Exercises, *a manual of discernment for the pilgrim journeying to God. After studying at the University of Paris, Ignatius, Francis Xavier (1506–1552), and other friends made vows of chastity and poverty, determining to travel to Jerusalem. When this became impossible, they went to Italy. The Society of Jesus (the Jesuits), founded by Ignatius and his early companions, was officially recognized by Pope Paul III in 1540 as a new order directly under the papacy. Its spirituality would be expressed most prominently in teaching and missionary work. The letters of Ignatius evince a new form of Catholic spiritual expression that was active and apostolic in its orientation. It was less a "response" to Protestantism than a model for Catholic life and work. Along with the works of other early Jesuits, it embodied a new spirit that so many had sought but not found in the late medieval church.*

CONDUCT AT TRENT: ON HELPING OTHERS, 1546

Our main aim [to God's greater glory] during this undertaking at Trent is to put into practice (as a group that lives together in one appropriate place) preaching, confessions and readings, teaching children, giving good example, visiting the poor in the hospitals, exhorting those around us, each of us according to the different talents he may happen to have, urging on as many as possible to greater piety and prayer. . . .

In their preaching they should not refer to points of conflict between Protestants and Catholics, but simply exhort all to upright conduct and to ecclesiastical practice, urging everyone to full self-knowledge and to greater knowledge and love of their Creator and Lord, with frequent allusions to the Council. At the end of each session, they should (as has been mentioned) lead prayers for the Council.

They should do the same with readings as with sermons, trying their best to influence people with greater love of their Creator and Lord as they explain the meaning of what is read; similarly, they should lead their hearers to pray for the Council. . . .

They should spend some time, as convenient, in the elementary teaching of youngsters, depending on the means and disposition of all involved, and with more or less explanation according to the capacity of the pupils. . . . Let them visit the almshouses once or twice a day, at times that are convenient for the patients' health, hearing confessions and consoling the poor, if possible taking them something, and urging them to the sort of prayers mentioned above for confession. If there are three of ours in Trent, each should visit the poor at least once every four days.

When they are urging people in their dealings with them to go to confession and communion, to say mass frequently, to undertake the Spiritual Exercises and other good works, they should also be urging them to pray for the Council.

From *Saint Ignatius of Loyola, Personal Writings: Reminiscences, Spiritual Diary, Select Letters, Including the Text of The Spiritual Exercises,* ed. and trans. Joseph A. Munitiz and Philip Endean (New York: Penguin Books, 1996), 165, 166, 230, 233–34, 257, 259, 262–63.

It was said that there are advantages in being slow to speak and measured in one's statements when doctrinal definitions are involved. The opposite is true when one is urging people
to look to their spiritual progress. Then one should be eloquent and ready to talk, full of sympathy and affection.

SPREADING GOD'S WORD IN A GERMAN UNIVERSITY, 1549

The aim that they should have above all before their eyes is that intended by the Supreme Pontiff who has sent them: to help the University of Ingolstadt, and as far as is possible the whole of
Germany, in all that concerns purity of faith, obedience to the Church, and firmness and sound-
ness of doctrine and upright living. . . .

They must be very competent in them, and teach solid doctrine without many technical
terms (which are unpopular), especially if these are hard to understand. The lectures should be
learned yet clear, sustained in argument yet not long-winded, and delivered with attention to
style. . . . Besides these academic lectures, it seems opportune on feast days to hold sermons on
Bible readings, more calculated to move hearts and form consciences than to produce learned
minds. . . . They should make efforts to attract their students into a friendship of spiritual quality, and if possible towards confession and making the Spiritual Exercises, even in the full form,
if they seem suitable to join the Society. . . .

On occasion they should give time to works of mercy of a more visible character, such as in
hospitals and prisons and helping other kinds of poor; such works arouse a "sweet fragrance" in
the Lord. Opportunity may also arise to act as peacemakers in quarrels and to teach basic Christian doctrine to the uneducated. Taking account of local conditions and the persons concerned,
prudence will dictate whether they should act themselves or through others.

They should make efforts to make friends with the leaders of their opponents, as also with
those who are most influential among the heretics or those who are suspected of it yet seem not
absolutely immovable. They must try to bring them back from their error by sensitive skill and
signs of love. . . . All must try to have at their finger-tips the main points concerning dogmas of
faith that are subjects of controversy with heretics, especially at the time and place when they are
present, and with those persons with whom they are dealing. Thus they will be able, whenever
opportunity arises, to put forward and defend the Catholic truth, to refute errors and to strengthen
the doubtful and wavering, whether by lectures and sermons or in the confessional and in con-
versations. . . .

It will be helpful to lead people, as far as possible, to open themselves to God's grace, exhorting them to a desire for salvation, to prayer, to alms, and to everything that conduces to receiving grace or increasing it. . . .

Let [the duke] understand also what glory it will mean for him if he is the first to introduce
into Germany seminaries in the form of such colleges, to foster sound doctrine and religion.

THE FINAL WORD ON OBEDIENCE, 1553, TO THE BROTHERS IN PORTUGAL

To form an idea of the exceptional intrinsic value of this obedience in the eyes of God Our Lord,
one should weigh both the worth of the noble sacrifice offered, involving the highest human
power, and the completeness of the self-offering undertaken, as one strips oneself of self, becoming a "living victim" pleasing to the Divine Majesty. Another indication is the intensity of the
difficulty experienced as one conquers self for love of God, opposing the natural human incli-
nation felt by us all to follow our own opinions. . . .

Let us be unpretentious and let us be gentle! God Our Lord will grant the grace to enable
you, gently and lovingly, to maintain constantly the offering you have made to Him. . . .

All that has been said does not exclude your bringing before your superiors a contrary
opinion that may have occurred to you, once you have prayed about the matter and you feel that

it would be proper and in accord with your respect for God to do so. . . . Such is the model on which divine Providence "gently disposes all things," so that the lower via the middle, and the middle via the higher, are led to their final ends. . . . The same can be seen upon the earth with respect to all secular constitutions that are duly established, and with respect to the ecclesiastical hierarchy, which is subordinated to you in virtue of holy obedience to select among the many routes open to you that which will bring you back to Portugal as soon and as safely as possible. So I order you in the name of Christ Our Lord to do this, even if it will be so as to return soon to India. . . . Firstly, you are well aware how important for the upkeep and advancement of Christianity in those lands, as also in Guinea and Brazil, is the good order that the King of Portugal can grant from his kingdom. When a prince of such Christian desires and holy intentions as is the King of Portugal receives information from someone of your experience about the state of affairs in those parts, you can imagine what influence this will have on him to do much more in the service of God Our Lord and for the good of those countries that you will describe to him. . . .

You are also aware how important it is for the good of the Indies that the persons sent there should be suitable for the aim that one is pursuing in those and in other lands. . . . Quite apart from all these reasons, which apply to furthering the good of India, it seems to me that you would fire the King's enthusiasm for the Ethiopian project, which has been planned for so many years without anything effective having been seen. Similarly, with regard to the Congo and Brazil, you could give no small help from Portugal, which you cannot do from India as there are not the same commercial relations. If people in India consider that your presence is important given your post, you can continue to act as superior no less from Portugal than from Japan or China, and probably much better. Just as you have gone away on other occasions for longer periods, do the same now.

▪ Discussion Questions

1. What does the Catholic life mean to Ignatius? What is innovative in his program for Catholic reform?
2. What advice does Ignatius give about dealing with the problem of heresy?
3. What role does Ignatius envision Jesuits playing throughout Europe and the rest of the world?
4. How does Ignatius think political leaders can be enlisted to support the aims of the reform movement?

40. Galileo Galilei, *Letter to the Grand Duchess Christina* (1615)

Italian-born and educated, Galileo Galilei (1564–1642) was among the most illustrious proponents of the new science in the seventeenth century. Early in his studies, he embraced Copernicus's theory that the sun, not the Earth, was at the center of the universe. Having improved on the newly invented telescope in 1609, he was able to substantiate the heliocentric view through his observations of the moon and other planets. Because Galileo's work challenged traditional scientific views, it sparked considerable controversy. In the letter excerpted here, written in 1615 to the Grand Duchess Christina of Tuscany, an important Catholic patron of learning, Galileo defends the validity of his findings while striving to separate matters of religious faith from the study of natural phenomena.

Stillman Drake, trans., *Discoveries and Opinions of Galileo* (New York: Doubleday, 1957), 175–86.

GALILEO GALILEI TO THE MOST SERENE GRAND DUCHESS MOTHER

Some years ago, as Your Serene Highness well knows, I discovered in the heavens many things that had not been seen before our own age. The novelty of these things, as well as some consequences which followed from them in contradiction to the physical notions commonly held among academic philosophers, stirred up against me no small number of professors—as if I had placed these things in the sky with my own hands in order to upset nature and overturn the sciences. . . .

Well, the passage of time has revealed to everyone the truths that I previously set forth. . . . But some, besides allegiance to their original error, possess I know not what fanciful interest in remaining hostile not so much toward the things in question as toward their discoverer. No longer being able to deny them, these men now take refuge in obstinate silence, but being more than ever exasperated by that which has pacified and quieted other men, they divert their thoughts to other fancies and seek new ways to damage me. . . .

Persisting in their original resolve to destroy me and everything mine by any means they can think of, these men are aware of my views in astronomy and philosophy. They know that as to the arrangement of the parts of the universe, I hold the sun to be situated motionless in the center of the revolution of the celestial orbs while the earth rotates on its axis and revolves about the sun. . . .

Now as to the false aspersions which they so unjustly seek to cast upon me, I have thought it necessary to justify myself in the eyes of all men, whose judgment in matters of religion and of reputation I must hold in great esteem. I shall therefore discourse of the particulars which these men produce to make this opinion detested and to have it condemned not merely as false but as heretical. To this end they make a shield of their hypocritical zeal for religion. They go about invoking the Bible, which they would have minister to their deceitful purposes. Contrary to the sense of the Bible and the intention of the holy Fathers, if I am not mistaken, they would extend such authorities until even in purely physical matters—where faith is not involved—they would have us altogether abandon reason and the evidence of our senses in favor of some biblical passage, though under the surface meaning of its words this passage may contain a different sense. . . .

The reason produced for condemning the opinion that the earth moves and the sun stands still is that in many places in the Bible one may read that the sun moves and the earth stands still. Since the Bible cannot err, it follows as a necessary consequence that anyone takes an erroneous and heretical position who maintains that the sun is inherently motionless and the earth movable.

With regard to this argument, I think in the first place that it is very pious to say and prudent to affirm that the holy Bible can never speak untruth—whenever its true meaning is understood. But I believe nobody will deny that it is often very abstruse, and may say things which are quite different from what its bare words signify. Hence in expounding the Bible if one were always to confine oneself to the unadorned grammatical meaning, one might fall into error. Not only contradictions and propositions far from true might thus be made to appear in the Bible, but even grave heresies and follies. Thus it would be necessary to assign to God feet, hands, and eyes, as well as corporeal and human affections, such as anger, repentance, hatred, and sometimes even the forgetting of things past and ignorance of those to come. These propositions uttered by the Holy Ghost were set down in that manner by the sacred scribes in order to accommodate them to the capacities of the common people, who are rude and unlearned. For the sake of those who deserve to be separated from the herd, it is necessary that wise expositors should produce the true senses of such passages, together with the special reasons for which they were set down in these words. This doctrine is so widespread and so definite with all theologians that it would be superfluous to adduce evidence for it.

Hence I think that I may reasonably conclude that whenever the Bible has occasion to speak of any physical conclusion (especially those which are very abstruse and hard to understand), the rule has been observed of avoiding confusion in the minds of the common people which would render them contumacious toward the higher mysteries. Now the Bible, merely to condescend to popular capacity, has not hesitated to obscure some very important pronouncements, attributing to God himself some qualities extremely remote from (and even contrary to) His essence. Who, then, would positively declare that this principle has been set aside, and the Bible has confined itself rigorously to the bare and restricted sense of its words, when speaking but casually of the earth, of water, of the sun, or of any other created thing? Especially in view of the fact that these things in no way concern the primary purpose of the sacred writings, which is the service of God and the salvation of souls—matters infinitely beyond the comprehension of the common people.

This being granted, I think that in discussions of physical problems we ought to begin not from the authority of scriptural passages, but from sense-experiences and necessary demonstrations; for the holy Bible and the phenomena of nature proceed alike from the divine Word, the former as the dictate of the Holy Ghost and the latter as the observant executrix of God's commands. It is necessary for the Bible, in order to be accommodated to the understanding of every man, to speak many things which appear to differ from the absolute truth so far as the bare meaning of the words is concerned. But Nature, on the other hand, is inexorable and immutable; she never transgresses the laws imposed upon her, or cares a whit whether her abstruse reasons and methods of operations are understandable to men. For that reason it appears that nothing physical which sense-experience sets before our eyes, or which necessary demonstrations prove to us, ought to be called in question (much less condemned) upon the testimony of biblical passages which may have some different meaning beneath their words. For the Bible is not chained in every expression to conditions as strict as those which govern all physical effects; nor is God any less excellently revealed in Nature's actions than in the sacred statements of the Bible. . . .

From this I do not mean to infer that we need not have an extraordinary esteem for the passages of holy Scripture. On the contrary, having arrived at any certainties in physics, we ought to utilize these as the most appropriate aids in the true exposition of the Bible and in the investigation of those meanings which are necessarily contained therein, for these must be concordant with demonstrated truths. I should judge that the authority of the Bible was designed to persuade men of those articles and propositions which, surpassing all human reasoning, could not be made credible by science, or by any other means than through the very mouth of the Holy Spirit.

Yet even in those propositions which are not matters of faith, this authority ought to be preferred over that of all human writings which are supported only by bare assertions or probable arguments, and not set forth in a demonstrative way. This I hold to be necessary and proper to the same extent that divine wisdom surpasses all human judgment and conjecture.

But I do not feel obliged to believe that that same God who has endowed us with senses, reason, and intellect has intended to forgo their use and by some other means to give us knowledge which we can attain by them. He would not require us to deny sense and reason in physical matters which are set before our eyes and minds by direct experience or necessary demonstrations. This must be especially true in those sciences of which but the faintest trace (and that consisting of conclusions) is to be found in the Bible. Of astronomy, for instance, so little is found that none of the planets except Venus are so much as mentioned, and this only once or twice under the name of "Lucifer." If the sacred scribes had had any intention of teaching people certain arrangements and motions of the heavenly bodies, or had they wished us to derive such knowledge from the Bible, then in my opinion they would not have spoken of these matters so sparingly in comparison with the infinite number of admirable conclusions which are demonstrated in that science. . . .

From these things it follows as a necessary consequence that, since the Holy Ghost did not intend to teach us whether heaven moves or stands still, whether its shape is spherical or like a discus or extended in a plane, nor whether the earth is located at its center or off to one side, then so much the less was it intended to settle for us any other conclusion of the same kind. And the motion or rest of the earth and the sun is so closely linked with the things just named, that without a determination of the one, neither side can be taken in the other matters. Now if the Holy Spirit has purposely neglected to teach us propositions of this sort as irrelevant to the highest goal (that is, to our salvation), how can anyone affirm that it is obligatory to take sides on them, and that one belief is required by faith, while the other side is erroneous? Can an opinion be heretical and yet have no concern with the salvation of souls? Can the Holy Ghost be asserted not to have intended teaching us something that does concern our salvation? I would say here something that was heard from an ecclesiastic of the most eminent degree: "That the intention of the Holy Ghost is to teach us how one goes to heaven, not how heaven goes." . . .

From this it is seen that the interpretation which we impose upon passages of Scripture would be false whenever it disagreed with demonstrated truths. And therefore we should seek the incontrovertible sense of the Bible with the assistance of demonstrated truth, and not in any way try to force the hand of Nature or deny experiences and rigorous proofs in accordance with the mere sound of words that may appeal to our frailty. . . .

To that end they would forbid him the use of reason, divine gift of Providence, and would abuse the just authority of holy Scripture—which, in the general opinion of theologians, can never oppose manifest experiences and necessary demonstrations when rightly understood and applied. If I am correct, it will stand them in no stead to go running to the Bible to cover up their inability to understand (let alone resolve) their opponents' arguments.

■ Discussion Questions

1. What is Galileo's goal in writing this letter to the Grand Duchess?
2. What is the basis of the attacks by Galileo's critics?
3. According to Galileo, what role should the Bible play in scientific inquiry?
4. Historians have credited Galileo for helping to popularize the principles and methods of the new science. How does this document support this view?

CHAPTER 13
State Building and the Search for Order, 1648–1690

The wars over religion not only left bitter memories in late-seventeenth-century Europe but also ruined economies and weakened governments. Politically, the quest for order fueled the development of two rival systems of state building: absolutism and constitutionalism, with France (first document) and England (third document), respectively, taking the lead. Despite their differences, rulers in both systems centralized their power and expanded their bureaucracies, casting an increasingly wide net over their subjects' lives. The second document indicates that not everyone submitted willingly to the expansion of state power, but such resistance was typically fruitless.

41. Louis de Rouvroy, Duke of Saint-Simon, *Memoirs* (1694–1723)

A nobleman and godson of Louis XIV, Louis de Rouvroy, duke of Saint-Simon (1675–1755), was raised at the royal palace of Versailles. He began recording his life and impressions of the court at the age of nineteen and continued for almost three decades. The result was his multivolume Memoirs, *which paint an intimate portrait of the Sun King and the workings of the absolutist state. Saint-Simon was not an entirely objective observer. Never achieving great success within the court, he often viewed it through the lens of his own resentment. This excerpt provides insight into the reasons behind Louis XIV's move to Versailles and his method of rule there.*

Let me touch now upon some other incidents in his career, and upon some points in his character.

He early showed a disinclination for Paris. The troubles that had taken place there during the minority made him regard the place as dangerous; he wished, too, to render himself venerable by hiding himself from the eyes of the multitude; all these considerations fixed him at St. Germains soon after the death of the Queen, his mother. It was to that place he began to attract the world by fêtes and gallantries, and by making it felt that he wished to be often seen.

His love for Madame de la Vallière, which was at first kept secret, occasioned frequent excursions to Versailles, then a little card castle, which had been built by Louis XIII.—annoyed, and his suite still more so, at being frequently obliged to sleep in a wretched inn there, after he had been out hunting in the forest of Saint Leger. That monarch rarely slept at Versailles more than one night, and then from necessity; the King, his son, slept there, so that he might be more in

Bayle St. John, trans., *The Memoirs of the Duke of Saint Simon,* vol. II (Philadelphia: Gebbie and Co., 1890), 363–69.

private with his mistress; pleasures unknown to the hero and just man, worthy son of Saint Louis, who built the little château.

These excursions of Louis XIV. by degrees gave birth to those immense buildings he erected at Versailles; and their convenience for a numerous court, so different from the apartments at St. Germains, led him to take up his abode there entirely shortly after the death of the Queen. He built an infinite number of apartments, which were asked for by those who wished to pay their court to him; whereas at St. Germains nearly everybody was obliged to lodge in the town, and the few who found accommodation at the château were strangely inconvenienced.

The frequent fêtes, the private promenades at Versailles, the journeys, were means on which the King seized in order to distinguish or mortify the courtiers, and thus render them more assiduous in pleasing him. He felt that of real favours he had not enough to bestow; in order to keep up the spirit of devotion, he therefore unceasingly invented all sorts of ideal ones, little preferences and petty distinctions, which answered his purpose as well.

He was exceedingly jealous of the attention paid him. Not only did he notice the presence of the most distinguished courtiers, but those of inferior degree also. He looked to the right and to the left, not only upon rising but upon going to bed, at his meals, in passing through his apartments, or his gardens of Versailles, where alone the courtiers were allowed to follow him; he saw and noticed everybody; not one escaped him, not even those who hoped to remain unnoticed. He marked well all absentees from the court, found out the reason of their absence, and never lost an opportunity of acting towards them as the occasion might seem to justify. With some of the courtiers (the most distinguished), it was a demerit not to make the court their ordinary abode; with others 'twas a fault to come but rarely; for those who never or scarcely ever came it was certain disgrace. When their names were in any way mentioned, "I do not know them," the King would reply haughtily. Those who presented themselves but seldom were thus characterised: "They are people I never see"; these decrees were irrevocable. He could not bear people who liked Paris.

Louis XIV. took great pains to be well informed of all that passed everywhere; in the public places, in the private houses, in society and familiar intercourse. His spies and tell-tales were infinite. He had them of all species; many who were ignorant that their information reached him; others who knew it; others who wrote to him direct, sending their letters through channels he indicated; and all these letters were seen by him alone, and always before everything else; others who sometimes spoke to him secretly in his cabinet, entering by the back stairs. These unknown means ruined an infinite number of people of all classes who never could discover the cause; often ruined them very unjustly; for the King, once prejudiced, never altered his opinion, or so rarely, that nothing was more rare. He had, too, another fault, very dangerous for others and often for himself, since it deprived him of good subjects. He had an excellent memory; in this way, that if he saw a man who, twenty years before, perhaps, had in some manner offended him, he did not forget the man, though he might forget the offence. This was enough, however, to exclude the person from all favour. The representations of a minister, of a general, of his confessor even, could not move the King. He would not yield.

The most cruel means by which the King was informed of what was passing—for many years before anybody knew it—was that of opening letters. The promptitude and dexterity with which they were opened passes understanding. He saw extracts from all the letters in which there were passages that the chiefs of the post-office, and then the minister who governed it, thought ought to go before him; entire letters, too, were sent to him, when their contents seemed to justify the sending. Thus the chiefs of the post, nay, the principal clerks were in a position to suppose what they pleased and against whom they pleased. A word of contempt against the King or the government, a joke, a detached phrase, was enough. It is incredible how many people, justly or unjustly, were more or less ruined, always without resource, without trial, and without knowing why. The secret was impenetrable; for nothing ever cost the King less than profound silence and dissimulation. . . .

He liked splendour, magnificence, and profusion in everything: you pleased him if you shone through the brilliancy of your houses, your clothes, your table, your equipages. Thus a taste for extravagance and luxury was disseminated through all classes of society; causing infinite harm, and leading to general confusion of rank and to ruin.

▪ Discussion Questions

1. How did Louis XIV use court etiquette as a form of power?
2. Why did nobles reside at Versailles? What benefits did they gain?
3. What is Saint-Simon's attitude toward Louis XIV's style of governing?
4. In what ways did court life embody the principles of absolutism?

42. Ludwig Fabritius, *The Revolt of Stenka Razin* (1670)

Despite its geographical and cultural isolation from the rest of Europe, Russia followed France's lead down the path of absolutism. In the process, Tsar Alexei (r. 1645–1676) legally combined millions of slaves and free peasants into a single serf class bound to the land and to their aristocratic masters. Not everyone passively accepted this fate, however. In 1667, a Cossack named Stenka Razin led a revolt against serfdom that gained considerable support among people whose social and economic status was threatened by the tsar's policies, including soldiers of peasant stock. Razin's ultimate defeat at the hands of the tsar elucidates the close ties between the Russian government's enhanced power and the enforcement of serfdom. Ludwig Fabritius, a Dutch soldier who lived in Russia from 1660 to 1677 while employed as a military expert in the Russian army, wrote this account of one stage of the revolt.

Then Stenka with his company started off upstream, rowing as far as Tsaritsyn, whence it took him only one day's journey to Panshin, a small town situated on the Don. Here he began straightaway quietly gathering the common people around him, giving them money, and promises of great riches if they would be loyal to him and help to exterminate the treacherous boyars.[1]

This lasted the whole winter, until by about spring he had assembled 4,000 to 5,000 men. With these he came to Tsaritsyn and demanded the immediate surrender of the fortress; the rabble soon achieved their purpose, and although the governor tried to take refuge in a tower, he soon had to give himself up as he was deserted by one and all. Stenka immediately had the wretched governor hanged; and all the goods they found belonging to the Tsar and his officers as well as to the merchants were confiscated and distributed among the rabble.

Stenka now began once more to make preparations. Since the plains are not cultivated, the people have to bring their corn from Nizhniy-Novgorod and Kazan down the Volga in big boats known as *nasady*, and everything destined for Astrakhan has first to pass Tsaritsyn. Stenka Razin duly noted this, and occupied the whole of the Volga, so that nothing could get through to Astrakhan. Here he captured a few hundred merchants with their valuable goods, taking possession of all kinds of fine linen, silks, striped silk material, sables, soft leather, ducats, talers, and many thousands of rubles in Russian money and merchandise of every description. . . .

---

[1]**boyars:** Noglemen.

Anthony Glenn Cross, ed. *Russia under Western Eyes, 1517–1825* (London: Elek Books, 1971), 120–23.

In the meantime four regiments of *streltsy*[2] were dispatched from Moscow to subdue these brigands. They arrived with their big boats and as they were not used to the water, were easily beaten. Here Stenka Razin gained possession of a large amount of ammunition and artillery-pieces and everything else he required. While the above-mentioned *streltsy* were sent from Moscow, about 5,000 men were ordered up from Astrakhan by water and by land to capture Stenka Razin. As soon as he had finished with the former, he took up a good position, and, being in possession of reliable information regarding our forces, he left Tsaritsyn and came to meet us half way at Chernyy Yar, confronting us before we had suspected his presence or received any information about him. We stopped at Chernyy Yar for a few days and sent out scouts by water and by land, but were unable to obtain any definite information. On 10 July [*sic*: June] a council of war was held at which it was decided to advance and seek out Stenka. The next morning, at 8 o'clock, our look-outs on the water came hurriedly and raised the alarm as the Cossacks were following at their heels. We got out of our boats and took up battle positions. General Knyaz Semen Ivanovich Lvov went through the ranks and reminded all the men to do their duty and to remember the oath they had taken to His Majesty the Tsar, to fight like honest soldiers against these irresponsible rebels, whereupon they all unanimously shouted: "Yes, we will give our lives for His Majesty the Tsar, and will fight to the last drop of our blood."

In the meantime Stenka prepared for battle and deployed on a wide front; to all those who had no rifle he gave a long pole, burnt a little at one end, and with a rag or small hook attached. They presented a strange sight on the plain from afar, and the common soldiers imagined that, since there were so many flags and standards, there must be a host of people. They [the common soldiers] held a consultation and at once decided that this was the chance for which they had been waiting so long, and with all their flags and drums they ran over to the enemy. They began kissing and embracing one another and swore with life and limb to stand together and to exterminate the treacherous boyars, to throw off the yoke of slavery, and to become free men.

The general looked at the officers and the officers at the general, and no one knew what to do; one said this, and another that, until finally it was decided that they and the general should get into the boats and withdraw to Astrakhan. But the rascally *streltsy* of Chernyy Yar stood on the walls and towers, turning their weapons on us and opened fire; some of them ran out of the fortress and cut us off from the boats, so that we had no means of escape. In the meantime those curs of ours who had gone over to the Cossacks came up from behind. We numbered about eighty men, officers, noblemen, and clerks. Murder at once began. Then, however, Stenka Razin ordered that no more officers were to be killed, saying that there must be a few good men among them who should be pardoned, whilst those others who had not lived in amity with their men should be condemned to well-deserved punishment by the Ataman and his *Krug*. [A *Krug* is a meeting convened by the order of the Ataman, at which the Cossacks stand in a circle with the standard in the centre; the Ataman then takes his place beside his best officers, to whom he divulges his wishes, ordering them to make these known to the common brothers and to hear their opinion on the matter.] . . .

A *Krug* was accordingly called and Stenka asked through his chiefs how the general and his officers had treated the soldiers under their command. Thereupon the unscrupulous curs, *streltsy* as well as soldiers, unanimously called out that there was not one of them who deserved to remain alive, and they all asked that their father Stepan Timofeyevich Razin should order them to be cut down. This was granted with the exception of General Knyaz Semen Ivanovich Lvov, whose life was specially spared by Stenka himself. The officers were now brought in order of rank out of the tower, into which they had been thrown bound hand and foot the previous day, their ropes were cut and they were led outside the gate. When all the bloodthirsty curs had lined up, each

---

[2] *streltsy:* Sharpshooters.

was eager to deal his former superior the first blow, one with the sword, another with the lance, another with the scimitar, and others again with martels, so that as soon as an officer was pushed into the ring, the curs immediately killed him with their many wounds; indeed, some were cut to pieces and straightaway thrown into the Volga. My stepfather, Paul Rudolf Beem, and Lt. Col. Wundrum and many other officers, senior and junior, were cut down before my eyes.

My own time had not yet come: this I could tell by the wonderful way in which God rescued me, for as I—half-dead—now awaited the final blow, my [former] orderly, a young soldier, came and took me by my bound arms and tried to take me down the hill. As I was already half-dead, I did not move and did not know what to do, but he came back and took me by the arms and led me, bound as I was, through the throng of curs, down the hill into the boat and immediately cut my arms free, saying that I should rest in peace here and that he would be responsible for me and do his best to save my life. . . . Then my guardian angel told me not to leave the boat, and left me. He returned in the evening and brought me a piece of bread which I enjoyed since I had had nothing to eat for two days.

The following day all our possessions were looted and gathered together under the main flag, so that both our bloodthirsty curs and the Cossacks got their share.

■ Discussion Questions

1. What motivated Razin and his followers to take action?
2. Why were Razin and his forces able to defeat the tsar's soldiers?
3. What does this account suggest about the role of the military in the growth of the Russian government's authority?
4. With whom do you think Fabritius's sympathies lie, and why?

43. British Parliament, *The English Bill of Rights* (1689)

Louis XIV had many admirers in Europe, including King James II of England. Unlike Louis, however, James faced a major challenge to his power: Parliament. The king and Parliament had been at odds for decades over the nature of royal authority, and James's absolutist policies proved too much for Parliament to bear. As a result, in 1688 Parliament ousted the king and offered the throne to Prince William of Orange and his wife, Mary, the eldest of James's adult daughters. In exchange, William and Mary agreed to accept the Bill of Rights, which legally defined the role of Parliament as the monarchy's partner in government. The bill marked the victory of constitutionalism over absolutism in England and formed the cornerstone of the idea that government should ensure certain rights by law to protect citizens from the dangers of arbitrary power.

Whereas the said late King James II having abdicated the government, and the throne being thereby vacant, his Highness the prince of Orange (whom it hath pleased Almighty God to make the glorious instrument of delivering this kingdom from popery and arbitrary power) did (by the advice of the lords spiritual and temporal, and diverse principal persons of the Commons) cause letters to be written to the lords spiritual and temporal, being Protestants, and other letters to the several counties, cities, universities, boroughs, and Cinque Ports, for the choosing of such persons to represent them, as were of right to be sent to parliament, to meet and sit at Westminster upon the two and twentieth day of January, in this year 1689, in order to such an

Great Britain, *The Statutes*, rev. ed. (London: Eyre and Spottiswoode, 1871), vol. II, 10–12.

establishment as that their religion, laws, and liberties might not again be in danger of being subverted; upon which letters elections have been accordingly made.

And thereupon the said lords spiritual and temporal and Commons, pursuant to their respective letters and elections, being now assembled in a full and free representation of this nation, taking into their most serious consideration the best means for attaining the ends aforesaid, do in the first place (as their ancestors in like case have usually done), for the vindication and assertion of their ancient rights and liberties, declare:

1. That the pretended power of suspending laws, or the execution of laws, by regal authority, without consent of parliament is illegal.

2. That the pretended power of dispensing with the laws, or the execution of law by regal authority, as it hath been assumed and exercises of late, is illegal.

3. That the commission for erecting the late court of commissioners for ecclesiastical causes, and all other commissions and courts of like nature, are illegal and pernicious.

4. That levying money for or to the use of the crown by pretense of prerogative, without grant of parliament, for longer time or in other manner than the same is or shall be granted, is illegal.

5. That it is the right of the subjects to petition the king, and all commitments and prosecutions for such petitioning are illegal.

6. That the raising or keeping a standing army within the kingdom in time of peace, unless it be with consent of parliament, is against law.

7. That the subjects which are Protestants may have arms for their defense suitable to their conditions, and as allowed by law.

8. That election of members of parliament ought to be free.

9. That the freedom of speech, and debates or proceedings in parliament, ought not to be impeached or questioned in any court or place out of parliament.

10. That excessive bail ought not to be required, nor excessive fines imposed, nor cruel and unusual punishments inflicted.

11. That jurors ought to be duly impaneled and returned, and jurors which pass upon men in trials for high treason ought to be freeholders.

12. That all grants and promises of fines and forfeitures of particular persons before conviction are illegal and void.

13. And that for redress of all grievances, and for the amending, strengthening, and preserving of the laws, parliament ought to be held frequently.

And they do claim, demand, and insist upon all and singular the premises, as their undoubted rights and liberties: and that no declarations, judgments, doings, or proceedings, to the prejudice of the people in any of the said premises, ought in any wise to be drawn hereafter into consequence or example.

To which demand of their rights they are particularly encouraged by the declaration of his Highness the prince of Orange, as being the only means for obtaining a full redress and remedy therein.

Having therefore an entire confidence that his said Highness the prince of Orange will perfect the deliverance so far advanced by him, and will still preserve them from the violation of their rights, which they have here asserted, and from all other attempt upon their religion, rights, and liberties:

The said lords spiritual and temporal, and commons, assembled at Westminster, do resolve that William and Mary, prince and princess of Orange, be, and be declared, king and queen of England, France, and Ireland, the dominions thereunto belonging, to hold the crown and royal dignity of the said kingdoms and dominions to them the said prince and princess during their lives. . . .

Upon which their said Majesties did accept the crown and royal dignity of the kingdoms of England, France, and Ireland, and the dominions thereunto belonging, according to the resolution and desire of the said lords and commons contained in the said declaration.

■ Discussion Questions

1. In what ways does the Bill of Rights limit the powers of the crown?
2. What role does the Bill of Rights grant Parliament in government?
3. How does the Bill of Rights give weight to the attitude of members of Parliament who thought that they had "made" the king and queen, William and Mary?

CHAPTER 14

The Atlantic System and Its Consequences, 1690–1740

The growth of European domestic economies and overseas colonization in the eighteenth century infused Europe with money, new products, and a new sense of optimism. Yet, as the first document illustrates, the good times came at a horrible price for the millions of African slaves who formed the economic backbone of the colonial system. Changes were afoot on the political front, too, with the stabilization of the European state system. Consequently, states such as Russia shone more brightly over the political landscape while others lost their luster. The second and third documents reveal that intellectual circles were also ablaze with change as scholars and writers cast political, social, and religious issues in a new, critical light. Even women's traditional place in society was for the first time systematically called into question.

44. Olaudah Equiano, *The Interesting Narrative of the Life of Olaudah Equiano, Written by Himself* (1789)

The autobiography of Olaudah Equiano (c. 1745–1797) puts a human face on the eighteenth-century Atlantic slave trade and its tragic consequences. While historians debate whether he was born in what is now Nigeria or in the colonies, Equiano was captured by local raiders and sold into slavery in his early teens. He gained his freedom in 1766 and soon thereafter became a vocal supporter of the English abolitionist movement. Having learned English as a young man, he published his autobiography in 1789, a best-seller in its day, with numerous editions published in Britain and America. In this excerpt, Equiano recounts his experience on the slave ship that took him away from his homeland, his freedom, and his very identity. Millions of others shared this same fate.

The first object which saluted my eyes when I arrived on the coast was the sea, and a slave ship which was then riding at anchor and waiting for its cargo. These filled me with astonishment, which was soon converted into terror when I was carried on board. I was immediately handled and tossed up to see if I were sound by some of the crew, and I was now persuaded that I had gotten into a world of bad spirits and that they were going to kill me. Their complexions too differing so much from ours, their long hair and the language they spoke (which was very different from any I had ever heard) united to confirm me in this belief. Indeed such were the horrors of

Abridged and edited by Paul Edwards, *Equiano's Travels: His Autobiography* (London: Heinemann, 1967), 25–32.

my views and fears at the moment that, if ten thousand worlds had been my own, I would have freely parted with them all to have exchanged my condition with that of the meanest slave in my own country. When I looked round the ship too and saw a large furnace or copper boiling and a multitude of black people of every description chained together, every one of their countenances expressing dejection and sorrow, I no longer doubted of my fate; and quite overpowered with horror and anguish, I fell motionless on the deck and fainted. When I recovered a little I found some black people about me, who I believed were some of those who had brought me on board and had been receiving their pay; they talked to me in order to cheer me, but all in vain. I asked them if we were not to be eaten by those white men with horrible looks, red faces, and loose hair. They told me I was not, and one of the crew brought me a small portion of spirituous liquor in a wine glass, but being afraid of him I would not take it out of his hand. One of the blacks therefore took it from him and gave it to me, and I took a little down my palate, which instead of reviving me, as they thought it would, threw me into the greatest consternation at the strange feeling it produced, having never tasted such any liquor before. Soon after this the blacks who brought me on board went off, and left me abandoned to despair.

I now saw myself deprived of all chance of returning to my native country or even the least glimpse of hope of gaining the shore, which I now considered as friendly; and I even wished for my former slavery in preference to my present situation, which was filled with horrors of every kind, still heightened by my ignorance of what I was to undergo. I was not long suffered to indulge my grief; I was soon put down under the decks, and there I received such a salutation in my nostrils as I had never experienced in my life: so that with the loathsomeness of the stench and crying together, I became so sick and low that I was not able to eat, nor had I the least desire to taste anything. I now wished for the last friend, death, to relieve me; but soon, to my grief, two of the white men offered me eatables, and on my refusing to eat, one of them held me fast by the hands and laid me across I think the windlass, and tied my feet while the other flogged me severely. I had never experienced anything of this kind before, and although, not being used to the water, I naturally feared that element the first time I saw it, yet nevertheless could I have got over the nettings I would have jumped over the side, but I could not; and besides, the crew used to watch us very closely who were not chained down to the decks, lest we should leap into the water: and I have seen some of these poor African prisoners most severely cut for attempting to do so, and hourly whipped for not eating. This indeed was often the case with myself. In a little time after, amongst the poor chained men I found some of my own nation, which in a small degree gave ease to my mind. I inquired of these what was to be done with us; they gave me to understand we were to be carried to these white people's country to work for them. I then was a little revived, and thought if it were no worse than working, my situation was not so desperate: but still I feared I should be put to death, the white people looked and acted, as I thought, in so savage a manner; for I had never seen among my people such instances of brutal cruelty, and this not only shewn towards us blacks but also to some of the whites themselves. One white man in particular I saw, when we were permitted to be on deck, flogged so unmercifully with a large rope near the foremast that he died in consequence of it; and they tossed him over the side as they would have done a brute. This made me fear these people the more, and I expected nothing less than to be treated in the same manner. . . . At last, when the ship we were in had got in all her cargo, they made ready with many fearful noises, and we were all put under deck so that we could not see how they managed the vessel. But this disappointment was the last of my sorrow. The stench of the hold while we were on the coast was so intolerably loathsome that it was dangerous to remain there for any time, and some of us had been permitted to stay on the deck for the fresh air; but now that the whole ship's cargo were confined together it became absolutely pestilential. The closeness of the place and the heat of the climate, added to the number in the ship, which was so crowded that each had scarcely room to turn himself, almost suffocated us. This produced copious perspirations, so that the air soon became unfit for respiration from a variety of loathsome smells, and brought on a sickness among the slaves, of which many died, thus falling victims to the improvident avarice, as I may call it, of their purchasers. This wretched situation was again aggravated by the galling of the chains, now become insupportable, and the filth of the necessary tubs, into which the children often fell and were almost suffocated. The shrieks of the women and the groans of the dying rendered the whole a scene of horror almost inconceivable. Happily perhaps for myself I was soon reduced so low here that it was thought necessary to keep me almost always on deck, and from my extreme youth I was not put in fetters. In this situation I expected every hour to share the fate of my companions, some of whom were almost daily brought upon deck at the point of death, which I began to hope would soon put an end to my miseries. . . . At last we came in sight of the island of Barbados, at which the whites on board gave a great shout and made many signs of joy to us. We did not know what to think of this, but as the vessel drew nearer we plainly saw the harbour and other ships of different kinds and sizes, and we soon anchored amongst them off Bridgetown. Many merchants and planters now came on board, though it was in the evening. They put us in separate parcels and examined us attentively. They also made us jump, and pointed to the land, signifying we were to go there. . . . We were not many days in the merchant's custody before we were sold after their usual manner, which is this: On a signal given, (as the beat of a drum) the buyers rush at once into the yard where the slaves are confined, and make choice of that parcel they like best. The noise and clamour with which this is attended and the eagerness visible in the countenances of the buyers serve not a little to increase the apprehensions of the terrified Africans, who may well be supposed to consider them as the ministers of that destruction to which they think themselves devoted. In this manner, without scruple, are relations and friends separated, most of them never to see each other again. I remember in the vessel in which I was brought over, in the men's apartment there were several brothers who, in the sale, were sold in different lots; and it was very moving on this occasion to see and hear their cries at parting. O, ye nominal Christians! might not an African ask you, Learned you this from your God who says unto you, Do unto all men as you would men should do unto you?

▪ Discussion Questions

1. What are Equiano's impressions of the white men on the ship and their treatment of the slaves?
2. How does this treatment reflect the slave traders' primary concerns?
3. What message do you think Equiano sought to convey to his readers?
4. To whom do you think Equiano's book especially appealed?

45. Montesquieu, *Persian Letters: Letter 37*   (1721)

As Europe's economy expanded, so did its intellectual horizons with the birth of the Enlightenment in the 1690s. Charles-Louis de Secondat, baron of Montesquieu (1689–1755), was an especially important literary figure on this front. In 1721, he published Persian Letters, *in which he uses fictional characters to explore an array of topics with the critical, reasoning spirit characteristic of the period. Letter 37 points to one of his and other Enlightenment writers' main targets: Louis XIV and his absolutist state. Along with its criticism of the king's vanity, ostentation, and life at court, the letter implicitly passes even more serious judgment on the aging ruler in noting his esteem for "oriental policies." Montesquieu condemns these same policies elsewhere in the letters as inhumane and unjust.*

Charles-Louis de Secondat, baron of Montesquieu, *Persian Letters*, vol. I, trans. John Davidson (London: Privately printed, 1892), 85–86.

USBEK TO IBBEN, AT SMYRNA

The King of France is old.[1] We have no examples in our histories of such a long reign as his. It is said that he possesses in a very high degree the faculty of making himself obeyed: he governs with equal ability his family, his court, and his kingdom: he has often been heard to say, that, of all existing governments, that of the Turks, or that of our august Sultan, pleased him best: such is his high opinion of Oriental statecraft.[2]

I have studied his character, and I have found certain contradictions which I cannot reconcile. For example, he has a minister who is only eighteen years old,[3] and a mistress who is fourscore;[4] he loves his religion, and yet he cannot abide those who assert that it ought to be strictly observed;[5] although he flies from the noise of cities, and is inclined to be reticent, from morning till night he is engaged in getting himself talked about; he is fond of trophies and victories, but he has as great a dread of seeing a good general at the head of his own troops, as at the head of an army of his enemies. It has never I believe happened to anyone but himself, to be burdened with more wealth than even a prince could hope for, and yet at the same time steeped in such poverty as a private person could ill brook.

He delights to reward those who serve him; but he pays as liberally the assiduous indolence of his courtiers, as the labours in the field of his captains; often the man who undresses him, or who hands him his serviette at table, is preferred before him who has taken cities and gained battles; he does not believe that the greatness of a monarch is compatible with restriction in the distribution of favours; and, without examining into the merit of a man, he will heap benefits upon him, believing that his selection makes the recipient worthy; accordingly, he has been known to bestow a small pension upon a man who had run off two leagues from the enemy, and a good government on another who had gone four.

Above all, he is magnificent in his buildings; there are more statues in his palace gardens[6] than there are citizens in a large town. His bodyguard is as strong as that of the prince before whom all the thrones of the earth tremble;[7] his armies are as numerous, his resources as great, and his finances as inexhaustible.

Paris, the 7th of the moon of Maharram, 1713.

■ Discussion Questions

1. What contradictions does Usbek see in Louis's character, and what do they reveal about his method of rule?
2. In what ways does this letter reflect Montesquieu's general interest in the foundation of good government?
3. Having read this letter, why do you think that scholars regard Montesquieu as a herald of the Enlightenment?

---

[1]Louis XIV. was then seventy-five years old, and had reigned for seventy. [All notes are Davidson's.]

[2]When Louis XIV. was in his sixteenth year, some courtiers discussed in his presence the absolute power of the Sultans, who dispose as they like of the goods and the lives of their subjects. "That is something like being a king," said the young monarch. Marshal d'Estrées, alarmed at the tendency revealed in that remark, rejoined, "But, sire, several of these emperors have been strangled even in my time."

[3]Barbezieux, son of Louvois, Louis's youngest minister, held office at twenty-three, not eighteen; and he was dead in 1713.

[4]Madame de Maintenon.   [5]The Jansenists.

[6]At Versailles.   [7]The shah of Persia.

46. Mary Astell, *Reflections upon Marriage*   (1706)

Like Montesquieu, English author Mary Astell (1666–1731) helped to usher in the Enlightenment by surveying society with a critical eye. First published anonymously in 1700, Reflections upon Marriage *is one of her best-known books; it shows her keen interest in the institution of marriage, education, and relations between the sexes. Only the third edition (1706) divulged her gender, but still not her name. As this excerpt reveals, Astell held a dim view of women's inequality in general and of their submissive role in marriage in particular. She argues that one should abhor the use of arbitrary power within the state, and so, too, within the family. Among the book's principal goals was to present spinsterhood as a viable alternative to marriage. Perhaps not surprisingly, Astell herself never married.*

These Reflections being made in the Country, where the Book that occasion'd them came but late to Hand, the *Reader* is desir'd to excuse their Unseasonableness as well as other Faults; and to believe that they have no other Design than to Correct some Abuses, which are not the less because Power and Prescription seem to Authorize them. If any are so needlessly curious as to enquire from what Hand they come, they may please to know, that it is not good Manners to ask, since the Title-Page does not tell them: We are all of us sufficiently Vain, and without doubt the Celebrated Name of *Author,* which most are so fond of, had not been avoided but for very good Reasons: To name but one; *Who will care to pull upon themselves an Hornet's nest?* 'Tis a very great Fault to regard rather who it is that Speaks, than what is Spoken; and either to submit to Authority, when we should only yield to Reason; or if Reason press too hard, to think to ward it off by Personal Objections and Reflections. Bold Truths may pass while the Speaker is Incognito, but are not endur'd when he is known; few Minds being strong enough to bear what Contradicts their Principles and Practices without Recriminating when they can. And tho' to tell the Truth be the most Friendly Office, yet whosoever is so hardy as to venture at it, shall be counted an Enemy for so doing.

Thus far the old Advertisement, when the Reflections first appear'd, A.D. 1700.

But the *Reflector,* who hopes *Reflector* is not bad English, now Governor is happily of the feminine Gender, had as good or better have said nothing; For People by being forbid, are only excited to a more curious Enquiry. A certain Ingenuous Gentleman (as she is inform'd) had the Good-Nature to own these Reflections, so far as to affirm that he had the Original M.S. in his Closet, a Proof she is not able to produce;[1] and so to make himself responsible for all their Faults, for which she returns him all due Acknowledgment. However, the Generality being of Opinion, that a Man would have had more Prudence and Manners than to have Publish'd such unseasonable Truths, or to have betray'd the *Arcana Imperii* of his Sex, she humbly confesses, that the Contrivance and Execution of this Design, which is unfortunately accus'd of being so destructive to the government, of the Men I mean, is entirely her own. She neither advis'd with Friends, nor turn'd over Antient or Modern Authors, nor prudently submitted to the Correction of such as are, or such as *think* they are good Judges, but with an *English* Spirit and Genius, set out upon the Forlorn Hope, meaning no hurt to any body, nor designing any thing but the Publick Good, and to retrieve, if possible, the Native Liberty, the Rights and Privileges of the Subject.

---

[1] Alas, Mary Astell never revealed the identity of this "Ingenuous Gentleman." [All notes are Hill's.]

Bridget Hill, ed., *The First English Feminist:* Reflections upon Marriage *and Other Writings by Mary Astell* (New York: St. Martin's Press, 1986), 69–76.

Far be it from her to stir up Sedition of any sort, none can abhor it more; and she heartily wishes that our Masters wou'd pay their Civil and Ecclesiastical Governors the same Submission, which they themselves extract from their Domestic Subjects. Nor can she imagine how she any way undermines the Masculine Empire, or blows the Trumpet of Rebellion to the Moiety of Mankind. Is it by exhorting Women, not to expect to have their own Will in any thing, but to be entirely Submissive, when once they have made choice of a Lord and Master, tho' he happen not to be so Wise, so Kind, or even so Just a Governor as was expected? She did not indeed advise them to think his Folly Wisdom, nor his Brutality that Love and Worship he promised in his Matrimonial Oath, for this required a Flight of Wit and Sense much above her poor Ability, and proper only to Masculine Understandings. However she did not in any manner prompt them to Resist, or to Abdicate the Perjur'd Spouse, tho' the Laws of GOD and the Land make special Provision for it, in a case wherein, as is to be fear'd, few Men can truly plead Not Guilty.

Tis true, thro' Want of Learning, and of that Superior Genius which Men as Men lay claim to, she was ignorant of the *Natural Inferiority* of our Sex, which our Masters lay down as a Self-Evident and Fundamental Truth.[2] She saw nothing in the Reason of Things, to make this either a Principle or a Conclusion, but much to the contrary; it being Sedition at least, if not Treason to assert it in this Reign. For if by the Natural Superiority of their Sex, they mean that every Man is by Nature superior to every Woman, which is the obvious meaning, and that which must be stuck to if they would speak Sense, it wou'd be a Sin in *any* Woman to have Dominion over *any* Man, and the greatest Queen ought not to command but to obey her Footman, because no Municipal Laws can supersede or change the Law of Nature; so that if the dominion of the Men be such, the *Salique Law*, as unjust as *English Men* have ever thought it, ought to take place over all the Earth, and the most glorious Reigns in the *English, Danish, Castilian*, and other Annals, were wicked Violations of the Law of Nature!

If they mean that *some* Men are superior to *some* Women, this is no great Discovery; had they turn'd the Tables they might have seen that *some* Women are Superior to *some* Men. Or had they been pleased to remember their Oaths of Allegiance and Supremacy, they might have known that *One* Woman is superior to *All* the Men in these Nations, or else they have sworn to very little purpose. And it must not be suppos'd, that their Reason and Religion wou'd suffer them to take Oaths, contrary to the Law of Nature and Reason of things.

By all which it appears, that our Reflector's Ignorance is very pitiable, it may be her Misfortune but not her Crime, especially since she is willing to be better inform'd, and hopes she shall never be so obstinate as to shut her Eyes against the Light of Truth, which is not to be charg'd with Novelty, how late soever we may be bless'd with the Discovery. Nor can Error, be it as Ancient as it may, ever plead Prescription against Truth. And since the only way to remove all Doubts, to answer all Objections, and to give the Mind entire Satisfaction, is not by *Affirming*, but by *Proving*, so that every one may see with their *own* Eyes, and Judge according to the best of their *own* Understandings, She hopes it is no Presumption to insist on this Natural Right of Judging for her self, and the rather, because by quitting it, we give up all the Means of Rational Conviction. Allow us then as many Glasses as you please to help our Sight, and as many good Arguments as you can afford to Convince our Understandings: But don't exact of us we beseech you, to affirm that we see such things as are only the Discovery of Men who have quicker Senses; or that we understand and Know what we have by Hearsay only, for to be so excessively Complaisant, is neither to see nor to understand.

---

[2]Possibly a reference to William Nichols, D.D., *The Duty of Inferiours Towards their Superiours in Five Practical Discourses*, 1701, in which he argued that man possesses "a higher state of natural perfection and dignity, and thereupon puts in a just claim of superiority, which everything which is of more worth has a right to, over that which has less" (pp. 87–88).

That the Custom of the World has put Women, generally speaking, into a State of Subjection, is not deny'd; but the Right can no more be prov'd from the Fact, than the Predominancy of Vice can justifie it. A certain great Man has endeavour'd to prove by Reasons not contemptible, that in the Original State of things the Woman was the Superior, and that her Subjection to the Man is an Effect of the Fall, and the Punishment of her Sin. And that Ingenious Theorist Mr. *Whiston*[3] asserts, That before the Fall there was a greater equality between the two Sexes. However this be 'tis certainly no Arrogance in a Woman to conclude, that she was made for the Service of GOD, and that this is her End. Because GOD made all Things for Himself, and a Rational Mind is too noble a Being to be Made for the Sake and Service of any Creature. The Service she at any time becomes oblig'd to pay to a Man, is only a Business by the Bye. Just as it may be any Man's Business and Duty to keep Hogs; he was not Made for this, but if he hires himself out to such an Employment, he ought conscientiously to perform it. Nor can anything be concluded to the contrary from St. *Paul's* Argument, *I Cor. II.* For he argues only for Decency and Order, according to the present Custom and State of things. Taking his Words strictly and literally, they prove too much, in that *Praying and Prophecying in the Church* are allow'd the Women, provided they do it with their Head Cover'd, as well as the Men; and no inequality can be inferr'd from hence, their Reverence to the Sacred Oracles who engage them in such Disputes. And therefore the blame be theirs, who have unnecessarily introduc'd them in the present Subject, and who by saying that the *Reflections* were not agreeable to Scripture, oblige the Reflector to shew that those who affirm it must either mistake her Meaning, or the Sense of Holy Scripture, or both, if they think what they say, and do not find fault merely because they resolve to do so. For had she ever writ any thing contrary to those sacred Truths, she wou'd be the first in pronouncing its Condemnation.

But what says the Holy Scripture? It speaks of Women as in a State of Subjection, and so it does of the *Jews* and *Christians* when under the Dominion of the *Chaldeans* and *Romans*, requiring of the one as well as of the other a quiet submission to them under whose Power they liv'd. But will any one say that these had a *Natural Superiority* and Right to Dominion? that they had a superior Understanding, or any Pre-eminence, except what their greater Strength acquir'd? Or that the other were subjected to their Adversaries for any other Reason but the Punishment of their sins, and in order to their Reformation? Or for the Exercise of their Vertue, and because the Order of the World and the Good of Society requir'd it?

If Mankind had never sinn'd, Reason wou'd always have been obey'd, there wou'd have been no struggle for Dominion, and Brutal Power wou'd not have prevail'd. But in the laps'd State of Mankind, and now that Men will not be guided by their Reason but by their Appetites, and do not what they *ought* but what they *can*, the Reason, or that which stands for it, the Will and Pleasure of the Governor is to be the Reason of those who will not be guided by their own, and must take place for Order's sake, altho' it shou'd not be conformable to right Reason. Nor can there be any Society great or little, from Empires down to private Families, with a last Resort, to determine the Affairs of that Society by an irresistible Sentence. Now unless this Supremacy be fix'd somewhere, there will be a perpetual Contention about it, such is the love of Dominion, and let the Reason of things be what it may, those who have least Force, or Cunning to supply it, will have the Disadvantage. So that since Women are acknowledg'd to have least Bodily strength, their being commanded to obey is in pure kindness to them and for their Quiet and Security, as well as for the Exercise of their Vertue. But does it follow that Domestic Governors have more Sense than their Subjects, any more than that other Governors have? We do not find that any Man

---

[3]William Whiston (1667–1752), divine, mathematician, and Newtonian. Author of many works including *A New Theory of the Earth* (1696). He succeeded Newton as the Lucasian Professor and did much to popularize Newton's ideas. In 1710 he was deprived of his chair for casting doubt on the doctrine of the Trinity.

thinks the worse of his own Understanding because another has superior Power; or concludes himself less capable of a Post of Honour and Authority, because he is not Prefer'd to it. How much time wou'd lie on Men's hands, how empty wou'd the Places of Concourse be, and how silent most Companies, did Men forbear to Censure their Governors, that is in effect to think themselves Wiser. Indeed Government wou'd be much more desirable than it is, did it invest the Possessor with a superior Understanding as well as Power. And if mere Power gives a Right to Rule, there can be no such thing as Usurpation; but a Highway-Man so long as he has strength to force, has also a Right to require our Obedience.

Again, if Absolute Sovereignty be not necessary in a State, how comes it to be so in a family? or if in a Family why not in a State; since no Reason can be alledg'd for the one that will not hold more strongly for the other? If the Authority of the Husband so far as it extends, is sacred and inalienable, why not of the Prince? The Domestic Sovereign is without Dispute Elected, and the Stipulations and Contract are mutual, is it not then partial in Men to the last degree, to contend for, and practise that Arbitrary Dominion in their Families, which they abhor and exclaim against in the State? For if Arbitrary Power is evil in itself, and an improper Method of Governing Rational and Free Agents, it ought not to be Practis'd any where; Nor is it less, but rather more mischievous in Families than in Kingdoms, by how much 100000 Tyrants are worse than one. What tho' a Husband can't deprive a Wife of Life without being responsible to the Law, he may however do what is much more grievous to a generous Mind, render Life miserable, for which she has no Redress, scarce Pity which is afforded to every other Complainant. It being thought a Wife's Duty to suffer everything without Complaint. *If all Men are born free*, how is it that all Women are born slaves? as they must be if the being subjected to the *inconstant, uncertain, unknown, arbitrary Will of Men*, be the *perfect Condition of Slavery*? and if the Essence of Freedom consists, as our Masters say it does, in having a *standing Rule to live by*? And why is Slavery so much condemn'd and strove against in one Case, and so highly applauded, and held so necessary and so sacred in another?

■ Discussion Questions

1. According to Mary Astell, what is women's customary status in society, and why?
2. What evidence does Astell present to challenge this status?
3. What does the language Astell uses reveal about her style of thinking and basic intellectual beliefs?
4. Why do you think scholars characterize *Reflections upon Marriage* as a "feminist" work?

Acknowledgments (continued)

The Book of Exodus, Chapters 1–24 (Tenth to Sixth Centuries B.C.). From *The Holy Bible*, Authorized King James Version. Copyright © 1960 by Oxford University Press. Reprinted with the permission of Oxford University Press.

Tyrtaeus of Sparta and Solon of Athens. *Poems* (Seventh to Sixth Century B.C.). From *The Greek Polis*, edited by Arthur W. H. Adkins and Peter White. Copyright © 1986 by The University of Chicago. Reprinted with the permission of The University of Chicago Press.

Sappho of Lesbos. *Poems* (Sixth Century B.C.). "To Aphrodite," "When I look at you," "Anactoria," "Parting," "Remembering the girl Atthis," and "The wedding of Hector and Andromache" from *Women's Life in Greece & Rome*, Second Edition, edited by Mary R. Lefkowitz and Maureen B. Fant. Copyright © 1992. Reprinted with the permission of The Johns Hopkins University Press.

Chapter 2

Lysias. *A Husband Speaks in His Own Defense* (c. 400 B.C.). From "On the Killing of Eratosthenes of Seducer in *The Murder of Herodes and Other Trials from the Athenian Law Courts* by Kathleen Freeman. Copyright © 1946. Reprinted with the permission of Hackett Publishing Company. All rights reserved.

Plato. *The Apology of Socrates* (399 B.C.). From *Dialogues of Plato*, translated by Benjamin Jowett and edited by J. D. Kaplan. Copyright © 1950. Reprinted with the permission of Pocket Books, a division of Simon & Schuster.

Thucydides, *The Funeral Oration of Pericles* (429 B.C.). From *Thucydides, The Peloponnesian Wars*, translated by Benjamin Jowett, revised and abridged by P. A. Brunt. Copyright © 1963. Reprinted with the permission of Simon & Schuster, Inc.

Chapter 3

Zenon, Egyptian Official. *Records* (259–250 B.C.). Letters 88, 89, 90, 92, and 93; Memoranda 170, and 171; Agenda 179, and 180; Accounts and Lists 181, and 182, excerpted from *Select Papyri, Volume I: Private Affairs*, translated by A. S. Hunt and C. C. Edgar. Reprinted with the permission of Routledge.

Funerary Inscriptions and Epitaphs, (5th–1st Centuries B.C.). Excerpts from *Women's Life in Greece & Rome: A Source Book in Translation*, Second edition, edited by Mary R. Lefkowitz & Maureen B. Fant. Copyright © 1992. Reprinted with the permission of The Johns Hopkins University Press.

Polybius. *The Histories* (Second Century B.C.). From *Polybius: The Histories*, translated by W. R. Paton, vol. VI. Copyright © 1960. Reprinted with the permission of Harvard University Press.

Chapter 4

Roman Women Demonstrate against the Oppian Law (195 B.C.). From *Livy: Volume IX*, Loeb Classical Library Volume #L295, translated by Evan T. Sage, Cambridge Mass: Harvard University Press, 1935. The Loeb Classical Library ® is a registered trademark of the President and Fellows of Harvard College. Reprinted with the permission of the publishers and The Trustees of the Loeb Classical Library.

The Twelve Tables (451–449 B.C.). From *Ancient Roman Statutes*, translated by Allan Chester Johnson, Paul Robinson Coleman-Norton, Frank Card Bourne. Copyright © 1961. Reprinted with the permission of the University of Texas Press.

Cicero. *On the Commonwealth* (54 B.C.). From *The Treatises of M. T. Cicero or The Nature of the Gods; on Divination; On Fate; On the Republic; On the Laws; and On Standard for the Consulship* translated and edited by C. D. Yonge. Published by Henry G. Bohn (1853).

Chapter 5

Augustus. *The Accomplishments of Augustus* (A.D. 14). From *Roman Civilization: Selected Readings, Vol. I, The Republic and the Augustan Age, Third Edition*, edited by Naphtali Lewis and Meyer Reinhold. Copyright © 1990 by Columbia University Press. Reprinted with the permission of the publishers.

Notices and Graffiti Describe Life in Pompeii (First Century A.D.). From "Real Estate Transactions," "Election Notices," and "The Humble Townspeople." From *Roman Civilization Selected Readings*, Vol. II: *The Empire*, Third edition, edited by Naphtali Lewis and Meyer Reinhold. Copyright © 1990 by Columbia University Press. Reprinted with the permission of the publishers.

Pliny the Younger. *Letters* (A.D. 111–113). From *Rome: Late Republic and Principate*, Vol. II, translated by Peter White. Edited by Walter Emil Kaegi, Jr., and Peter White. Copyright © 1986 by The University of Chicago. Reprinted with the permission of the University of Chicago Press.

Chapter 6

St. Jerome. *Letter 107* (A.D. 403). From *Select Letters of St. Jerome,* translated by F. A. Wright. Copyright © 1963 by the President and Fellows of Harvard College. Reprinted with the permission of Harvard University Press.

The Burgundian Code (c. 475–525). Translated by Katherine Fischer Drew. Copyright © 1972 by the University of Pennsylvania Press. Reprinted with the permission of the Publishers.

Procopius. *Buildings* (c. 533–554). From *Procopius,* Vol. VII, translated by H. B. Dewing. Copyright © 1961 by the President and Fellows of Harvard College. Reprinted with the permission of Harvard University Press.

Chapter 7

Islamic Terms of Peace. (633–643). From *Islam: from the Prophet Muhammad to the Capture of Constantinople,* Vol. I: *Politics and War,* edited and translated by Bernard Lewis. Copyright © 1974. Reprinted with the permission of Walker and Company.

The Life of Lady Balthild, Queen of the Franks (late Seventh Century). From *Late Merovingian France: History and Hagiography 640–720,* by Paul Fouracre and Richard A. Gerberding. Copyright © 1996. Reprinted with the permission of Manchester University Press.

Pope Gregory the Great. *Letters* (598–601). From *A Select Library of Nicene and Post-Nicene Fathers of the Christian Church,* Second Series, Vol. XII: *Leo the Great, Gregory the Great,* and vol. XIII, Part II: *Gregory the Great, Ephraim Slaves and Aphrahat,* translated and edited by Philip Schaff and Henry Wace. Published by the Christian Literature Company (1898).

Chapter 8

Digenis Akritas: The Two-Blood Border Lord (10th or 11th Century). Translated by Denison B. Hull. Copyright © 1972 by Ohio University Press. Reprinted with the permission of the publishers.

Ahmad al-Ya'qubi. *Kitab al-buldan* (Ninth Century). From *Islam: from the Prophet Muhammad to the Capture of Constantinople,* Vol. II: *Religion and Society,* edited and translated by Bernard Lewis. Copyright © 1974. Reprinted with the permission of Walker and Company.

General Capitulary for the Missi., (c. 802). From *Translations and Reprints from the Original Sources of European History,* Vol. VI, edited by Dana Carleton Munro. Published by the University of Pennsylvania Press (1898).

Chapter 9

Urban Charters of Jaca, Spain (c. 1077), and *Loriss, France* (1155). From *Medieval Iberia: Readings from Christian, Muslim, and Jewish Sources,* translated by Thomas N. Bisson and edited by Olivia Remie Constable. Copyright © 1997 by The University of Pennsylvania Press. Reprinted with the permission of the publishers. Excerpts from *A Source Book of Medieval History,* edited by Frederic Austin. Published by the American Book Company.

Emperor Henry IV and Pope Gregory VII. *Letters of the Investiture Conflict* (1076). From *The Correspondence of Pope Gregory VII: Selected Letters from the Registrum,* translated by Ephraim Emerton. Published by Columbia University Press (1912). Henry IV. "Letter 12" from *Imperial Lives and Letters of the Eleventh Century* (pp. 150–151), translated by Theodor E. Mommsen and Karl F. Morrison. Edited by Robert L. Benson. Copyright © 1962 by Columbia University Press. Reprinted with the permission of the publishers.

Hildegard of Bingen. *Selected Writings* (12th Century). From *Symphonia: A Critical Edition of the Symphonia armonie celestium revelationum, Second Edition,* translated by Barbara Newman. Copyright © 1998 by Cornell University Press. "Hildegard to the prelates at Mainz" from *The Letters of Hildegard of Bingen, Vol. I* (pp. 76–80) translated by Joseph Baird and Radd Ehrman. Copyright © 1994 by Oxford University Press. Reprinted with the permission of the publishers.

Saints Francis and Clare of Assisi. *Selected Writings* (13th Centuries) from *Select Historical Documents of the Middle Ages,* edited by Ernest Henderson. Published by Bell and Sons (1921). Excerpts from "The Testament of Saint Clare," from *Francis and Clare: The Complete Works,* translated by Regis J. Armstrong and Ignatius C. Brady. Copyright © 1982 by The Missionary Society of Saint Paul the Apostle in the State of New York. Reprinted with the permission of Paulist Press.

Chapter 10

Hadewijch of Brabant. *Letters and Poems of a Female Mystic* (1220–1240). From Ria Vanderauwera, "The Brabant Mystic: Hadewijch, 1220–1240," (pp. 193–95; 198–201), from *Medieval Women Writers,* edited by

Katharina M. Wilson. Copyright © 1984 by The University of Georgia Press. Reprinted with the permission of the publishers.

Medieval University Life (12th–Early 13th Centuries). Excerpts from *Translations and Reprints from the Original Sources of European History,* Vol. II, no. 3, edited by Dana Carleton Munro. Published by the University of Pennsylvania Press, 1898. Excerpts from *Wine, Women, and Song: Mediaeval Latin Students' Songs* (pp. 58–64), edited by John Addington Symonds. Published by Chatto and Windus, 1907.

Dante Alighieri. *Human and Divine Love* (Late 13th–Early 14th Centuries). From *La vita nuova,* translated by Barbara Reynolds. Published by Penguin Books (1980). Copyright © 1969 by Barbara Reynolds. Excerpts from *The Comedy of Dante Alighieri the Florentine, Cantica III: Paradise,* translated by Dorothy L. Sayers and Barbara Reynolds. Copyright © 1981 by Dorothy L. Sayers and Barbara Reynolds. Both reprinted with the permission of David Higham Associates, Ltd.

Chapter 11

The Black Death (14th Century). Translated and edited by Rosemary Horrox. Copyright © 1994. Reprinted with the permission of Manchester University Press.

Christine de Pisan. *Laments on the Evils of the Civil War* (1410). From *The Epistle of the Prison of Human Life with an Epistle to the Queen of France and Lament on the Evils of the Civil War,* edited and translated by Josette A. Wisman. Copyright © 1984. Reprinted with the permission of Garland Publishing.

Giovanni Pico della Mirandola. *Oration on the Dignity of Man* (1496). From *The Italian Renaissance Reader,* edited by Julia Conaway Bondanella and Mark Musa. Copyright © 1987 by Julia Conaway Bondanella and Mark Musa. Reprinted with the permission of Dutton Signet, a division of Penguin Putnam Inc.

Alessandra Strozzi. *Letters from a Widow and Matriarch of a Great Family* (1450–1465). From *University of Chicago Readings in Western Civilization, 5: The Renaissance,* edited by Eric Cochrane and Julius Kirshner. Copyright © 1986 by The University of Chicago. Reprinted with the permission of The University of Chicago Press.

Chapter 12

Argula von Grumbach and John Hooker. *Women's Actions in the Reformation* (1520s–30s). Excerpt from *The Dissolution of the Monasteries* by Joyce Youings. Copyright © 1971 by Joyce Youings. Reprinted with the permission of HarperCollins Publishers, Ltd.

Henry IV. *Edict of Nantes* (1598). From "The Great Pressures and Grievances of the Protestants in France," Edmund Everand. Saint Ignatius of Loyola. *A New Kind of Catholicism* (1546, 1549, 1553). From *St. Ignatius of Loyola: Personal Writings: Reminiscences, Spiritual Diary, Select Letters including the text of The Spiritual Exercises,* edited and translated by Joseph A. Munitiz and Philip Endean. Copyright © 1996 by Joseph A. Munitiz and Philip Endean. Reprinted with the permission of Penguin Books, Ltd.

Galileo, *Letter to the Grand Duchess Christina* (1615). *From Discoveries and Opinions of Galileo,* translated by Stillman Drake. Copyright © 1957 by Stillman Drake. Reprinted with the permission of Doubleday, a division of Random House, Inc.

Chapter 13

Louis de Rouvroy, Duke of Saint-Simon. *Memoirs* (1694–1723). From *The Memoirs of The Duke of Saint-Simon,* translated by Bayle St. John, Vol. II.

Ludwig Fabritius. *The Revolt of Stenka Razin* (1670). From *Russia Under Western Eyes 1517–1825,* edited by Anthony Glenn Cross. Copyright © 1971 by Anthony Glenn Cross. Reprinted with permission.

British Parliament. *The English Bill of Rights* (1689). From *The Statutes:* revised edition, 1871, vol. II.

Chapter 14

Olaudah Equiano. *The Interesting Narrative of the Life of Olaudah Equiano, Written by Himself* (1789). From *Equiano's Travels: His Autobiography,* edited by Paul Edwards. Published by Frederick A. Praeger, 1966.

Montesquieu. *Persian Letters: Letter 37* (1721). Translated by John Davidson, Vol. I.

Mary Astell. *Reflections upon Marriage* (1706). Excerpt from *The First English Feminist: Reflections Upon Marriage and Other Writings,* edited by Bridget Hill. Copyright © 1986 by Bridget Hill. Reprinted by permission.

Badinerie
Nocturne

Mozart Aria